GROWING UP DISABLED IN AUSTRALIA

GROWING UP DISABLED IN AUSTRALIA

EDITED BY CARLY FINDLAY

In places, this book contains ableist language and references to suicide and self-harm, homophobia, intergenerational trauma, medical trauma and other themes that may be distressing.

Published by Black Inc.,
an imprint of Schwartz Books Pty Ltd
Level 1, 221 Drummond Street
Carlton VIC 3053, Australia
enquiries@blackincbooks.com
www.blackincbooks.com

9781760641436 (paperback)
9781743821374 (ebook)

A catalogue record for this book is available from the National Library of Australia

Cover art by Wendy Dawson
Cover and typesetting by Akiko Chan
Text design by Tristan Main

Contents

Introduction

Carly Findlay OAM

Like some of the other contributors to this anthology, I didn't grow up disabled. Even though I have a severe lifelong skin condition, I rejected the term 'disabled' because I thought it had negative connotations and I didn't see how it related to me. The only time I saw disabled people in the media was when they competed in the Paralympics, or when a tabloid TV show was painting their life as a tragedy. And I didn't see anyone like me. I thought disability looked a certain way. And I didn't fit that.

Because I didn't identify as disabled, I wasn't able to advocate for the support I needed in school, nor recognise or speak up against discrimination towards other disabled people. In hindsight, it's clear that I had internalised ableism. By insisting I wasn't disabled, I was perpetuating the 'othering'. And I lacked a sense of pride and community.

It wasn't until I was in my mid-twenties, when I mentored young people with chronic illness, that I realised how much we had in common – serious lifelong conditions that required many specialists at the hospital, extended absences from school and work, and encountering attitudinal barriers from ignorance or discrimination. These young people allowed me to work through that internalised ableism and showed me that I could embrace the term 'disabled'.

I began writing publicly about life with ichthyosis, which led to work in the mainstream media and presenting on a disability-led TV show called *No Limits*. I got to know more chronically ill and disabled people and came to understand the social model of disability. This model acknowledges the physical, attitudinal, communication and social barriers faced by people with impairments. It challenges these obstacles by arguing that society should accommodate impairment as an expected aspect of human diversity. I felt safe to embrace the label of 'disabled' because of the writing and friendship of other disabled people. And this meant I could finally advocate for myself and for others.

I now identify as a proud disabled woman, not wanting to hide my disability and chronic illness. And I want to help be the change in the media, so that young disabled people can see themselves and what's possible for them.

I hope that this book can be a friend to people who need it, because it's a friend I needed when I was younger.

This book will change history. It's the first of its kind in Australia. And I hope it won't be the last. Publishers – both literary and news – need to commit to publishing work by disabled people. We deserve better representation in literature.

From 2010 to 2014, Stella Young edited *ABC Ramp Up*. It was a place for disabled people to write about our own experiences, advocate for policy change and celebrate disability pride. The government defunded it in 2014, and there hasn't been a dedicated place for Australian disability writing online since. While *Growing Up Disabled in Australia* has a finite number of stories and will never replace *Ramp Up*, I am glad to have helped provide a writing space for disabled people to tell their stories. I am forever thankful for Stella's work, and I read and reference her writing regularly.

We had over 360 submissions to *Growing Up Disabled in Australia*. It was such an honour reading through the submissions – one of the best jobs I've ever had. The quality of writing is extraordinary, and there is a definite hunger from disabled people to tell their stories (and to read the stories of others).

Choosing the contributors was a hard task – I wish we could have included many more. I'm proud of everyone who submitted and encourage those who didn't get into this anthology to keep writing and find other opportunities for their work.

This anthology shows the diversity of disability – not just in terms of impairments, but also experiences. I took an intersectional approach when selecting the work. The people in this book are disabled, chronically ill, mentally ill and neurodiverse, and inhabit the city, regional and rural regions and Aboriginal communities. They span generations – some are elders and some are still growing up – and genders, cultures and sexualities. Not everyone in the book sees disability as part of their identity, but some are waving the pride flag loudly; both responses are valid. Some people have chosen to use a pseudonym, such is the stigma or fear of speaking out about disability.

I hope this book creates a sense of identity, pride and belonging to a community – for the contributors and for readers.

I can't wait to see these writers fly.

A note on the social model of disability

Growing Up Disabled in Australia is based on the social model of disability. People with Disability Australia describes this as follows: 'The social model sees "disability" is the result of the interaction between people living with impairments and an environment filled with physical, attitudinal, communication and social barriers. It therefore carries the implication that the physical, attitudinal, communication and social environment must change to enable people living with impairments to participate in society on an equal basis with others."

A social model perspective does not deny the reality of impairment nor its impact on the individual. However, it does challenge the physical, attitudinal, communication and social environment to accommodate impairment an expected incident of human diversity.'

Question Marks and a Theory of Vision

Andy Jackson

I didn't grow up disabled. My body and its place in the world seemed normal to me. Why wouldn't it?

I grew up in Bendigo, a goldfields city in central Victoria, a city small enough to safely ride around on a bicycle unsupervised, but large enough to have a shopping mall and the first Myer in Australia. We lived in a relatively new suburb, with clusters of mid-century quarter-acre homes surrounded by former quarries that had become vacant lots. In the imaginations of the children who lived there, they were far from vacant. As soon as I could ride a bike, I was out there on those hillocks and dunes, daydreaming places where I could escape myself and belong at the same time.

My father was a salesman, tall and unusually shaped, with a prosthetic leg. I only learnt this latter detail later on. Mum was stoic and uninterested in focusing on the negatives. In photographs from the time, Dad wore white business shirts and had slicked-down hair. My brother and I clambered around him, his posture suggesting love, albeit undemonstrative, and mild disinterest. To remember him, I only have these photos, because when I was two, before my brain had the chance to develop the capacity for long-term memory, he had some kind of cardiac event, was rushed to hospital and died.

We lived halfway between the showgrounds and the hospital, and that now seems fitting. As it would turn out, I spent quite a bit of time being examined by medical specialists, on show.

*

My mother tells a story – I don't remember this, so you'll have to take her word for it – that on my first day of school she wasn't sure how I'd handle it socially. I was quiet, sensitive, bookish. So she told the teacher to keep half an eye on me. At some point, I disappeared from the playground. Soon enough, the teacher found me in the library, in a corner, reading to a small circle of other kids. Mum tells this story, as parents do, to show just how unusual, how precocious I was. But somewhere at the centre of that reading circle is someone preparing to put themselves on show – like being a poet, where the focus is both me and not me.

*

I didn't grow up disabled. Disabled was other people. People different from me. Pale-blue Spastic Society buses that drove haltingly through our neighbourhood, picking up and dropping off kids whom I had nothing to do with. They went to a special school. The air between us was charged and strange. There was so much I didn't understand about bodies, so many things that could go awry.

In late primary school, my best friend and I decided that we should start a private detective agency. We'd read lots of books, especially adventures and mysteries that could be solved with the right combination of confidence and intelligence. For some reason we thought Bendigo must have an abundance of unsolved riddles and problems that prepubescent boys could unravel. We placed a hand-drawn advertisement on the noticeboard of our classroom, which no one responded to. There was nothing special about us.

*

Around the age of twelve, I entered a growth spurt, and suddenly this blond-haired, pale-skinned, slightly gawky child began looking deformed. My spine bent and curved under the pressure. It pressed outwards and tilted me to the side. Unbeknown to me, my mother had been watching for years, wondering, quietly worried that I might have inherited something that would catapult me towards – what, exactly? A stareable body? Disability? My father? My spine was a kind of question mark.

Mum took me to an orthopaedic specialist in Melbourne, who said confidently, 'Yes, we really must operate soon.' Severe spinal curvature, especially if left unchecked, can cause great pressure on the internal organs. I needed to be stabilised, corrected. I thought 'soon' meant that very afternoon, that I'd be whisked into the Royal Children's Hospital nearby, home of the annual Good Friday Appeal, tragedy and sympathy, and within hours I'd be under anaesthetic, being fixed. In fact, the surgery would occur about two months later.

*

On my first night in hospital, after I was admitted, I watched Mum leave the ward with my older brother, who was fourteen at the time, walking beside her. She seemed quieter than usual, less upright, more uncertain. Unusually for him, he placed his arm around her, as they disappeared out of view. I know now he was telling her everything would be okay.

Later, Mum would tell me how fascinating it was that the sickest kids in the hospital, shadowed by cancer or aflame with burns, tended to be the least complaining, while the kids with minor ailments were endlessly pressing the button to summon the nurse, for painkillers, for attention. By implication, I wasn't one of *those* kids.

Another memory: standing exposed in a windowless room somewhere in the hospital, my clothes in a neat pile on a shelf. The click-flash of the camera, me in my underwear, an expression on my face that might be called blank but is more awkward, ambiguous. I might be hiding my embarrassment, or just hoping it will be over soon because it's cold there. I am standing as upright as I can, but this skeleton's version of normal is cursive.

*

The operations were, as is often the case, not entirely successful. The curvature was slightly corrected but continued with a vengeance as I grew. I have the same genetic condition my father had, Marfan syndrome, a heritable disorder of connective tissue. This means, apart from my visible difference, the valves of my heart will always be at risk of fraying and tearing. So far it's fine, thanks to medication and annual check-ups. When I was first diagnosed, the medical consensus was that a lifespan of over forty years was unlikely. I'm now forty-eight, almost the age my dad was when he died. These days, most people with Marfan – in Western countries anyway – will live until old age. Although mortality is always there, a companion, it doesn't loom quite so menacingly.

There's no doubt it's reassuring to have a name for your difference. And medicine can make life more manageable, can even save your life. But you always have to leave the hospital or the clinic, face the world and its hostility to question marks.

*

In my teenage years, was I disabled? I was Hunchback. Quasimodo. Someone to stare at, or shout things at as you drove past. Someone to pick on, or pity. A classmate with a Yorkshire accent as thick as his glasses, sitting in the bus seat in front of me on a school excursion, taunted me the entire two-hour trip. A young apprentice in overalls sped past me on his bike, asking, 'What's under your shirt, hunchy?' As I walked from English to Chemistry, I overheard one of the cool girls joking to her friend that I was someone she wanted as a boyfriend. Laughter isn't always contagious. And being stared at is a strange kind of fame. I absorbed it all, quietly, not knowing what to do with it. Well, I wrote some things in exercise books, but I didn't show anyone.

*

Plato had a theory of vision that now seems scientifically absurd but makes a lot of sense to some deep part of me. Instead of light coming into the eye, which is then interpreted by the brain, the idea was that the eye sent out a kind of 'fire' that then brought back information about what it encountered. A fire within each of us, lighting our way. This was the dominant theory until only a few centuries ago. Stories – especially ones that rely on their being a source of light inside us – are hard to shift. In fact, recent research suggested that around 50 per cent of adults believe in some version of the theory, even now.

We have all felt that uncanny sensation that someone is watching us. We can't see them, but we feel something over our shoulder, their intense gaze. It's as if their eyes are sending out tiny, tangible sparks of light, which tickle or singe our skin. To be physically different is to be continually assailed by these missiles of looking. Those of us who are stareable absorb these sparks into our bodies. We carry burn marks and develop scar tissue. We are tense, bracing ourselves for unwanted attention. We doubt ourselves, our beauty. These fires disable. They can even spread out beyond the hearth to burn others. At the same time, harnessed, they can warm and sustain.

*

One more memory: an open-mic poetry session in the back room of a Brunswick pub, early 2000s. A small circle of writers and those who hoped they could be. I'm around thirty years old. Grown up, but still green. I've been reading my poems in public for a few years now but haven't yet really written – or spoken – directly about my bodily difference. The MC says my name and I walk to the stage, a slight tremor of nerves fanning the embers in my chest.

I begin: 'I have a hunch / that curvature / can be aperture / given that light, like water, / does not travel in a straight line …'

A stunned, warm silence fills the room. When I finish the poem and the applause fades, I rush to the men's bathroom to cry in relief. I then pull myself together and emerge into a slightly different world.

For me, poetry is a way of affirming that bodily difference is a source of insight. It asks questions. It is an opening. It suggests another way of being together.

The same is true of saying *I am disabled*, as I do now.

Forever Fixing

El Gibbs

No one told me when I first got sick that I had abruptly joined a community, one with a history, and theories, and ways of being. Instead, I was told to relentlessly search for a cure, and an exit, no matter the cost – to wage war on my diseased self.

I had become disabled – not just by my disease, but by the way the world treated me. When I found that out, everything changed.

*

It all started with a few spots on my arm one summer day. A few red, flaky spots that I ignored. I had drinking to do, drugs to take, bands to see, chaos to create.

But the spots had their own agenda. They joined together and spread down my arm, and then all over my body. Various doctors peered at me and pronounced that it was nothing to worry about. 'Here's a cream that will fix you.'

Three months later, I was covered from head to toe in crimson, weepy, flaking, hot, sore skin. It cracked every time I breathed in or out, and I bled on everything. By now, the doctors had agreed that a cream probably wouldn't fix me and that I had to go to hospital. For a few days, right? No, they said. For a few weeks. I was nineteen.

Each morning in hospital, I would stand on sheets in my undies while two nurses painted my skin with a paste, then wrapped me in bandages. The next day, the paste would be scrubbed from my skin, and after a bath in tar it would be reapplied. Repeat. Repeat. Repeat.

My skin responded to this with the same aggressive rebellion as I did. After three weeks, the doctors gave up, discharging me to have outpatient treatment somewhere else. My body hadn't done what the textbooks said it should; I'd failed the treatment, they said.

My chaotic sharehouse didn't know what to do with me when I got home. I hadn't been given any pain management, so I took things into my own hands, careening from pub to dealer and playing loud records to hide my frightened sobbing. When I started uncontrollably shivering, and this went on for several days, a housemate convinced me that it couldn't be a normal part of whatever the fuck was happening to me and that I should tell Outpatients how bad I felt. He drove me to the hospital, and I can still remember the worry on his face.

I must have looked as bad as I felt, because once I got there, it seemed like lots of things happened very quickly. I was rushed from doctor to doctor, and there was a lot of yelling. 'How was this allowed to happen?' And then I don't remember much else.

*

The medical model of disability says that I am broken because my body has a disease and it doesn't work the way a so-called 'normal' body does. There is this normal body, you see, that doctors learn about, described in medical textbooks. When things go wrong with this fictional body, medicine is applied and the body returns to its normal state. All better now. Any deviation from this path is abnormal, aberrant, an exception to the rule.

This model of disability, with its focus always on the individual disabled person, reigned for a long time. It argues for containment, for institutionalisation. It thinks normal people need to be sheltered from the 'freaks'. We couldn't possibly have a place in the world just as we are.

*

Psoriasis is an immune system disorder where the skin gets stuck in healing mode, forever fixing what isn't broken – its own medical model of disability. I had erythrodermic psoriasis, covering my entire body. This meant I could not control my body temperature, hydration or blood pressure, and all my hair fell out. My skin had become infected as well, so I was in a bunch of trouble.

I have flashes of memory from that time. Hot, painful, terrifying, baffling, and oh god so sore.

Sometime after this crisis, I was in a general ward, with doctors surveying my recalcitrant self. Each day a gaggle of physicians would peer at me from the end of the bed. I'd react with sarcasm or hostility, or I'd ignore them altogether. Each day it was the same: more wet dressings, more creams, and no, they had no idea how long this would go on for.

At the end of the ward was a fire escape. Outside the building, on the landing, was a table where I would sit late at night, peering out at the world that seemed to be passing me by. I'd smoke bongs and play music and cry so hard that the skin on my face would bleed.

In the end, I was put on the first of many drug trials, and it worked well enough to get me out of hospital after numerous weeks.

When I landed back in the world, life was different. Everyone around me was so glad it was over, that I was better now. But I would have flashbacks to the period in hospital that were so severe I'd stop in the street, gasping and overwhelmed. My peer group and family had very little understanding of what this meant, and I hardly understood it myself, nor did I have a clue how to deal with it.

I decided that taking a lot of drugs, being incredibly angry and not talking about what had happened was the best way to handle it, so that's what I did. I yelled 'Leper!' and 'Unclean!' at people on the tram who stared at me. I was so afraid that I thought the fear would swallow me whole.

The years that followed were tough. I made several suicide attempts, and spent some time in a mental health facility, where I worked out fairly quickly that I really needed to stop taking drugs. Detox, rehab and years of sobriety came next, where I cycled in and out of hospital every few months, the psoriasis raging all over my body.

I was diagnosed with arthritis when I was twenty-two, pain shooting up my back and down my legs. Now it was not just my skin but also my bones that groaned and ached, refusing to cooperate with my need to run away from the world.

I focused hard on fixing myself, on repairing the damage from raging around. I blamed myself for everything. I wrote affirmations every day for five years, convinced that if I could just start to think differently, the psoriasis would go away. People around me said that my condition was a reflection of my self-hatred, that if I loved myself I would get better. So I worked on liking myself, but my disease got worse.

For a long time, I was told that the only way to treat my disease, to cure myself, was to be in hospital for weeks or months at a time. So I complied, spending so much time there that I had the 'El room', decorated with a cardboard cut-out of Princess Leia and posters of space. I wrote essays for uni, did my community work, edited magazines and smoked with friends out on the balcony, pretending that this was all utterly normal.

And in a weird way, it was. It was my normal to spend months in hospital, and even after being discharged to still have to go there every day. It was my normal to be on a first-name basis with all the new doctors my own age, and for the nurses to fuss over me like the parents they kind of were. I knew every shortcut between different parts of the large hospital, the underground tunnels and where to get chocolate and milkshakes late at night.

The treatments would work for a while. They painted my body with pastes and lotions, wrapped me in bandages, zapped me with UVB light every day. After a month or so, my disease would retreat to a socially acceptable norm, and all the medical staff would gather at the end of my bed, congratulating themselves on their cleverness. I was just a passive recipient of their wisdom, with no agency or knowledge of my own.

For years, I asked them what was going to happen next. Would I always be like this? What would happen to me in the future? How would my disease progress? Each time I asked, they said that I just had to try this next treatment and we'd talk about all that later. I would leave the hospital in tears, directed to take yet another leap of faith with no parachute.

Eventually, the treatments stopped working. My body refused to react like the doctors' textbooks said it should, revelling in its proliferation of disease. I looked burnt, my skin bright red and weeping, shedding flakes everywhere I went, like a kind of bread crumb trail tracing the way home. I existed in a haze of pain, my bones singing their hurt throughout my body, which felt like an enemy, hostile territory.

Every few months, I'd be asked to try something new. Drugs would be flown in from overseas and injected into my disobedient body. Some worked amazingly well, washing away my disease in a few weeks, leaving me blinking in astonishment as I suddenly looked just like everyone else. People stopped staring at me, and I wasn't in pain. But the drugs would inevitably stop working, or be withdrawn suddenly because of emerging side effects, and I'd be left broken-hearted, and once again so, so sick. My disease would roar back, even worse than before, shattering me with pain and despair.

Each time the doctors asked me to try a new drug, they were so certain. Armed with piles of studies that showed this would work for sure, they never stopped to listen to what I actually wanted or needed. Every effort was focused on 'getting me well', no matter the consequences.

What I wanted was certainty, or at least a little honesty. I wanted any one of the doctors to level with me about what was happening, to be real about what my future would be, to offer me a sliver of space to get my head around that. But every time I tried to discuss being disabled, to talk about disability, about living my life well as a sick person, I was told that I was being defeatist, giving up, that it wasn't the time yet to have that conversation.

Instead, I had that conversation with the nurses, snot-crying that I couldn't do it anymore. I couldn't undergo another round of treatment. I couldn't stand the uncertainty. I just wanted things to be the same for a while. I couldn't cope at home without help, but I couldn't face coming into hospital again.

The nurses were immensely kind, patting my shoulder gently and passing me tissues, and saying yes, this would probably be for the rest of my life, and yes, that wasn't fair, and no, it's not unusual to find hospital so awful, and yes, you need more support at home. Yes, I was disabled.

But what did being disabled mean? Both for me, and for how I fitted into a world that had little room for the way my body worked. Did it mean being an inspirational Paralympian, or raising money for a cure? Did it mean being isolated and always in hospital? Was I too disabled to work, or study, or love, or dance? Was I disabled enough to get assistance?

I had no one to answer any of those questions. The medical folk all understood my impairments through the medical model of disability. My illness wasn't something to be accepted or accommodated, but an entity in its own right to be fought through their collective cleverness.

I didn't know any other disabled people, or know any other ways of thinking about disability. There was no handy booklet about how to be disabled, to guide me through my emergence into a disabled life.

The medical model sets strict rules – apply this treatment and this will be the result. There is little room for the vagaries of an individual body, or any acknowledgement that treatments work differently for different people, and sometimes not at all. The doctors would often stare down at me, berating me for treatments that didn't work or looking upon me as a puzzle to be solved.

They never contemplated, even as a remote possibility, that I was enough, with my disease, with my disfigurement, with my limp, with it all. They never considered me saying no, or enough, or oh god, would you all just fucking stop.

*

When I found the social model of disability, it was like an explosion went off in my brain.

I'd been part of the disability system for a long time – on the Disability Support Pension, using the disability employment service, getting disability supports – but I didn't understand disability as a political or social issue. My disability was all about what was wrong with me and how I didn't measure up to 'normal' people. It was about what I couldn't do, how broken I was, how aberrant and weird my body was.

The social model of disability, unlike the medical one, puts the onus on the world to change, not the individual disabled person. It says that what disabled me wasnot my particular impairments, but rather the barriers of an ableist society. In this model, the problem with how I looked became about attitudes to difference, not me being a freak; the problem with public transport was the lack of stairs and seats, not that I couldn't climb up to the station or stand up for the trip; the problem with employers was their attitudes and inflexibility, not the way I looked or the pain I was in being 'too much' for a workplace.

This model also offered me a connection to the wider world of disability, and disabled people. I was now part of a community that had a history of fighting for their rights and freedoms. My individual battle – for the right to make decisions for myself, to have some control over what happened to me, to have a say about my life – was echoed in a million other battles.

The social model of disability gave me a framework for understanding my chronic illness, but it sometimes had little room for my actual experience of being sick. I had to find a way to reconcile my knowledge that disability was about structural barriers with the reality of my impairments. Was there space for both disability pride and finding my disabled body literally hard to bear? Sometimes it *was* my impairments that stopped me from accessing the world, not just the obstacles in that world. I could engage in political action and break down external barriers all I liked, but my skin was still raw and bleeding, and I was still in pain and exhausted. Did this mean that the medical model was right? That I had to focus on finding a cure? What did it mean if I decided not to try any more treatments? What would happen when there were no more treatments to try? What if I wanted the pain to stop? Would this mean I was a failure as a disabled person?

*

Working through all these questions has been vital for how I now understand myself as a disabled person, and the disabled life that I live. I'm not sure what my teenage self would make of that life, of the disabled world I'm part of. I live outside the city now, in a small town. I use a walking stick and can't walk far. My skin is still red, sore, flaky and bleeding, and my joints are crumbling and so, so sore.

But I sit much easier with all of this. I've got to an equilibrium of sorts, where I have enough treatment to smooth the harsher edges of my impairments, and the rest I just leave and the world can deal with it. I drop skin flakes on the train and at work and don't feel ashamed or obliged to apologise. I expect accessibility, and the necessary adjustments to do my job, and I have the help I need to keep me living at home.

I don't often have any of those old, terrible feelings about being a burden, or broken, or that my disease makes me less than non-disabled people. I find the pain tough going, though, and occasionally I'll even tell people that.

I have a community of disabled people that I belong to, and dear friends who I share this disabled life with. We connect from around the country and across the world, uniting in the effort to make the world less hostile to us. I value this more than I can say.

I wish I could tell that isolated, terrified teen – sitting on the hospital fire escape, sobbing and feeling so alone – that one day she won't feel that way. She will find a place in the world where every part of her belongs, and where there is no need to hide. And she can do this while still being sick, still being sore and still looking different.

Selected Epistles

Olivia Muscat

Dear PE teachers,

I know physical activity is important. But you didn't need to try to convince me I was good at athletics. I was never going to believe you. I knew coming second out of two isn't actually a mark of talent. It just made me feel like shit. I like to win because of effort and skill, not because I'm the only competitor. And also, I really, really, *really* hate shot-put.

Sincerely yours,

The least enthusiastic potential shot-put champion that ever attended an athletics carnival,

Olivia

*

Dear creepy man on the train platform (or on the train, bus, tram, or in the shop, or wherever),

It is no concern of yours how I get dressed in the morning, how I look after myself or if I have a boyfriend. Please take the hint when I move away from you, and don't follow me to ask if I live on my own. I don't have to answer your creepy questions and I am under absolutely no obligation to be polite to you. Kindly get lost.

Regards,

You don't need to know my name, so stop asking

Dear person at Flinders Street Station,

I don't know what part of me walking straight towards the escalators makes you believe I don't know that the escalators are ahead of me. Don't grab my arm and try to drag me on. It's dangerous and pretty fucking rude.

Yours truly,

Just trying to get where I need to go

*

Dear random street people,

No, I am not the person you know who looks nothing like me but also happens to use a cane or have a guide dog. And no, I don't know them … probably.

Best wishes,

Olivia. Not Ashleigh or Claire or Christine or Tess or Michaela or Jordie or Cassie or Emma-Mae

*

Dear Drama teacher,

It was astonishingly hurtful when you would not let me audition to be a member of the chorus in the Year 8 school production – when you offhandedly told me you hoped I wouldn't come to the audition. I'm not sure if you realised how soul-crushing that was. Well, let me tell you: it was one of the most upsetting things that happened to me in a really terrible year.

Thank you for seeing the error of your ways (once my parents pointed it out to you, mind) and for becoming more open to creativity and improvisation, and for going on to cast me in several major roles in musicals and plays that involved me dancing and running and throwing myself across a stage. You turned out to be one of my favourite people and a truly amazing teacher and director.

Playing Ida, Malvolio and Nancy was some of the most fun I have ever had. And when people came up to me afterwards and told me that they didn't realise I was blind, it was a testament to both of us. There were some hairy moments, but that never stopped us from giving anything a go. I'm a better performer and person because of you and what you encouraged me to achieve.

In Year 12, you completely made up for that first, heartbreaking non-audition by informing me that with my acting and singing abilities, there was no other choice for the role of Nancy in *Oliver!* You just casually said it in the corridor one day and it made everything worth it. So many people would have chosen the next best actor and singer because it would have just been easier with a sighted person. You didn't, and if I do say so myself, I crushed it. We crushed it!

With gratitude and appreciation,

Olivia

*

Dear Jemima,

For so long I was reluctant to take the plunge and get a guide dog, but you are one of the best things that has ever happened to me. I'm no longer fearful of travelling independently to places I've never been before because you're crazily good at your job. And though I might occasionally get us a bit lost, I know you'll stick by my side and keep me safe. You have an uncanny ability to know exactly what I need you to find before I've even given you a command, which is a bit spooky but often comes in handy.

We've conquered so much of Melbourne, and even cities we don't live in, together. And although you do shed that blonde hair of yours everywhere and you have some pretty gross habits – and I really hate talking to random strangers about dogs – you've changed my life and expanded my world. You are 100 per cent worth any compromise.

I will love you always, my girl,

Olivia (that's me, Ma)

Dear fellow blind person,

Just because we're both blind doesn't mean we will be friends.

If we have things in common, and get on, and enjoy each other's company, we can absolutely be friends. I look forward to it. But our mutual blindness doesn't equal automatic best friendship. I will ignore that Facebook friend request, no matter how many mutual friends we have, until we have actually met in person, or at least had a conversation, because that's my policy, and being a fellow blindy doesn't exempt you from that. It's not a secret society.

'Till we meet,

Olivia

*

Dear every visiting teacher I ever had,

Thank you for insisting that I learn braille even though I still had enough vision to read print. Although I don't use it all the time, it comes in useful pretty often. It's a great skill to have, despite all the fancy tech that exists these days.

I apologise for being so resistant at times, and I know I'd probably be a faster braille reader now if I'd worked harder at it then. It's in my nature to be stubborn, and I couldn't predict the future. I didn't want to imagine that my vision would go and I'd need to rely on braille; I was a kid and that thought was scary. But here we are, and I'm grateful for your perseverance.

Apologies and thanks,

Olivia

*

Dear kids at school,

Primary school, high school – it doesn't matter. I know there were those of you who were completely pleasant to my face but laughed or scoffed behind my back. I don't know if you thought I couldn't tell or that I was too brainless or naive to realise, or too scared to confront you about it. But honestly, I just didn't care. It's no concern of mine if you think being blind made me somehow worthy of mockery. And guess what, I probably mocked you right back. I didn't give a shit about your approval anyway.

Bye!

*

Dear well-meaning people,

Chances are, unless I've asked you outright, I don't want, need or appreciate your advice.

Thanks in advance,

P.S. Yes. I know scientists are working on bionic eyes.

*

Dear even more random street people,

Don't touch me without my permission. Don't grab my cane. Don't pat my dog. And definitely don't argue with me if you do pat my dog and I ask you politely not to. If you say something about my cute puppy and I don't respond, don't get shitty. I've probably had a long day. If you offer me a seat on public transport and I say thanks but no thanks, don't call me an ungrateful bitch. I have my reasons. If I walk onto crowded public transport and ask whether there's a seat close by, don't just ignore me until I give up and go stand somewhere, desperately trying to both keep my balance and keep my dog from getting trampled.

Just because I don't see you, it doesn't mean I don't know you're there. When you advance on me in some misguided attempt to tie my shoelace and I pull away and tell you I've got it, don't act like I've done something wrong. *You've* invaded my personal space and made assumptions about me. I'm not in the wrong here.

Cheers,

Member of the public who deserves just as much respect as you do

Dear teachers, of music and other subjects,

I appreciate all the time and effort and energy you put into making me a good musician. I really do. It seemed like the easiest road, didn't it? I was a talented singer, and music is one of those pre-tread, ready-to-follow blind paths that appear to have the fewest hurdles. But this unwavering assumption that music was my future led me to think it was my only option, especially after I went totally blind. I cut off many other possible pathways because everyone told me music was my future. And when I got to university and found out that studying music made me want to curl up in a ball and never do anything again, I had the most enormous crisis of confidence imaginable. Every tutorial, every lecture, every singing lesson filled me with dread. I felt constantly on the verge of throwing up. And of course I pretended everything was fine.

Everyone's expectations that I would become a musician weighed heavily on me, and it was a huge struggle to wriggle my way out from underneath them. It almost completely crushed my spirit.

So, while you meant well, I wish you hadn't implied music was my only option. Because it wasn't. You took something I loved and twisted it into something compulsory, something that caused me terrible pain and fear. And only after that horrible year did I realise I had other talents, other interests, other pathways, and I was able to forge a new, more fulfilling future for myself.

Yours, in relief and regret,

Olivia

*

Dear word police,

I don't know how many times I have to tell you that it's okay to refer to me as totally blind. That's what I am. I'm not 'vision impaired'; my vision is non-existent. I'm not 'partially sighted'; there's no partial about it. I have no sight. It's gone, dead, caput.

There's no need to get flustered when I say 'totally blind'. That's how I refer to myself, because it leaves no room for interpretation. It's final. Totally blind means I can't see anything. *Because I really can't see anything* and it's kind of important for people who I interact with to know that. It's a fact, like saying I have brown hair, or size seven feet, or naturally great eyebrows. I'm not offended by it, so I don't see why you should be either.

Kind regards,

Totally blind Olivia – yes, totally

*

Dear people who assume that because my eyes don't work my mind doesn't either,

Fuck. You.

Best wishes,

None of your damn business

*

Dear Mum,

I don't think I will ever know all the things you did for me. All the battles you fought when I was too small, too scared or too sad to fight them myself. All the opportunities you made sure I was able to take advantage of. All the times people tried to knock me down and keep me out: dance lessons, Japanese classes, 'dangerous' excursions, school productions. The government told you I couldn't stay at my school if I wanted support after I lost my remaining sight. You went in there and gave them absolute hell until I got what you believed I deserved. You always did it with such poise and professionalism, and with your signature brand of take-no-bullshit attitude.

Watching you do all that on my behalf set me up to become someone who isn't afraid to demand what she deserves. To call out injustice where she sees it. And to take absolutely zero bullshit. Of all the many gifts you gave me, this one might be the best.

You put fire and steel into my head and heart when I needed to take charge of my life and stand up for myself. But you also knew when I just needed you to wrap me up in a hug and not let go.

Because of everything you did for me while you were here, I am able to do it on my own now that you're gone. I know you're cheering me on inside my heart, and that means everything to me.

I never sit around and wish I wasn't blind. It isn't a good use of my time. And most of the time I hardly even notice that I'm down 20 per cent of my five senses. Sometimes I genuinely have to remind myself that other people get most of their information visually.

But those weeks spent sitting beside you in that hospital bed, when we knew you were dying, and you could barely bring yourself to speak. When we couldn't have our passionate, ridiculous, funny conversations, or arguments, depending on the day. Then. Then, I would've given anything to see you for just five minutes. To look into your eyes and memorise every detail of your beautiful, precious, fierce face. The face that raised me, the body that held me, that was about to be wrenched from me forever.

We will never sit down and discuss all the battles you fought for me, all the times you felt that the system was beyond broken but you kept fighting anyway, all the times you came up against sheer ignorance and prejudice but you didn't back down because you loved me and believed I had something to offer the world.

I will never hear those stories from you. Yet somehow, I don't need to hear them, because they are in my blood. They live with your unending spirit inside my soul. They course through my body and spill out into every decision I make – and will continue to make.

I love, honour and treasure you with everything I have.

Forever yours,

Your first daughter,

Olivia

To Lake Nash and Back

Dion Beasley and Johanna Bell

This is an edited extract from the illustrated memoir *Cheeky Dogs: To Lake Nash and Back* by Dion Beasley and Johanna Bell (Allen & Unwin, 2019).

Alice Springs. 1991.
My mum came in on the back road from Lake Nash.
Rough, rough, bumpy, bumpy.
Me in her belly.

After I was born, she took the same road back.
Straight past Utopia, all the way to Lake Nash.
We stayed there for a bit.

Everywhere the earth was red. Plenty, plenty dogs.

All of us in a brown house and a blue house too.
All of us together – Mum, Dad, me and my sister
standing in the doorway with her thumbs sticking up.
Tall trees out the back.
Two small and two big beautiful trees.
Cooking outside.
Eating damper with strawberry jam.
Dad turning kangaroo in the coals.
How did he catch that kangaroo?
Gun? No. Spear? No.

A brown dog in the grass
chasing, chasing.
Teeth in the meat
straight on the fire.

My legs worked back then.
Walking walking everywhere.
Strong feet. No shoes.

My grandmother tells a story about when I was small, four,
maybe five.
My dad gone somewhere and me
looking, looking.
Out of the house, down the road
walking, walking.
Hot sun, dry mouth
tired, tired.
They found me where the bullocky drink
a long, long way from home.

I'm three, maybe four.
I walk to the shop to buy flour.
Three big angry dogs are following me.
Hair up. Sharp teeth.
I am screaming, scared.
Looking, looking
for somewhere to hide.
The sign outside the shop says
No dogs allowed!

*

My mum is a Morton and my dad is a Beasley
but now I live with the Boulters – Tony and Joie.
Our house is on Fazaldeen Road.
Drive south. Turn right. Go straight.
If you get to the dump you've gone too far.

*

At Lake Nash there are two rivers.
Big ones – Rankin and Georgina.
Lots of small ones too like snakes running into the lake.

When I was little, four maybe five, it rained and rained
and it didn't stop.
The rivers grew big. The snakes disappeared.
The sky was on the ground, clouds in the lake.
The water coming up, up, up.
My dad was there. He picked me up.
Strong arms
and carried me across.

*

We got stuck in a river once, me, Tony and Joie.
Tony was driving the big white car.
Don't cross the river, Joie said.
But Tony had a different idea.
Too deep! Too deep!
Car lifting up, spinning around.
Water coming in up to our feet
our legs, our waists!
Me floating, floating.
Joie swimming out, holding onto the bull bar.
Seatbelt off, Joie pulling me out.
Water, water everywhere. Mud on my feet.
We were very lucky, Joie said.
Tony wasn't. He lost his thong.

We fight sometimes, Tony and me.
I like playing tricks that make him cross.
When he's asleep I wheel into his room
quiet, quiet
and switch on all the lights!
Tony makes big eyes. He has to get out of bed.
Me gone by then, laughing, laughing.

I play other tricks too.
I turn my fingers into dogs at the dinner table.
Backwards and forwards they run
knocking over plates and spilling the ginger beer.
Burp!
Don't you be doing that, Tony says.

I hide Tony's favourite saltshaker and the eye drops he got from the doctor.
Sometimes I pull the toilet roll off and turn it into a road.
All the way to Lake Nash.
Rough, rough, bumpy, bumpy.
Seven hours from here, it takes
and you can only go after the big rains stop.

One day, I'm going back to Lake Nash with Angela and Damilia.
Her eyes don't work and I can't hear.
We're a funny bunch, Joie says.
I want to take my scooter but I need a special trailer for that.
Tony will make me one he says.
And Angela will pull it over the bumps.
Rough, rough, bumpy, bumpy
all the way back to my family
in Lake Nash.

*

I talk with my hands
signing, signing.
Wendy taught me first
and Anna and my friend Kristie
and Dan the policeman too.
If we can't find a sign, we just make it up.
Dog two pats on the leg
Fox sign for F + sign for snout
Wolf sign for W + sign for snout
Hyena sign for H + sign for snout
African hunting dog sign for wild + sign for dog

*

Every year the show comes to Tennant Creek.
Big rides going dizzy fast.
Flipping, dipping, whizzing past.
Dizzy chairs. Motorbikes.
Sideways shaker. Cage of Death.
BOYS WITH LEGS THAT DON'T WORK AREN'T ALLOWED.
That's what the man who sells the tickets says.
I go on the dodgems instead.
Cars bouncing this way and that.
Zipping, racing, bumping, biting.
Just like the dogs at Mulga Camp.
Fighting, fighting, always fighting.
No crashing allowed! says Joie.
But I look the other way so I can't see her hands.
Bang, bang, crash, crash.
My hat flies off.
I watch it get squashed
and I smile.

*

I was scared
when I was small, four, maybe five.
Walking to the shop.
Three angry grey dogs.
Hair up. Sharp teeth.
Me on the ground.
Their teeth in my skin.
A man was there, picking me up.
What would have happened if he was not?

*

This year, I'll be going back.
Rough, rough, bumpy, bumpy.
All the way to Lake Nash.

Past the place with no trees. Completely flat.
Past the little rivers like snakes sliding into the lake.
More than seven hours on a bumpy road
dust flying out the back.

To the brown house where we used to live.
Mum, Dad, my sister and me.
Making damper, cooking kangaroo.
Swimming down near the bridge with the kids.
Splashing. Laughing. Slapping the water.

Watching the dogs.
Black dogs brown dogs white dogs red.
Mothers, brothers, father dogs.
One eye open. One ear up.
Always only half asleep.

Riding on my scooter to the shop for a drink.
Cold one – orange, lemon, red.
The dogs will be there.
Big ones with sharp teeth.
Hair up, ready to fight.
I remember teeth in my skin.
I feel the scar on my stomach, long and thin.

No! Not this time!
I'm big now and strong.
They can't get me.

I buy my fizzy orange drink.
Stop and wait.

Family in the shade, dogs at my feet.
Opening it. Cold can on my lips.
Down, down, down it goes.
Eyes closed, waiting for the air rushing up.
Rumbling, rumbling, stomach then throat.
Burp!

Everybody looks.
Mothers. Fathers. Brothers. Cousins.
Even the dogs.
Everybody.
Laughing, laughing.
It feels good to be home again
with family in Lake Nash.

The Eleventh House

Sam Drummond

Mum came up to us, holding a limp figure.

'She's still breathing,' she said.

The mountain looked down at us with pity. The surrounding orchard gathered around to watch the drama. House Eleven had known all along that trouble was coming.

She was alive but motionless. Blood trickled out of her nose.

Tears streamed down my face. I thought back to everything that had led to where we were.

Surgery One

A picture can tell a thousand lies. My inaugural school photo shows a couple dozen middle-class white kids surrounded by suburban bush, smiling with the innocence that comes with embarking on a journey of every opportunity. Front and centre is a beaming kid. The only perceivable difference between him and the others is that he is a bit smaller and sitting in a wheelchair.

'Keep smiling, Sam,' people would say. So I did, hiding my confusion at the transformation that had just occurred.

I don't remember my parents' initial worry and confusion at my diagnosis.

I don't remember the arguments they had about whether there was something wrong with me.

I don't even really remember what life was like before they got divorced, except for the birth of my brother.

All I remember is wanting to chase a ball around. Like a neurotic dog who drops a slimy tennis ball at your feet and then, on being ignored, picks it up and puts it slightly closer to your feet, I was obsessed with anything vaguely spherical.

By the time the letter from the Royal Children's Hospital arrived, Mum, my younger brother and I had moved into House Four – a two-bedroom unit on a main road, built from dark-brown brick that looked as if it could have been cardboard. For all I know, it was.

The letter confirmed a date for surgery to both legs. While there was no question in my newly separated parents' minds about whether to go ahead, there was also no explanation of what was going to happen in a way that a five-year-old could understand. At least, not that I can remember.

Even now, when I look through photos with Mum from before Surgery One, we see different images. Mum sees my bowed legs. I see my untouched innocence.

In the slideshow of my memories, that carefree kid woke from a general anaesthetic, legs encased in plaster, at the same time that he began to wake from his childhood.

I screamed from unimaginable pain. Our family quickly discovered that if you want your own room in the public system, the best way is to break decibel records. The doctors said everything was fine. But the screaming didn't stop.

It didn't stop for food or drink. It didn't stop for well wishes from family – sympathetic but ultimately pointless phrases like 'You're being so brave' and 'We wish we could go through the pain instead of you'. It didn't even stop for a celebrity visit from *Full House*'s John Stamos, who was in town for the Logies and pulled an I'll-just-sign-this-photo-and-move-on manoeuvre on me.

It wasn't until my feet went purple that the doctors started taking notice of their patient. The plaster was cutting off my circulation. They wheeled me straight back into surgery for something that should have been done right the first time.

The second round of plaster came off after six weeks. Recovery consisted of sitting in the lounge room of House Four and kicking a balloon over and over again.

I found solace in handling our pet budgerigar, Budge. We had found Budge strolling along our driveway in House Three. I would later walk out the back of House Eight to find Budge in his cage with his head mysteriously severed from his body. He wasn't a real pet like the other families had. For now, though, he was my friend. Animal friends didn't make assumptions or judgements.

I returned to school with a brave face.

'You've been through all this and you're still smiling,' the adults said. 'Keep smiling, Sam.'

So I did. I learnt how to smile like a five-year-old. But my eyes grew the weariness of someone who knew pain earlier than they should have.

Surgery Two

One theory of why time speeds up as we age is that our perception changes in proportion to the time we have already spent alive. So four years for a ten-year-old is the equivalent of twenty years for a fifty-year-old.

Any way you look at it, a lot happened over the next four years.

After Husband Two and Divorce Two, we made it to House Seven. House Seven was showing signs of years of neglect. The weatherboards had greyed from exposure to endless peak-hour traffic jams out front. The willow tree in the backyard was felled after its roots began to strangle the sewerage pipes. The home was held together by rotting wooden stumps, Centrelink, child support payments and Mum's five casual jobs.

The back room began to smell after I started making a bit of pocket money from breeding mice and selling them to the local pet store. The cost of the upkeep was probably more than the pittance I received for the litters, but Mum didn't let on. I stopped the business after I learnt that my tiny friends weren't being sold as pets but dropped into heated glass tanks as food for snakes.

House Seven had the advantage of being over the road from school. It was just on the wrong side of the road for our unconventional family to be fully accepted into the established classes.

The houses on the right side of the road didn't run out of petrol on the hill down to the petrol station. The houses on the right side of the road could leave their doors open without fear of burglary, even though their belongings were worth much more. Our thieves were fools. The houses on the right side of the road didn't have to put up with surgery.

I can't remember walking to school on weekdays, but I clearly recall the click of plastic studs as I ambled down to the school oval on Saturday mornings, dressed as a miniature James Hird, for Auskick.

Doctors had always recommended non–weight bearing exercise. They would suggest swimming and cycling. Every time. Swimming and cycling. Swimming came naturally but required regular access to a pool. Putting me on a bike was a bit like trying to get a penguin to fly. I dreaded the school's annual bike ed day like most kids dread the dental van.

Later in life, when I had finally found a bicycle that vaguely fit my design, I would triumphantly announce to a doctor that the torn muscles in my knee and hips were from the very non–weight bearing exercise of riding a bike.

But for now, I was set on ball sports. Aussie rules, in particular. I might have only got a kick here, a handball there, but I was doing what I loved.

At the time, a lot of change was happening in the Victorian school system. While nearby schools were closing because of Kennett's cutbacks, my school was reaping the benefits. Its population boomed with students from increasingly diverse backgrounds, and the extra funding brought the best teachers and facilities from around the leafy suburbs.

We got the news that Surgery Two was needed just after Mr Howard started the stint of conservatism that would shape the progressivism of my generation.

To distract me from what was to come, Dad used his share of the school holidays to drive my brother and me to the Red Centre in an old mustard Ford Falcon. Our young minds were aware of the cultural contrast, as people who had been there for millennia waved at us from shopping centres in Alice that had only just popped up.

A hundred kilometres from Uluru, Dad pointed to a rising red mound in the distance. Astonished that we could see the famous landmark from such a long way away, we pulled over to take pictures with our disposable Kodak.

Dad started talking to a fellow traveller.

'You know, some of the international tourists think this is Uluru itself,' said the traveller. 'Unbelievable.'

Dad nodded his head in agreement. 'Unbelievable,' he repeated while sidling over to us.

'Come on, kids,' he said out of the side of his mouth. 'Let's get going.'

Once we got to the real thing, we could not escape the feeling that we were simply an inconsequential blip in the Earth's long story.

Despite this insight, it still seemed like the years since Surgery One should have been long enough for doctors to figure out a few things. It helped that only one leg needed to be operated on this time. Also, that no plaster would be required, meaning there would be no chance of the circulation being cut off.

As I left for the hospital, I was confident about the next steps. I had endured countless appointments being poked and prodded by dozens of doctors and medical students. They seemed excited by the opportunity I presented, using words like 'abnormality' and 'mutation'. I knew it wasn't like *X-Men* or *Teenage Mutant Ninja Turtles*, but the message got through: my body needed fixing, and I was ready.

There is something about doctors and normality. Doctors are trained to identify abnormality and to problem-solve until it vaguely resembles their understanding of its reverse. It is little wonder that parents who have always been surrounded by depictions of what is normal are seduced by the idea of fixing abnormality. It is no surprise that children who are taught about the doctrine of abnormality want to satisfy their adults by getting rid of it.

From the very first breath, one might enquire 'Is the baby healthy?'

'Ten fingers, ten toes,' might come the answer.

Why, though, but for normality?

Several hours after arriving at the hospital with the goal of resembling normality, I woke with a medieval torture device on my left leg. Seven metal pins held the broken limb together.

Over the months to come, our family woke from any delusions that the normal world was designed for us.

For Mum, life's difficulty level was raised, as if we were playing the outdated version of *Donkey Kong* I had been given as a get-well present. Adding full-time carer to full-time worker and full-time parent needed a circuit breaker.

That circuit breaker came with a knock from a door-to-door salesman, who gave us the cursed gift of pay TV. The first month of the six-month subscription was free, but the screen addiction affected our lives for the next decade.

The TV became our entertainment, our educator and parent. The ability to quote every episode of *The Simpsons*' golden era is a given for many millennials. But knowledge of cartoons that have ended up in animation graveyards, such as *Wacky Races* or *Dastardly and Muttley*, has limited use outside the occasional trivia night.

We would also flick on the news and see Pauline Hanson blaming our national predicaments on my newly arrived schoolmates and the nice locals from our Centralian adventure. But even a ten-year-old could see through that, and we would quickly change the channel back to the Cartoon Network.

Minimal exercise and poor diet left me unhealthy and laid the groundwork for my brother's childhood of obesity.

One night, as Mum lifted me from my chair to the couch, she heard the crack in her back that would put her on the Disability Support Pension fifteen years later. Disadvantage continues and compounds for years and generations.

The entry of the pins into the skin needed constant cleaning. My blanket became soaked with a deathly mixture of blood, Betadine and pus. The wounds became infected.

Once, I screamed at the world, 'Why me?', tears soaking my pillow.

The world did not answer.

At the age of ten, that would be the last time I let myself cry from physical pain.

Surgery Three

Mum found a path to escape Husband Two by following the father she had spent twenty years also escaping, who in turn had spent his adult life escaping the horrors of World War II. We moved to the country – our soundtrack 'Peaches' by The Presidents of the United States of America. We didn't see any peaches, though, just apples and eucalypts starting to feel the effects of the Millennium Drought.

Mum wanted a slower lifestyle and that is what we got.

We were confronted by a choice of schools: the sentimentality provoked by the gold rush–era school buildings had protected them from being consolidated like their city siblings. While teachers' strikes had been a rarity in the city, they were common in the regions.

I survived the change of pace at school by joining a Grade 5/6 composite class and finishing the more senior work a year early.

My final year of primary school was defined by strikes, coursework I had already completed, and constant jibes, comments and laughter about my disability from younger students who had never seen anything like me outside fairytale portrayals.

I entered the maturity of high school with a sigh of relief.

Husband Two returned, Houses Eight, Nine and Ten went by, Husband Two left again.

House Eleven was meant to be another new leaf for our compact family. The yellowed weatherboard farmhouse was surrounded by apple orchards on three sides and a road too close for comfort in such a rural setting. This all stood at the foot of a mountain, whose face was contorted with the colonial tension between ancient eucalypts and the invading, enchanting oak forest. Mum's love of mysticism intensified – perhaps she was trying to find a permanent escape route. Candles and oils filled the rooms. There was a natural remedy for everything. One day, a man with a sword came around, claiming he was Arthur reincarnated and his artefact was Excalibur itself. My brother and I simply shrugged.

House Eleven left no doubt about our isolation, with the road our only connection to civilisation.

Still, Mum fought hard for us to stay connected, even convincing the school bus company to move the designated stop to our driveway. It saved me the walk but forced Jane from down the road to walk an extra 200 metres.

By House Eleven, a fourth member of our family had arrived: Maggie.

There is every chance Maggie had been planned for a while. For us kids, though, her entry into our lives seemed magical.

A labrador–cocker spaniel, she had a dopey smile, long black hair with a white front and a single white paw. She did not judge any scale of normality. She was the real pet I had longed for.

But a competition began between brothers to be Maggie's favourite. Aged nine and thirteen, the four-year gap between us had never felt so wide. The fighting intensified. A younger brother was a convenient scapegoat. I blamed him for everything, even for life itself. Maggie became the rope in our tug of war.

He would feed her a fish finger from his dinner plate.

I would sneak her into my bedroom and hide her under my doona on the bitter winter nights.

He would walk her through the orchards.

I would throw a ball for her to fetch until after dark.

He would call her for pats. I would call her for more pats.

Back and forth it went.

A truce was called the day that dreaded letter with 'RCH' printed in the corner came in the mail. A date had been set for the next surgery.

Health care for a disabled kid in the country adds another level of disruption. Just a simple appointment requires a full day off for both child and parent. The cost of travel skyrockets. Operations require complex logistics to find accommodation for parents as well as finding minders for siblings.

The entourage of medical staff assured me they had some ideas to make the process easier, but it was little comfort.

My trepidation was profound, and I was surprised to wake from Surgery Three without any external apparatus holding my leg together – just a large chunk of metal inserted along my thigh bone.

I was given the autonomy of a button to release morphine. After I refused to press the button enough for their liking, the doctors took that option away and prescribed regular doses.

I returned to House Eleven to find blossoms on the apple trees.

On the Saturday after returning, I sat in the sun in my wheelchair as two contests with seemingly foregone conclusions took place: the Victorian state election and the AFL first preliminary final between Essendon and Carlton.

I was far more invested in the latter.

As the day progressed and inevitability was replaced by incredulity, commentators were asking two questions: why had no one seen the Kennett backlash that was coming from the bush, and why, oh why, did Dean Wallis try to take on Fraser Brown in the dying seconds?

The Bombers lost by one point. Steve Bracks's Labor would eventually form government by one seat.

I listened on the wireless as Carlton's Justin Murphy marked and the final siren sounded. I stared at the foot of my wheelchair with a tear in my eye.

Watching me inquisitively was the black-and-white furball of Maggie.

'What are we going to do?' I asked, only half rhetorically.

She turned to look down the path that led past the verandah, then back at me.

I released the chair's brake and put the radio on a nearby table. She got up, wagging her tail expectantly. She looked again down the path.

I pushed along from the side door, rolled down the path, followed the verandah, did a 180-degree turn at the water tank, and came back around the verandah to the side door.

Maggie followed the whole way, barking with the pure joy of someone dancing with nobody watching.

And so began our races.

Out the side door, down the path, follow the verandah, 180 at the water tank, back around the verandah, touch the side door, with Maggie going paw-to-wheel with the chair.

I started timing it. 1 minute, 20 seconds. 1 minute, 10 seconds. 1 minute, 5 seconds. I broke the minute with a 58-second run. Then down to 53 seconds – world records falling thick and fast.

Maggie and I would get our exercise every day I was at home in the wheelchair. At the end of each session, she would lap up some water, go inside and sit at the foot of my chair for the rest of the night. I would sit smiling to myself. It wasn't the fresh air, or the exercise, or the quicker recovery, although those were probably factors. But I had won the battle – I was Maggie's favourite.

*

Once my wounds had healed and I was out of the wheelchair, we were posed with a quandary.

'Maggie's looking a bit pudgy,' said Mum, pointing out what we had all been thinking. She turned to my brother. 'Can you take her out on your bike for some exercise?'

I'll give my brother this: he tried. But as soon as he started pedaling, his bike started moving, Maggie would bark and chase the wheels to the point of forcing him to fall.

She had developed a love of running alongside the wheelchair, but when we swapped four wheels for two, she went into attack mode. Her hatred of bikes was Orwellian: four wheels good, two wheels bad.

Eventually, my brother reluctantly got off his bike and walked her through the orchard.

*

Human memory is a remarkable thing.

My brother and I had not talked about that morning in detail for two decades. It turns out we remember each moment with parallel precision.

Each moment, that is, except for how it begins.

In my mind, we are standing out the front of our house, waiting for the bus with Jane from down the road. A cyclist rides by. Maggie takes chase. She starts to return with a look of triumph.

In my brother's mind, we are also standing out the front of our house, waiting for the bus with Jane from down the road. One of us throws a tennis ball over the road. Maggie takes chase. She picks it up and starts to return with a look of triumph.

From there the memories align.

A tiny car comes speeding around the corner.

We yell at Maggie, begging her to stop.

She is completely unaware of anything but her success. Time, for a fleeting moment, stands still.

Time resumes as the car hits her at full speed.

I stand frozen as Mum runs out on the road. The car pulls up 50 metres downwind. A woman gets out and walks towards us.

'I'm sorry,' she says. 'I have to get to work.'

The woman gets back into her car and speeds off.

Mum comes up to us, holding a limp figure.

'She's still breathing,' she says.

The mountain looks down at us with pity. The surrounding orchard gathers around to watch the drama. House Eleven had known all along that trouble was coming

Maggie is alive but motionless. Blood trickles out of her nose.

Tears stream down my face. I think back to everything that has led to where we are.

It is the smell that sticks with you the most. The smell of fear. The smell of trauma. The smell of impending death.

We put her on a tarpaulin in the car boot and race into town to the vet.

As we lie her down on the surgery table, the vet gives us the news we have been dreading: there is no saving her. She mentions the price of euthanising her. It is more than Mum has in the bank.

Mum looks into Maggie's eyes. She looks back. And, as if giving one final gift, she takes a drawn-out final breath.

The vet puts her stethoscope to Maggie's heart. 'She's gone,' she confirms.

But then, as if on a hunch, she places the stethoscope on Maggie's stomach. She looks up with astonishment. 'Did you know she's pregnant?'

We stare at each other, not knowing what to say.

She feels the belly. 'There are four. They're very young.'

'Can we save them?' Mum asks.

'We could operate,' says the vet, 'but they won't survive.'

Mum looks at us. We shake our heads.

'No,' Mum says. 'Let them go.'

A tear rolls down my cheek.

It is the final tear of my teenage years.

Wired for Sound

Fiona Murphy

'These glasses will help you hear,' the audiologist says as he hands me a set of thick black frames. The year is 1997, and everyone – including Mel B of The Spice Girls – is wearing glasses with thin wire frames.

The audiologist notices me frowning. 'I know that the glasses seem a bit big, but the frames need to be thick enough to house all the wires that will transmit sound,' he explains.

Despite their bulk, I hold the glasses gingerly, afraid that I will drop them or accidentally press one of the buttons. There are hearing aids built into each arm and a dial to modulate volume.

'Go on, put them on. I'm sure you'll look fine,' Mum says, nudging me gently.

I tuck my hair out of the way and slide them on. The lenses are plain plastic, so the room doesn't shift and blur like it does when I try on my friend Jennifer's glasses. Instead they just sit heavily on the bridge of my nose.

'Now, make sure that the tube is inside your ear,' instructs the audiologist.

I push the plastic tube in tight. It feels like an earplug. I can hear crackling in my right ear, like a poorly tuned transistor radio. It takes me a moment to realise that it is my hair brushing over the microphone.

'How does it sound?' Mum asks. Her voice is full and bright.

I turn towards her in surprise. 'Your voice is so loud.'

'I bet you can't wait to go to school,' the audiologist says.

*

I spend the weekend standing in front of the bathroom mirror. My new glasses overwhelm my eight-year-old face. They make me look serious, like an accountant or a bureaucrat. I flash my teeth in the mirror again and again, trying to get used to the feeling of my cheeks pushing my glasses upwards when I smile.

*

Despite the mild weather, my lenses keep fogging up. My face feels hot and sweaty. I take my glasses off and wipe them clean on the corner of my school shirt.

'Careful, you might scratch them,' Mum says, glancing from the road to me. 'Use that black cloth from your glasses case.'

I polish the lenses with the soft cloth. My hands are shaking. Most of my classmates don't know that I'm deaf. Today, my deafness will become visible.

Three years earlier, my Grade 1 teacher advised Mum that I should be tested to see if I have a learning disorder, as I could not spell even the most basic words. It was then Mum realised that I'd memorised all the picture books at home, and had been dutifully parroting them to her whenever she asked me to read. After a series of tests, I was diagnosed as profoundly deaf in my left ear.

'Most deaf children have difficulty learning to read,' explained the doctor to Mum and me. 'All the sounds get muddled up.'

'So, what can we do?' asked Mum. 'Does she need hearing aids?'

'No, there aren't any hearing aids powerful enough for her left ear. Fiona will just have to figure out how to match letters with their sounds,' said the doctor with a shrug.

So Mum sat with me each night, and together we worked through the alphabet by tapping, clicking and clapping the sound of each letter. Eventually we moved on to combinations of letters. She made flashcards of phonics, visual representations of sound, which we would practise for hours. And still, three years on, I am at the bottom of my class.

This year, when I started Grade 4, the school cautioned Mum that I would need to make big improvements to stay in the mainstream class. The thought of being in a Special Ed class, without any friends, is terrifying. A few weeks ago, Mum had a chance encounter with an old gentleman who was wearing hearing glasses.

She went through the Yellow Pages and found an audiologist in Sydney who makes them. The audiologist explained that the glasses wouldn't allow me to hear anything with my left ear, but they would transport sounds from the left side of my body to my right ear.

I keep polishing my glasses, thinking about the school day ahead. Perhaps nobody will notice the buttons and batteries? And if they do, maybe I could tell them that spies like James Bond wear these glasses? As we near the school, I slide them on and take a deep breath. I squeeze my hands to stop them from shaking.

'Are they switched on?' Mum asks once she's parked.

'Yup.' My voice comes out in a squeak. I reluctantly open the car door and make my way towards the school gate.

*

'They look huge.'

A classmate is pointing at my glasses.

I quickly look down at my desk and pretend to organise my pencil case.

'Seats, everyone. Pens and paper out, it's test time.' Ms Hull raps on her desk.

Everyone dives into their seats. My glasses amplify the rustling of copybooks and the unzipping of pencil cases. I want to turn down the volume, but I don't want any of my classmates to see the hearing aids.

'Everyone ready?' asks Ms Hull.

Ms Hull starts each day with a spelling test. In the school holidays she travels to Asia and Africa, climbs mountains and hikes through dense rainforest. I wish she would tell us those stories instead of testing our spelling.

'Okay, the first word is "fridge",' Ms Hull announces. She is exceptionally tall and straight-spined, and her voice normally wafts high above my head. Today, it sounds loud and clear in my right ear. My chest expands with hope – maybe these glasses will make me as quick and smart as everyone else.

For the next ten minutes, my head bobs up and down as Ms Hull reads out the list of words. I look closely at her face as she says each word, hoping that the way she is moving her mouth will give me some hint about what letters to write down. I silently mouth the word, trying to break it up into syllables before gluing it back together.

'Alright, pencils down,' says Ms Hull.

Despite trying hard, my copybook is still mostly blank. My few attempts are written in tight, nervous script. I sink down in my chair; the glasses haven't magically helped me to spell.

*

By the end of the school day my ears ache, not from the sounds travelling through the plastic frames, but from the weight of the glasses. The tops of my ears have turned red and tender.

*

Each day continues much the same. Everyone bows their heads as Ms Hull reads out lists of words and we attempt to spell them; I bob my head, trying to make out the sounds from her lips. My pencil continues to shake with self-doubt as I muddle through each word.

After each test, Ms Hull gets us to swap our copybooks with a partner. Correcting each other's work, she tells us, will help us become better spellers. I always push my copybook towards my neighbour with eyes downcast.

Ms Hull writes out the words on the blackboard. During the solemn silence, as we check if our classmates are correct or not, my shame feels heavy and immense.

*

I'm responsible for maintaining my glasses. It requires a steady pincer grip to slot the small, round batteries into the back of each arm. The plastic tube that sits in my right ear gets clogged with wax; I use a small brush to clean it out, though mostly I accidentally push the wax up higher, into the bend of the tubing. The lenses collect fingerprints and tiny scratches; I run the soft cloth over them again and again. Sometimes I smudge the prints so that I have to squint to see through the smears.

Each night I place my glasses in a large black case, my face and ears finally unencumbered as I sleep.

*

'The next word is "recycle",' announces Ms Hull. '"Re-*cy*-cle."'

I scrawl my answer with quick, assured strokes.

Afterwards, I look at my page in quiet wonder, taking in all the big ticks.

*

As the year goes on, my body start to change in small ways. Shorts become more difficult to pull up, as my legs have started to thicken around my sides and bottom. It takes me awhile to realise that I am growing hips. Then, t-shirts begin to cling to my chest. I am becoming aware of my body in ways that are disorientating and worrisome.

By the start of the next school year I am awkward, tubby and beginning to collect pimples. I haven't worn my glasses over the summer and feel uneasy as I put them on for the first day of Grade 5. They are so big, so obviously mechanical, and draw more attention to me and my uncooperative body.

*

'That's a tall pile of books,' says the school librarian. 'They will keep you busy.'

I smile at the thought of the hours I'll spend reading them. Reading is no longer a terrifying ordeal; it has become a pleasure. The sweet shock of understanding every word on a page sends me on a mission to find more books to read. Nearly every lunchtime I sit in the cool, still air of the library. It feels comforting to be surrounded by books. I work my way through shelf after shelf of stories that carry me up and away: away from the thoughts of starting high school next year; away from the growing pains of puberty; away from the feeling of being known as 'the deaf girl'.

*

One day, halfway through Grade 6, a basketball wallops me on the side of my head and knocks off my glasses. I pick them up, and one arm dangles. They are broken. I feel guilty, and glad. These glasses represent a version of myself that I don't want to be – slow, effortful and stupid. By now reading and writing feel comfortable. Perhaps I don't need these glasses anymore? I leave them in their case, relieved that no one will know I am deaf when I start high school.

*

Now, at the age of thirty-one, after two decades of hiding my deafness, I've developed a strong sense of Deaf Pride. This wasn't a swift process, nor an inevitable one. It was only when I encountered Deaf culture in my late twenties that I learnt I could celebrate my deafness, rather than feel like my body is broken. Even though my life is now at an exquisite and arresting moment of self-acceptance, it took me years to unlearn the negative internal dialogue I had with myself about my body. And while I haven't worn hearing glasses since I was ten years old, I make my deafness visible in other ways. Sometimes I wear a jumper with the words 'The future is accessible' emblazoned across the front. I usually tell people that I am deaf, as I know that it is my right to have access to events, information and opportunities.

Recently, I read a story about a teacher with a hard-of-hearing student. In the classroom the boy communicated in English, but the teacher discovered that he had begun to learn Auslan at home. Having noted his unease with spelling tests – the way he squirmed and hooked his arm around his worksheet, she decided to try incorporating some basic signs into the next lesson. The teacher began the next spelling test by reading a list of words aloud. The boy scored four out of ten. Knowing the crushing weight of shame that can descend on someone after receiving a low score, the teacher encouraged the boy to play for ten minutes – to jump and stretch and move, allowing the frozen block of fear to melt and his small body to shake off any discomfort. Then she sat him down and repeated the test, only this time she signed each word in Auslan. He sat up straight and watched her hands, before taking his pencil to the page with clear, clean strokes. Afterwards, he passed the sheet back for marking – he had got every word right. This teacher, though obviously chuffed by the boy's result, didn't gloat over her cleverness; instead, she wished that she had realised sooner how hearing-centric her teaching methods had been. She was now determined to learn Auslan.

For hundreds of years, signing was widely considered no more than a series of gestures and pantomime. It was thought to be so primitive, so dangerous, that most health professionals and educators believed it stunted brain growth. In 1880, at the Second International Congress on the Education of the Deaf, it was declared that all deaf students must be taught using the Pure Oral method exclusively. This effectively banned the use of sign language in schools worldwide, and deaf students had to rely on lip-reading their teachers.

While the ban is no longer operating, attitudes regarding sign language continue to prevail, with many considering it the 'last resort' when educating a child. According to the World Federation of the Deaf, only 1 to 2 per cent of deaf people across the world access education through sign. And while Australian Sign Language was recognised as a community language in 1987, it took until 2016 for the government to finalise the first Auslan curriculum. Before then, teachers had had to rely on the general frameworks for languages, such as the ones created for French or Japanese, to teach sign language. I think about all the deaf and hard-of-hearing children around Australia who are in mainstream classes without the support of sign language, as well as the teachers who do not have the time or resources to learn and teach in Auslan, and it makes me ache with rage and sadness. My relationship with reading and writing began so anxiously. This feeling has never left me. Despite having developed a deep love of and need for reading and writing, my anxiety resurrects itself whenever I need to write in company, such as on a whiteboard or even on a birthday card. A small part of me worries that other people will jeer at any error I make.

Since my late twenties, my hearing has steadily decreased. When I was diagnosed with otosclerosis, a condition that is causing the bones of my ears to harden, the news wasn't devastating. While it means I will lose my hearing completely – a thought that used to make my heart seize with fear – this doesn't fill me with terror now that I am learning sign language. Having a language that fits my body and allows me to converse unguardedly is a joy and an utter, profound relief.

Hippotherapy

Alistair Baldwin

Whenever I meet someone else who grew up disabled in Australia, there's only one key thing I want to know about them. I go through the small-talk motions, I feign interest in how their day went, I wait a respectful amount of time before I derail the conversation with the question I've been dying to ask.

'Hey, did you have to ride horses too?'

It is one of life's great tragedies that 'hippotherapy' has nothing to do with hippos. Had I, at age eight, received hippo-riding lessons, I think I would have grown up to become a very different man. More confident. More self-assured. Khaki would probably feature more prominently in my wardrobe.

The boring reality is that hippos have to do with horses (*hippopotamus* derives from the Ancient Greek word for 'river horse'), and it's horses that have to do with hippotherapy.

When it comes to treatment options for a young boy with a congenital muscle disease, one's mind doesn't instinctively jump to horses. Yet therapeutic horse-riding, or hippotherapy, got an emphatic tick of approval from my neurologist, my physio and my occupational therapist.

Such is its popularity that in every state and territory of Australia you can find Riding for the Disabled Association (RDA) centres – made moderately affordable to non-aristocratic disableds through government subsidies. Owing to both ubiquity and these subsidies, I've found that Australian adults with a disability are nearly as likely to have grown up horse-riding as Australian adults who were child actors on *The Saddle Club*. Which is to say, quite likely.

My local centre in Perth was called RDA Capricorn. Its stables and paddock were located next to Perry Lakes Stadium, the multi-purpose sports complex specially built for the 1962 Commonwealth Games. It was a somewhat ironic neighbour. Perry Lakes was where my able-bodied classmates played basketball, where inter-school athletics carnivals I couldn't compete in were held. I doubt many people knew that within limping distance, hidden among eucalyptus trees and down a discreet dirt road, was a bunch of adolescent cripples on horses.

I would go to the centre once a week, wearing knock-off R.M. Williams on my tiny, flat feet. I'd head inside, to where they kept the helmets, and try to find one that fit well. Then I'd go through to the back, my boots digging into wood mulch, where there was a series of ramps leading to platforms of different heights.

The platform you used depended on which horse you were riding that day. Rather than attempt hoisting themselves onto a horse with strength they didn't have, each child would walk or roll their wheelchair up to a platform approximately matching the height of their assigned horse. You'd get into the saddle with the help of a volunteer, who would almost invariably be a horse-obsessed teenage girl whose time and generosity were rewarded with the opportunity to ride for free after all the disabled kids went home.

In my first year or so, I always rode Albert. He was an old pony, relatively low to the ground, white with mottled grey specks. Later, as I gained confidence and skill, I rode Apollo – a proper horse, much taller and more muscular, with a chestnut coat.

In each session we would ride around the rectangular paddock a couple times, then crisscross from corner to corner, weave in and out of traffic cones and jump over small obstacles.

There was something exhilarating about turning your steed with the slightest pull of the reins, nailing a jump, shifting gears into a fast trot. What I enjoyed most was the sheer novelty of it. I was, finally, in control of an able body.

The jury's out, though, on just how much riding a horse can really help disabled people.

One of the first recorded people to posit the health benefits of horse-riding was Hippocrates (also nothing to do with hippos), circa 400 BC, who called it a 'natural exercise' that benefited the body, mind and spirit. However, in a separate scroll, Hippocrates wrote that for those with a passion for riding, 'the constant jolting on their horses unfits them for intercourse'. As someone who once landed wrong on the downbeat of a trot, I can say (in a slightly high-pitched voice) this assessment has some basis in reality. If I were a conspiracy theorist, I'd say that's why the government pays for it – it's all part of a long game to stop us invalids infecting the gene pool with our subpar DNA.

A cursory google search tells me another key horse-therapy believer was Lis Hartel, a Danish dressage champion who contracted polio in 1944 at the age of twenty-three. Paralysed below the knees, she continued competitive dressage against medical advice, becoming the first woman to win a silver medal in an Olympics event open to men and women. She credited horse-riding with improving her polio symptoms, and began advocating for hippotherapy for disabled people after she retired from sport.

The official RDA website states that hippotherapy helps develop 'postural control, equilibrium reactions, balance, coordination and spatial orientation'. A 2015 medical article tells me that it has been used to treat 'autism, cerebral palsy, arthritis, multiple sclerosis, head injury, stroke, spinal cord injury, behavioural disorders and psychiatric disorders', although 'the effectiveness of hippotherapy for many of these indications is unclear'.

What do I think? The truth is, I don't know if it helped me. In theory, it probably improved my core strength, in the same way that sitting on a yoga ball improves core strength – the shifting stability awakening deep, moth-eaten muscles in my abdomen. But I certainly didn't notice this at the time. It's hard to assess progress or decline from inside a disability, especially as a child. It's near impossible to compare yourself to how you were six months ago, because all you want to do is compare yourself to your friends and your bullies – and that's all they want to do right back.

My mum did declare countless times that horse-riding had helped my posture, that I began sitting on couches as though I were a vigilant security guard. To this day she still brings it up. She was a fan of the whole thing because I'd finally found a physical activity I was okay at. My older brother was a sporty kid, playing both footy and basketball, and he received ribbons, trophies and

Most Valuable Plater certificates semi-regularly, placing them on a shelf above his bed. As part of her tireless efforts to ensure I never felt I was living a diluted version of childhood, Mum went to a shop to custom-order horse-shaped trophies for me (marked 'achievement' of a nondescript variety), and she would award these biannually. The shelf above my bed soon looked as shiny as my brother's, until I got to the age where showing off my mum-ordered, store-bought trophies for 'achievement' in a prescribed therapy became supremely embarrassing. Then I took them all down and put them in a box.

When I decided to stop horse-riding for good, I think Mum was more upset than I was. But she respected my autonomy, and she agreed that the freak event that drove the final nail into the coffin of my horse-riding career – an event as traumatic as it was bizarre – was a good enough reason to call it quits.

Western Australia does not have daylight saving. The matter has been the subject of four state referendums – in 1975, 1984, 1992 and 2009 – and was rejected by Western Australians all four times. I remember it being, inexplicably, the defining debate of my youth. It provided local talkback radio with countless hours of content, as a divided population went into bat for either saving time or experiencing it as nature intended.

It's the 2009 referendum I want to talk about – or, specifically, the years leading up to it. In 2006, a three-year trial of daylight savings began, so that people could try it on for size before buying it for good. The event that led me to quit horse-riding happened a week after we all, sceptically, put our clocks one hour back.

I had my afternoon session as usual. Everyone got the memo and arrived on time. It was a nice, peaceful day. Then, halfway through, we all heard it.

Click. Hissss …

The Perry Lakes Stadium grounds that the paddock bordered relied on an automatic sprinkler system – those powerful, pressurised ones that always seem to pop out of the ground just as you've laid down your picnic blanket. The system was scheduled to come on at 5.30 p.m., partly so the sun didn't instantly evaporate the water as it sprayed out, and partly because Perry Lakes had been informed that these powerful jets of water spooked the RDA horses, so it was best they didn't go off during a hippotherapy session. But unfortunately, Perry Lakes had not recived the daylight savings memo.

Time slowed down. In the millisecond after the *click-hiss*, Apollo got sucker-punched in the face with water. Before I realised what was happening, I was halfway across the paddock.

Riding horses have four main gaits, ascending in speed like gears in a car. At RDA we only used two: 'walk' and 'trot'. 'Canter', graceful and smooth as it is, was above our abilities. When the sprinklers went off that day, every single horse instinctively shifted into their fourth gear: 'gallop', a gait you may recognise from watching a horse race. In an instant, a dozen tiny, disabled children were flung into the atmosphere.

Apollo's speed suddenly threw me back into the saddle, my spine slamming onto his rump. One leg began waving in the wind like a flag as he charged from one end of the paddock to the other. The other foot remained in the stirrup, and my hands somehow kept hold of the reins.

Apollo was making a dash for the paddock gate, which was shut during sessions, and it was his graceful, speedy jump over it that finally dislodged me from the saddle and sent me down into the mulch with a thud. I fractured two ribs, and couldn't attend the school excursion to the movies the next day.

It's easier to get back on the horse when it's not literally a horse. It's easier when it's pilates, or a daily sudoku, or any other activity with an almost non-existent risk of injury.

I knew you shouldn't let one setback stop you pursuing something you enjoy. I recovered pretty quickly, as did my fellow horse-riders; we were all roughed up a little, but the incident didn't make any of us more disabled than we already were. But I was scared it would happen again, or something else would, something worse. The odd confluence in my injury of daylight savings and sprinkler systems made me fear even the most banal things, like how it's impossible to look at a stapler or a rake the same way after watching the *Final Destination* movies. As a little disabled kid, in and out of hospitals, in a body that's constantly discussed in terms of its weakness and frailty, it's easy for your mind to jump to death as a consequence for almost anything, even when your specific condition isn't immediately terminal.

I asked my parents if I could study Italian, and going to a weekend class soon became my extracurricular activity. Then, a year or so later, RDA Capricorn moved its facilities from Perry Lakes to Pinjar, a much longer car trip away, so even if I had decided to return to riding it would have been inconvenient.

My dad had been on the volunteer board at the centre in his spare time, and continued to do so even after I stopped riding. He would occasionally update me about their new programs or sleepover camps. He eventually left too. The last thing I remember hearing about the centre was that Albert, the first horse I regularly rode, had died.

Despite their unfortunate and abrupt end, I look back on my horse-riding days with fondness.

Even now, I feel a strange affinity for horses. Partly because of the afternoons I spent with them as a child, and partly because, as with humans, a horse's value to society is inextricably, albeit unfortunately, linked to its abledness. It doesn't take much more than a vague grasp of history and a little imagination to see that, if they could, abled people would melt the lame down into glue.

Beyond that, I'm just glad I was lucky enough to grow up doing something, anything, surrounded by other disabled kids. 'Sail-ability' was a popular kid's maritime activity recommended by my occupational therapists, as was Surfing for the Disabled. In another life, I'd be writing a charming short story about how daylight savings set off a sequence of events that nearly led to me drowning at sea.

At school, all my friends were abled (as were my enemies). I put so much effort into trying to hide the gap between our abilities. In horse-riding, I never had to disguise the odd way my shoulders rounded, my strange gait, the weird way my hands grasped things. It's exhausting to fight the way you naturally exist. The spaces and moments in which you can relax into how your body truly is are sacred. And that's what horse-riding gave me.

That's why I like asking other disabled people if they did horse-riding too. In a world where you can feel impossibly different to everyone around you, there's comfort in finding people you share a perspective, an identity, a diagnosis or an experience with.

'Life Goes On' and 'The Blue Rose'

Kerri-ann Messenger

Written while attending a Have Your Say Conference in Geelong. I took part in a workshop involving people who have lived in institutions.

Life Goes On

What is happening to me?
Do you feel what we feel?
Why do our hearts keep on beating?
Why do our eyes cry when we don't have a voice?
When it makes me cry, it scares me,
overwhelms me.
Don't you know it's the end of the world
when we are trapped in institutions,
and getting teased
because we have a disability?
It's like we don't have a right to exist.
What can I say when it hurts so much?
But life goes on.
Don't they know it's the end of the world
when they hurt us like that?
Once hurtful words touch me,
my soul is burnt.
I sit alone and begin to cry.
Rain pours from my eyes.
And my heart is breaking.

Written after my parents and I discussed my birth and the encouraging words of a nurse when she realised I had Down syndrome.

The Blue Rose

Every special garden should have a Blue Rose,
and they picked me.
I was placed in their arms
and as I looked up into their eyes
I brought sunshine into their lives.
I felt them holding me,
knew love was coursing through their veins.
One nurse said,
'Walk away and let the government look after her –
she probably won't say more than one word.'
I proved that nurse wrong!
The other nurse said,
'Think of it as being lucky, like having a Blue Rose in
    your garden.
A very rare and beautiful thing. Every garden should
    have one.'
With my smile, I can make you feel good.
That makes it all worthwhile.
I can speak to your heart
even by saying nothing at all.
That is just the way it is.
I can melt your heart with just a smile.
The Blue Rose is a symbol.
A symbol of the heart.
A symbol of the soul.
The Blue Rose reaches the coldest of hearts,
the homeless, the downhearted, and
the people who do not understand disabilities.
The Blue Rose only wants to be your friend.
The Blue Rose is the heart of us all.
We only want to join in and have fun.
We do not want to be left out of things,
or stand outside the fire.

Please do not steal our hearts.
All we want to do is reach out to you,
and give our heart as a gift.
I want to give you the greatest gift of all.
It is a blue rose – it's rare and beautiful
and everyone should have one.
That's what friends are for!
To hear this lonely teardrop speak,
it would tell you of the dreams and wishes
that never come true.
But when we need someone, we reach out
to touch love.
Oh, please describe the meaning of love!
Do you feel what I feel, the unconditional love and
the warmth?
And life goes on.

Falling in Love, Fanfic, and Bone Fusion

Kit Kavanagh-Ryan

Expectations are weird. Mum raised me on a steady diet of the love letters between Virginia Woolf and Vita Sackville-West, but when I told her about my first girlfriend she drove into a tree.

'You're not gay,' she said as we sat in the car, bits of it beeping and flashing orange while the tree creaked its reproach. 'Kitty, you're making things terribly hard.'

I didn't say, 'Actually, I'm bi,' because even though I wasn't much for nuance at seventeen, she was way less so, and the conversation was already going down a path I'd thought reserved for afternoon kids' TV.

I'm not sure what I did say. Probably something like: 'Are you surprised?' or: '*You're* the massive Vita–Virginia shipper.'

She would have been crying before I was halfway done explaining what 'shipping' was.

I do remember asking her, seatbelt cutting into my neck, what exactly she meant by 'hard'.

My girlfriend and I fell in love from my parents' dining room in Melbourne and her mum's kitchen in North Carolina. We wrote stories for each other – the most delightful, nerdiest courtship. There were dragons in human form with water allergies, a misanthropic cartoonist who lived in the woods, and girls who knew the Names of things. These characters had lived in our heads from when we were thirteen; I'd read Ursula K. Le Guin that year. There was a queen and a diplomat who wrote lots (and lots) of passionate love letters across an endless ocean, at least three kidnapping plots, and, as our end-of-high-school exams approached in both Australia and the United States, a lot of bad French.

Falling in love felt effortless. We'd done it. We'd declared it. What, apart from international phone roaming in the mid-2000s, was *hard* about this, Ma?

'You can't be a lesbian *and* disabled,' she wailed. 'Why would you do that to yourself?'

*

For me, growing up disabled in Australia was just your average Tuesday. Nothing too bad happens on a Tuesday. I went to school, loathed Maths, eye-rolled my way through English and pondered why all the queer people in books kept dying. I listened to The Smiths on repeat, before realising that Morrissey is the actual worst.

I wondered when breasts would ever show up, then hated them once they did. I also had a massive, multi-level surgery when I was thirteen, which did put a sad crimp in my Year 8 social life – but that's what the internet is for.

While I discovered Yahoo Groups, met *both* my future romantic partners online and played long-running RPGs where many of my characters died heroically of heart failure, I also had various tendons swapped around.

My muscles were stretched out of their preferred places, and some very clever people built new arches for my feet out of a large chunk of my right left hip. This created a body that hyperextended more than it flexed, which in English means I'm less likely to curl forward into a top-heavy question mark. Surgeons also hammered out a lot of the deformities in my feet so that I could weight-bear and wear shoes.

Alright. So maybe my average Tuesday was a bit metal for a while.

'Hi,' I said, on a forum for the fantasy author Tamora Pierce in November 2000, only with more chatspeak than I'm going to replicate here. 'My name is Kitty and I sort of can't walk. Isn't Daine/Numair amazing?'

'That's really interesting!' came one reply. 'You know, it might be a bit OOC, but I have this *evil* plotbunny for the next thread ...'

While I spent months IRL with metal hooks sticking out of my big toes or hauling myself to school on crutches and awkwardly explaining to the vice-principal for the fifth time that I wasn't *trying* to fail PE, but at the same time I fell into a safe online space with blessedly few expectations.

No one particularly cared that I had cerebral palsy, because they were busy with school or family or their own grief and the general ridiculousness of being thirteen. Plus, I was Australian with an Irish name amid a crowd of nerdy Americans.* Faking cool was *easy*. I had an accent.

It's only as an adult that I realised one of the things which drew me to Tamora Pierce's work at the time was that so many of her characters *fall down*. Surgery rehabilitation is a little bit like knight training, only less glamorous and with far fewer horses. You work, you stretch, you hurt, you break things.

You do it again.

Those characters were the closest I could get to crip representation that didn't resemble Very Special Episodes. Most 'disabled' books I read growing up made disability – always physical disability, usually paralysis – seem like a punishment. I didn't feel punished. I felt like talking to dragons and learning how to spin magic into thread. I wasn't *suffering*, even if Ms Ecconomides kept calling me brave.

People on the internet didn't call me brave. Mostly, they said I was a good writer, even if I did use way too many commas.

They were the people I talked to when I was sick of physio, when I was happy, when I wondered if my parents were disappointed that, though the last round of surgeries seemed to be keeping me *walking*, my body was still lopsided, jarring and sore.

I poured my anxieties about arthritis into grizzled assassin characters, and made evil queens out of my anger at Annie's mother when she told me, tears in her eyes, that she wished *her* daughter would work 'just a little bit harder' to 'get herself' out of her wheelchair.

Annie had cerebral palsy too, along with film-star-perfect teeth. We were matched up at school as fellow crips for years and we hated each other's guts because of it, but I still want to push her mother down some stairs. I shared all this with the internet, and also wrote a lot of poetry.

You know, expected adolescent stuff. Only with more metal.

*

---

* + 1 Canadian. Sorry, Hez!

Expectations ache, and not just because I'm about to talk to a man about calf lengthening.

There's nothing quite like sitting in the consulting rooms in D North (Orthopaedics) at the Royal Children's Hospital as an allegedly adult patient. I feel almost as on display as the meerkats in the new building.

Not because of the kids. They've got better shit to do than gawk at some round, awkward so-and-so with a walking stick. But there are some parents whose eyes turn bright and fixed, and I feel pawed at before any surgeon comes at me with a Sharpie.

I watch as these parents watch. There is a kid on the floor, and her dad's worried eyes catch on the small things we share: curled hands, lopsided posture. He looks from her tiny, kicking legs in (amazing) pink and purple ankle-foot orthoses to my own atrophied calves, exposed by 'gym clothes' that I wear in hospitals way more than at the gym.

Yep, I bite back silently, trying to focus on the lurid yellow wall art and the questions I need to ask my surgeon, *we do grow up*.

The transition from child to adult services for people with cerebral palsy is abrupt and expensive. In my case it means a lot of surreal moments being a childless adult in a parent–child space, because my main surgeon still only sees patients – adult and child alike – in the children's hospital.

'Excuse me,' someone says.

I manage not to wince at the feel of a hand on my knee. I look down. She's wearing teal nail polish, cracking in all the corners. At the front desk, someone is asking about estimated anaesthesia costs with the upticked, breathless apology-voice of the newly and publicly panicked.

I blink. The hand on my knee is still there. I look up. 'I'm sorry?'

'No, I'm sorry,' the woman says. 'I just ... do you have diplegia? My son has diplegia and ...' She swallows. 'You're walking. That's so good. Well done you.'

'Yeah,' I say, hoping that her son is doing something far more interesting than listening to adults being uncomfortable with each other. 'I walk, but that was mostly luck, you know. Some surgery, sure, but a lot of luck. It's mostly my balance that's the issue —'

'I just . . .' She shudders.

I've been trying not to look at her face, because I can feel her eyes on me and I don't know what my expression is going to say back. Still, I see her lip caught between her teeth. There's an orange stain on a soft blue shirt. She's wearing jasmine perfume, and the scent sits heavy in the back of my mouth.

'I just want him to walk and be happy. You understand, don't you?'

*

I don't shout at those parents.

I don't tell them that I'm not a blueprint, that my ability to weight-bear is, quite honestly, the least interesting thing about me.

Because it does, literally, get me places.

I can haul myself upstairs and reach ATMs, and most of the time I get handed the adults' menu in restaurants where my body, patched and fused and lopsided as it is, fits through the door. I'll never pass that weird American sobriety test in films where the inebriated walks steadily along a straight line – physios love that test too, you know! – and I've been kicked out of a few pubs for drunkenness before taking a drink. But I can walk.

And that is, in many ways, a gift. Not God's gift or even the surgeon's gift – but something my body achieves that allows me a privilege and a seat at a lot of tables, so long as the seat isn't a barstool. I understand wanting what's 'best' for someone you love, but you need to think about how 'best' is built.

Although I don't shout at those parents, this piece is an attempt to haul my way to a seat at their table. An attempt to use some of the words that a load of far-flung teenagers gave me to answer back Annie's mum, along with the family who love me but often grieve for a life I wouldn't know how to live, because I'm busy living this one. My life is neither a miracle nor a tragedy, but I've been bruised by expectations. Mostly my own, but they came from *somewhere*.

I want to ask parents to look at their kids and see what they can do *now* – how warm or empathetic or funny or vivid they are as their own uncorrected selves.

Sometimes, surgery might help them navigate this world a little better. A lot of the time, it won't do everything they – or you – hope. And that's fine.

But don't make us wear your hopes.

We all have our own.

Noisy Silence

Anna Whateley

Letter, age five:

Dear Father Christmas. Please bring me a Curly-Wurly, a Barbie and a bike. I will leave you some wine. I am a little Australian Girl. Love from Anna Whateley.

My family were driving through the outback when we pulled over so my father could wallop me on the bum. I was talking again – unrestrainable talk, endless words tumbling out. My father would say, 'Empty vessels make the most noise,' and 'Engage your brain before your mouth.' I didn't understand what he meant, and couldn't oblige even once I did. I can still feel the brittle ground by the side of the road, and then being unable to sit when I got back in the van – hovering half suspended over the seat, silent tears streaming.

Report card, age five:

Anna talks fluently, at great length and in minute detail. Anna does not always show a considerate and caring attitude towards others. Anna has rapid and careless work habits. Anna is very confident. Anna needs to remember to clean her fingernails. Anna is an untidy worker.

I was rehearsing with my class for the school carnival. We'd learnt the square dances and now we were gathered at the front of the room, practising a piece about the bushranger Ben Hall. We were singing the verses written up on the blackboard when my teacher, who I completely loved, bopped me on the head. I write 'bopped' to make it seem lighter than it actually felt. You know that gag where you pretend to splat an egg on someone's head, but it's really your hand? Like that.

But it wasn't a joke. It hurt. And there was no eggy ending. He just bopped me out of sheer frustration at the persistent talking. I'd been excited, energised, and I couldn't stop the words spilling out.

Report card, age six:

I would like to see Anna apply her abounding energy to producing the standard of written work I know she is capable of, and to give her oral capabilities a well-earned rest!

My primary school had less than one hundred students and, for all its faults, was a loving community. Formal corporal punishment was being phased out, although it was still legal at the time. Kids had been caned by the previous principal and the memory makes my fingers sting. Given the choice, my own teacher opted to pat kids on the bottom with a metre-long ruler that had red chalk crosses on the end, a bit like the XXXX brand of beer (but he did three). The unlucky kid then had to walk around the school with the chalk marks as a sign of their disobedience. My teacher objected to the cane. But he hit me: just me, just that once, because I couldn't stop talking.

These are the two occasions I recall being physically reprimanded as a child, and both times were to stop the words. Twice in my childhood, trusted and important men silenced me with their hands.

Diary, age twelve:

This morning we went rollerskating, and I did backward crossovers in both directions for the first time!! Rebecca and I stopped playing with each other on Friday because she went off with Petrina, the BITCH, and I went off with Cheryl, who is very nice.

I was irrepressibly bubbly in these early years. When I was on my own, I shuffled cards for hours, trying to design the perfect randomness. I also wrote in my diaries daily – first as a running commentary of friendship changes and crushes, and later in the form of poetry and drawings. In every photo of me from that time, I have a giant smile, fingers up my nose, or a look of sheer delight as I brandish my Kylie Mole binder.

When I had stitches, they broke open and the wounds healed poorly – three months on crutches instead of one. I mucked around in the bath and split my head open, making all the water turn blood red. 'Attention seeking', they chided after each injury.

I was the only member of my family who was left-handed, who had red hair and who *talked*; the genetic dumping ground, they said. I was born in Thailand, so there were jokes that I was the 'postman's daughter', but given my lack of Asian appearance or family members, these jokes always ended with a disappointed 'but probably not'.

I began to expect everyone I met to treat me with disdain, and they usually did. They so desperately wanted me to be quiet, and I so desperately couldn't be.

Diary, age twelve:

I've had a lot of trouble sleeping. Like getting to bed at 8:30 and falling asleep at 11.00.

If I were a child in the current education system, I would be referred for assessment. I would be diagnosed with attention deficit hyperactivity disorder (ADHD), autism, sensory processing disorder (SPD) and Ehlers-Danlos syndrome (EDS). But back in the '80s, they diagnosed me with 'chatterbox', 'people pleaser', 'fussy', 'never reaching her potential' and 'clumsy'.

I flooded everyone with words for reasons similar to those that, nowadays, motivate people to use social media: I was constantly checking in, trying to understand, decipher and connect. Everyone else seemed to have the instruction manual, but I had to compile my own based on how people reacted to my words. Like a sonar system, navigating pathways and detecting objects underwater. How do they know when to finish a joke? How do they run without hurting themselves? How do they make truly *best* friends? They, they, they. It was always them and me.

Diary, age thirteen:

Well, things are getting better, you could say. We went to church. Lynn's kids came so I spent most of the time keeping them occupied. Then we had lunch and they put on a timer and I wasn't allowed to talk for ten minutes. Then we decided to go to the drive-in. It was an all-nighter!

My family loved movies and television. Confusingly, the few characters I observed to be 'like me' didn't elicit the same admonition. Everyone loved Anne Shirley from *Anne of Green Gables*. Yes, she got into trouble, but she grew up into a sensible person within a couple of hours. Hawkeye from *M*A*S*H* said inappropriate things, but he saved lives and was funny, so no one minded. Maria in *The Sound of Music* (I'm sure a 'flibbertigibbet' is a primitive attempt at a name for ADHD) was lauded as a talented, caring person.

I conclude that, when it came to me, it was my very being that was annoying. My words, presence, thoughts and desires – myself – were so exasperating they drove even a pacifist teacher to assault.

Diary, age thirteen:

I put in a new tampon in the morning about one and a half hours before school, but had to change it at 9 a.m. I only brought the one extra, so I spent the rest of the day with toilet paper in my pants, suckful.

I devoted page after page in my diaries to worrying over 'average Australian Girl things', including who asked who out, periods and what Nicole did behind the PE shed. I had a constant stream of boyfriends, albeit often for just a few hours, or perhaps a week. My mum started taking us rollerskating and I found it was something I could do – a sport that was not hot and sweaty on the oval, or loud with echoes at the pool. The breeze as I skated was always the right temperature, and it was perfectly acceptable to skate alone. I did figures and dance but wasn't keen on dancing with an actual partner because they often smelled bad. My ankles were weak, and I didn't like competitions. Even so, I mastered the basics, and for a few years my family had a space where we felt at home. Our actual home was falling apart.

Diary, age thirteen/fourteen:

We went shopping and I got a badge that said, 'I killed Laura Palmer'! How cool! (It's a TV show) ... Oooh arrrh, I feel like screaming and crying. The social was tonight. Ben can't dance for shit! But we slow danced after a while. He's really good at that. Then I went to the toilet. After that things got worse. I told him nothing was wrong, and then I gave him the cold shoulder. I don't know how I feel anymore. I want to die. Anna?

My grades in high school were excellent. I played the flute and avoided sport. Privately, I developed an eating disorder. Bubbly Anna now lacked any deep sense of belonging, and sadness grew in the quiet places of her mind. I'd left behind familiar teachers, my primary school and every known part of my life. My parents were divorcing. Boyfriends had become more complicated. My new uniform was an excruciatingly itchy hessian sack.

In the early '90s I couldn't style my hair in a way that was remotely acceptable. When I cut it short, they chimed 'Annie' down the port racks. After finding a picture of the orphan character, I saw that, yes, I looked like her, but the accuracy of the resemblance didn't make it hurt any less. Nothing was normal. Every day was painful. High school had so many students I felt lost. Two rice cakes with Vegemite, before a tiny morsel at dinner. Perhaps I stopped eating properly in a search for control. We had a big family, so no one noticed.

Diary, approx. age fifteen:

If there were words
put into the silent places
in my heart
in my soul
they would be magic.
Magic to tell
to help me understand
to open the flood
the rush of freedom
magic words
like wind

can feel them
can't grasp them
always just out of reach
their effect untold.

My weight dropped, and people said I looked good. I wanted to be invisibly normal – not 'Annie' – and being thin was normal. So I became very thin. Never enough to get really sick, but enough to know I was getting one thing right. I couldn't control what came out of my mouth, but I could control what went in.

The starvation made me giddy and talking became even harder to regulate. I lost marks for misspelling my name as I rushed to submit assessments. One day, I touched some equipment at the wrong time in Maths class. The teacher yelled so forcefully that spittle came flying over and hit the desk. I had been trying to listen and understand, my fingers reaching out to feel the shapes as he described them, but they weren't supposed to be touched. He compared me to my well-behaved, top-grade-scoring older siblings: why was I, in contrast, such a disappointment?

I rollerskated twice a week, soothed by wheels turning, music thumping and colourful lights flashing. I remember more about the rink than school in those years. We did 'The Time Warp', and I wore my comfortable bike pants and t-shirt. Mum bought me my own expensive leather skates (I still have them in my cupboard). I cleaned the wheels and watched them spin and spin when the ball bearings were oiled. At thirteen, I met a boy who took me on my first real date, to see *Look Who's Talking Too*. At fifteen, I had an inappropriate six-month relationship with a skating coach eight years my senior.

Diary, age fifteen:

It feels like I'm in a tin can, and people keep knocking on it and the sound echoes in my head. I won't cry.

I left high school after three years and started a senior certificate at TAFE. The divorce was now complete, and we had a new home. The skating rink had been turned into a bingo hall. The total lack of rules in the TAFE system gave my small group of new friends a sense of unity. We learnt independence and self-reliance. We experimented with how we looked, our bodies playthings to change at our own will. These freedoms suited me. I cut off my hair again, this time into a crew cut, and dyed it mulberry. I increased my food intake, now including dim sims and Burger Rings. I could wear comfortable clothes and Dr Martens. When it was cold, we would huddle together on the benches and play cards. There were no loud bells, no shouting teachers, and there was no standing still on parade. There was less for me to get wrong, and I was less wrong.

Diary, age fifteen:

> *A bird that cannot talk*
> *only repeat what it is told*
> *forever silenced for inability*
> *to find the words to tell the*
> *untellable to those who can*
> *only hear themselves.*
> *You see me, a mirror, careful –*
> *Don't look too close, distortions*
> *may appear.*

There's a difference between rules and responsibilities. Rules can be broken, and 'fixed' through punishment; responsibilities tap into something deeper. At college they didn't chastise or shame us for being late; they made sure we had a bus ticket and gave us the class notes we'd missed out on. Lessons were informal. My English teacher explained to me, patiently and privately, that if I answered all the questions posed in classes, my friends might not learn. She gave me an A before the due date, and it became easy for me to keep my answers to myself because she and I were a team, and I sensed the value she saw in me. In Maths, I wasn't 'calling out' – I was contributing enthusiastically to the discussion. We were allowed to have food on the table and munch quietly throughout classes, like people do at work sometimes, to maintain their focus.

It was far more comfortable, and yet, despite my external world becoming more in line with my needs, my diaries became darker. I struggled with what was probably depression.

Diary, age fifteen:

I suddenly feel very lonely, like everything is material and fake, and I'm becoming just like everything else. I can feel the emptiness. Emotions are running through me that I can't interpret, understand, or that I want.

The bubbly little Australian Girl loved her fluid, bisexual tomboy self, but was no longer writing to Santa. My grades were erratic, and there was a distinct possibility I wouldn't complete my senior certificate. I had chronic headaches and fell into unhealthy, sometimes violent, relationships – one after another.

My friends and teachers pulled me through, helping with assignments and understanding that life was complicated. A lot of things went wrong in these years, and they weren't my fault. I talked less and less. At home, I retreated into the lyrics of Pearl Jam, doing jigsaw puzzles and watching TV for days at a time.

Report card, Maths, age sixteen:

Given some of the sounds you make in class and the fact you've got this result, maybe you are a cat! Let me explain: cats are lucky, and given your sporadic efforts this semester, you are fortunate to have scraped a pass. The frustrating part of the equation is that I believe you are quite talented, you just aren't disciplined enough in your approach to study.

After finishing school at seventeen, I scored a ticket from my estranged father to travel to the UK. There, I felt a sense of freedom once more, the chance to start again. No one knew my history or assumed I would behave in a certain way. I made mistakes and they were blamed on my foreignness. I felt comfortable asking about social rules because I wasn't expected to know them, and this offered an easy way to make friends without awkward small talk.

I travelled back and forth between countries for a decade, always seeking the chance to be new, to have that excuse for not fitting in. I attended various universities – Brisbane, Yorkshire, Scotland, Brisbane, London, Hertfordshire, Brisbane – never finishing a course before I moved on again. I failed for a while, and then one day, in Uxbridge, something clicked. I cracked the code of how to write assignments, to understand the theory. For this

I thank my friendship with a mature age student who understood the course material as deeply as the lecturers. He took the time to talk me through how theory worked, from Marxism to postmodernism, while I formatted his assignments. My mind soared with the concepts, and I turned the theories into threads I could weave into an analysis. We both graduated with first-class honours.

Growing up didn't end, for me, with adulthood. I hid under a semi-mastered conformity to become a typical twenty-something. I didn't write diaries, or poetry; I did teaching, marriage and children. Becoming a parent took away my easy escapes, and after a few years I stopped coping so well. I began to suffer seemingly unconnected physical ailments. I couldn't talk, unless I was sticking my foot in my mouth. How could I parent children when I myself hadn't grown up? My mask was slipping.

After a decade of misdiagnoses and wrong medications, and with my third child playing games on the psychiatrist's floor, I was diagnosed with ADHD at thirty-eight years of age. I was given the correct medication; it prevented my dopamine crashes and granted me a blessed moment of pause. In that small space I could finally, magically, choose whether to speak.

The diagnosis helped, but it didn't fix everything. After a particularly stressful semester of university teaching, my body crashed. The osteoarthritis I'd had since my twenties worsened, and they diagnosed me with fibromyalgia. More recently, they diagnosed me with Ehlers-Danlos syndrome, a genetic disorder affecting collagen and connective tissue that I'm still trying to understand. One thing was clear: my body's pain and malfunction wasn't a mental health issue after all. My body aged too fast, and it still felt like my mind hadn't grown up.

Diary, late teens:

> *Don't keep tearing out the sutures*
> *I so carefully put in place.*
> *I need them, or my self might escape.*

Last year, I started seeing a new psychiatrist. She told me a story to explain how she understood my labels. She knew I'd been diagnosed with ADHD, and that I was questioning whether I was autistic. She said she didn't believe in these labels, only trauma. The labels, she said, are like calling yourself a mermaid – covered with beautiful scales, only able to swim and play in the water (if you'll forgive her gendered analogy). My family and friends were humans, dwelling on the land, and even though we talked and laughed, I couldn't walk among them. I could remain happy in the water, preening my scales, never quite able to get close to those humans – or, she said, I could *grow some legs*. I could fight the temptation to hide behind my label, work through the trauma, and emerge.

Our time ran out. I didn't know quite what to think of the vision she'd offered. Was she calling me a chicken? A mermaid chicken? A traumatised mermaid chicken? It took me a while to decode the analogy, but ultimately I decided that I loved being a mermaid. There are, in fact, shitloads of mer*folk*, and we have a wondrous world that all the leggy people are quite curious about.

Psychological assessment, age forty-one, 2019:

Given the severity of Anna's social communication difficulties and her restricted, repetitive behaviours, she is considered high functioning and therefore her current severity is at level one, 'requiring support'. Anna is an insightful and intelligent woman, which indicates a very hopeful diagnosis.

Determined, I found a psychologist who specialised in adult women with autism. I was upfront that my life had included a history of complex trauma, and that I needed her to see beyond that somehow. When she said I clearly met the criteria for autism spectrum disorder, my relief – my glee – recalled the little Australian Girl who laughed so hard at her Kylie Mole binder. The psychologist said I was in the top 1 per cent for matrix reasoning, explaining my love of puzzles and cards and my fascination with how things connect. On the flipside, I 'process slowly' and have the typical ADHD inability to disregard irrelevant detail. She explained that my obsession with words put me in the top 2 per cent for verbal skills. Not verbose, but possessing a genuine ability. She suggested that these skills are the reason I have 'passed' as neurotypical.

I can see that 'passing' has come at a cost. I was high functioning, until I was low functioning. Those terms describe how we appear, not how we *feel*, more privately, less obviously. Could we say 'extreme masking' or 'openly neurodivergent' presentation? I don't know. I'm at the beginning of my journey to understanding my autistic self, and I don't know if I'll ever disentangle ADHD from that understanding. But I feel confident to poke my head above water and show my beautiful scales; to let someone in, and not swim away. The labels give me acceptance and community. I'm learning to use the word 'disability' positively – validating and full of strength.

Diary, late teens:

The problem with time
only forward.
Deeds are never undone
every moment remembered
the past echoes forever
cease the sound.

No one would dare hit me now, and I've become protective of merfolk at risk. I recognise the trauma of growing up disabled without support, and I'm doing my best to work through it. My childhood was traumatic because they kept throwing me onto the land and wondering why I couldn't walk. More serious traumatic events occurred in my teens, ones for which I still have no words, though I recognise that these were able to unfold upon an existing foundation of early reprimands, and the conditioning that encouraged me to accept abuse and remain silent about it.

Trauma isn't the same thing as autism or ADHD. I still don't have the social rule book. I do have a husband who talks *with* me, and children who cackle at my bad puns as we play with words together. I have a sense of belonging among writers and other neurodiverse people. Quiet times aren't so silent. Instead of following the rules, I wrote a story, a whole novel. It doesn't have all the answers, but it has words for anyone stuck in a noisy silence. It's full of merfolk.

Letter, college farewells:

Dear Anna, You have been a friend, a supportive rabbit, and a pretty scaly fish. I wish you luck in the future.

Ben Hall, the bushranger, broke the rules, the laws, and we celebrated his life as I was bopped on the head for speaking out of turn. Neurotypicals, I've learnt, don't follow the rules, though I'm not sure they always realise. This was a revelation for me: that they get it wrong and they don't seem to care.

My father may have found the sound of my talking painful to his sensitive ears. That's as nice as I can be about that day in the van. I expect he doesn't remember, but my silent sobbing, suspended above the seat, will never leave me. These early reprimands made it clear to me I was meant to be punished, to seek forgiveness or tolerance for my disability.

They were wrong in what they did. If anyone had truly listened to my talking, and valued my passion and special interests, my childhood could have been different. There was an Anna constructed through report cards and grades. But her writings, her poetry, show anguish and exuberance in the face of constant criticism.

That little Australian Girl who wrote to Santa now has more ways to sign her name, more letters, including 'PhD'. I'm as proud of 'doctor' as I am of 'autism', 'ADHD' and 'EDS'. The letters and labels tumble out just as my words once did, but they're mine; they're my beautiful scales and they give me access to an entire world under the water.

Don't fear the labels. They can mean the difference between being voiceless on land or singing among an ocean chorus. A label or two as a child and I could have more readily found a community, a group of disabled people to make into an 'us' and a 'we'. A simple pronoun changes everything.

You Are Enough

Jordon Steele-John

This chapter is the result of an interview between Greens senator Jordon Steele-John and emeritus professor Chilla Bulbeck.

My family emigrated from the UK when I was a baby. And we did that in quite an unusual way: instead of it just being Mum and Dad and me and Harry, the whole family moved. So, me, Harry, Mum, Dad, Nanna, Poppa, Aunty, Uncle and Great-Grandma all moved to Western Australia, and for the first five or so years of my life we lived more or less together in the same house. That gave me a really interesting perspective on the intergenerational nature of a family unit, which I would later learn is quite unusual in this modern age. Because I was growing up around my grandparents and my great-grandma every single day, I had hundreds of years of history in one spot. It also meant that I had a very strong connection to my family.

There was a lot of trauma in my earlier life. My mum was diagnosed with an inoperable brain aneurism when I was six years old. She had a really bad headache one day and went to the hospital. They did an MRI and she didn't even get home before they rang her and said, 'It's not safe to drive. Come back immediately, we don't know what's going on.' So she had to pull over and turn around. And they found an aneurism in her head that was one of, at the time, only nine on record in Australia. It's kind of like having a medical grenade in your head. That was an incredibly traumatic experience for me, as a child. Then, later that year, my great-grandma passed away. That was my first experience with familial death. And then in 2001, a year to the day after Mum was diagnosed with an aneurism, my dad collapsed in front of me with a cerebral haemorrhage. They discovered three more aneurisms in his head, which triggered off a long recovery process for him and also involved a decline in his mental health.

Because we were a close family unit with intergenerational support built in, we managed to get through the trauma a lot easier. The practical reality of those medical conditions and issues involved many, many journeys up and down the Kwinana Freeway, before it was extended to Charlie Gairdner's in Nedlands.

In different circumstances, I might have had to go into day care. But Nanna and Pop could look after me while Mum went up and down and did the stuff, and Craig was around, my uncle. So we could pull together, in that way. It was a difficult time, but we also had more support than we otherwise would. And through all that, I was developing my sense of self as a person, and also coming into a conception of myself as a disabled person. In a close-knit family, brought closer together through hardship, my family's view of me as a disabled person was particularly important. And it fundamentally shaped my conception of my disability.

My mum always wanted to have kids, and never thought that she could. She has an incredible capacity for love, my mum, huge. My whole family have. My dad's not the same in that regard; he had a very, very difficult childhood, and that was something that never stopped affecting him. But for Mum and Mum's side of the family, showing love was not a problem. Me and my brother Harry, before we knew anything else as kids, we knew that we were loved. Thoroughly loved and cherished by the family we were part of. People spend a lot of time trying to pick apart what the nature of love ultimately is, but for me it's that you are enough. That just as a person, you are enough. You're more than enough, you're awesome, you're amazing. And that's not the same as spoilt brattishness, it's just a fundamental, core, 'we bloody love ya, there's nothing about you that's disappointing' kind of thing. That was part of the backdrop against which I started to form this sense of 'Okay, so I am enough as a human being, I'm loved and I'm a good person. I've got a disability. So what?' When I was little I didn't immediately think 'I've got a disability!' I thought: 'I can't walk like Harry does.'

Mum had been a social worker in the UK for twenty years – in child protection. Because of her, we were drenched in social justice and systems theories. A human rights or social justice perspective on life was always there, mixed with her deep belief in the autonomy of children. Mum's a big advocate for the idea that children are not the chattel of their parents, but independent human beings with their own rights. She created the space for me to come to my own view about myself as a person, and then my cerebral palsy as a subset of that aspect of personhood.

There was never a thought that I was broken, which I've come to understand is a common thought that a lot of kids have as they grow up disabled. I never had that thought about myself. I have gone on a kind of journey with my self-conception of disability, enabled by the space that Tracey gave me as a parent, and the boundless affection of my grandparents and my brother. They were constant pillars of love and support, and Tracey gave me an intellectual framework in which to think. Not *how* to think, just 'this is the space you can think in'. I could ask 'What is this cerebral palsy? Like *really*?' And she'd say, 'Well what do you think it is?' And I'd say, 'Well, I can't walk like Harry does, instead I crawl about.' It's like you go to walk but there's something not happening there. We used to say my brain telephone doesn't ring up my legs properly. And I was totally happy explaining that to other people. Relatively recently I've learnt how comparatively little I know about cerebral palsy, because I've not been medicalised. It's not necessary – what I need to know is what it means for me. Again, I've learnt that this is rare, not to be medicalised from a very early age.

My family believed I was deserving of love, respect and autonomy, and that I was a good person. And that gave me the space to think, 'Okay, well, I might not be able to walk, but I'm not broken, I'm still okay. Let's journey with this thing and see where we go.' That carried me a long way through my childhood. I always used to talk about journeying with disability. I conceptualised it as having this thing I wasn't ashamed of. I wasn't broken, I kind of travelled alongside it. And in that process, it shaped and moved me, and I shaped and moved it. From a very secure sense of self – I made my way with it.

I wouldn't say that I *didn't* identify as a disabled person, but as I moved more into the world of disability activism and identity, I noticed something. In one of his memoirs, Obama talks about being a black man raised by a white mother and white grandparents in Hawaii in the '60s, and he reflects on what that did to his racial identity and how unique his experience was. He had people who supported him, encouraging him to engage with his identity as a black man. He says he never felt he needed to choose between Black America and White America; he felt able to legitimately live in both those spaces. That chimed with me: that sense of living a really unusual childhood that allows you to embody two things comfortably. Until I started getting involved in disability activism, I could have said with conviction that there is no disabled Australia and non-disabled Australia, there is only the Australian community.

When I got involved in disability activism, it was like I was three-quarters of the way there, but the fourth bit hadn't slotted in yet. The big problem with that statement of Obama's is that there *is* a Black America and a White America. He is just one of a very small number of people who feel their personal lives transcend that. And, there's a lot of argument in black literature about whether that is a form of self-delusion. Personally I felt like I was finally breaking a self-delusion by getting involved in the disabled community. I even used to claim that while disability was part of who I was, it did not define me – I'd say that proudly. And then I had this lightbulb moment: What are you saying when you say that? It's not about whether it defines *you*; you are defined by society, by *it*!' And you can either claim your identity as a member of a group within society that is treated differently because of an impairment, and understand the social model of disability – its emphasis on the collective creation of the negative aspects. Or you can pretend to yourself that this is an individual thing, that you just get to journey with!

It was a bit of an epiphany moment: like, actually you *have* been individualising this, and when you say 'it's part of who I am but it does not define me', it's like saying 'I have got this disease, but I won't let it change who I am'. It's *not* a negative thing. You have an impairment, but you are a disabled person because that is how you self-identify – you claim back that power. As somebody who is a member of a group subject to discrimination, but also as part of a community of people. And then we get to disabled culture, which is kind of a new concept in Australia.

I feel so much more settled in myself since I had that moment of understanding.

I think I had fooled myself into thinking that because I didn't define myself as disabled, I could transcend the discrimination faced by disabled people. I had it impressed upon me less than so many other people because I avoided school (I was home-schooled). But still it's there. And it doesn't mean that I haven't had, in my life, moments of frustration or anger. Sometimes the inaccessibility and ableism of the world in which we live really gets you down. And I'm sure that's the same for everybody. There are moments when you can respond to that with eloquence and logic, and sometimes you just go 'arghhhh'. I've had my share of 'arghhhh', as we all have. But I feel so much more comfortable with who I am, and wonderfully connected to the four million other disabled Australians. The prize for liberating myself from the illusion of not being defined as a disabled person is to come into a sense of collective community with other disabled people. And that's incredibly affirming and wonderful.

I joined the Greens the minute I could, when I was sixteen. I still remember getting the Hogwartian letter through the post to say that my application had been received and someone was going to ring me. And I remember the first conversation with the membership officer: 'Have I passed the test?' I was hugely nervous about it.

I was a candidate in an election soon after. I was seventeen when I was preselected and I would turn eighteen in October. I was the candidate for Warnbro, where I lived. I never thought I would do anything like that. I was terrified, bloody terrified, but what pushed me to do it was hearing of people wanting to be a politician because they think it will be a cool career. I've never thought of politics as a career. For me politics is a vocation, and the aim is to ensure the voices of people who aren't often heard and yet are incredibly affected by the decisions made in politics, are actually heard and empowered in that space. So I was shit-scared but it was an opportunity for young people to have a voice, for a disabled person to talk about disability issues and youth issues. As scared as I was, I wanted to give it a go.

I'm a tragic political nerd and find it all interesting but I also love being part of grassroots movements. I love working alongside people and being part of something. Organising, planning events, how do we get more people involved? – I love that atmosphere. I want to be out there, in there, doing things. And I had a heightened awareness that, as a disabled person and a young person, much of our lives is shaped by decisions made in spaces where our voices are not heard. Our lives are shaped negatively because of that. Representative democracy doesn't function at its best unless it is representative of the community it's created to serve. And young people and disabled people are not heard enough in those spaces. We do not have the input or the control that we should have in decision-making. All the problems in the NDIS, why we're still abused and mistreated – all that can be linked to our lack of voice. So that's what drove me forward.

I had a very interesting experience when I was young – ten or eleven. I went to a new place that had just opened and they had an accessible car parking bay. We drove up to where it was supposed to be and it had been turned into a loading bay. I was pretty miffed about that, so I went to the centre administrator and said, 'Why the hell have you turned it into a loading bay?' And the woman said very patronisingly, 'Well, there are other car parking places, and we need that to unload material for paying customers.' And I was like, '*I* am a paying …' – well I wasn't, I was eleven. But the inference was that disabled people are something to be charitably given a bit of space if we feel like it, but not centrally included in the planning of a space.

I encountered a similar attitude when I entered parliament. This is a building that was built in 1988 and at the time they were patting themselves on the back for the number of accessible toilets they put in the public areas. But not a single piece of the working areas of Parliament House was built to be accessible, even by 1988 standards. When a man who used a wheelchair, Graham Edwards, was elected to the House of Representatives, they changed an office for him but nobody thought to change anything on the senate side of the building. Because again the thinking was, 'Oh, that's an anomaly, it will never happen again.' And the reaction to me entering Parliament House was, 'Oh crap, we haven't got an accessible office.' So far they've fixed things to the bare minimum for me. And I've been saying that it's not good enough, that you need a comprehensive accessibility plan for the building. How are you going to transform the way it works so that you are prepared for other disabled people to be elected? And I'm just met with blank stares.

In the two years I've been there, I've been banging the drum particularly about the lack of provision for a deaf person, if they were elected. In New Zealand, when Mojo Mathers was elected, it took eighteen months for her to be able to properly take her seat in parliament and participate because they had to figure out how to get enough interpreters for her to do her job, for her contribution to be incorporated into the minuting system and so on. One of my first conversations with the people at Parliamentary Services was, 'What's your plan?' They still don't have a plan, two years later. So, I think that says two critical things about our society. It says a lot about the role that we subconsciously or consciously have come to believe disabled people should play in Australia, which is, maybe to be taken to Parliament House on a day trip but never elected. And second, it says that when challenged to make a change our society does the bare minimum to remove the immediate pressure, at which point it stops again. And this led back to the social model of disability, and the understanding that disability is not something the individual has and which is therefore their responsibility, but instead is created through the interaction of their impairment or difference with barriers created and sustained in society by ableism, by presumptions. Addressing the discrimination that disabled people face is a *whole* of society issue – everybody has a responsibility for breaking down and changing it.

To me, the ideal is a world where the rights of disabled people are supported, and our equality, our fundamental humanity, is recognised and celebrated in all aspects of society. Disabled people will always claim – as is our right – an identity as disabled people. The goal for me is not to erase that, any more than the identity of a person of colour or what have you should be erased. And where we come to that in a legislative sense, in a political sense, is that the laws and our structures, whether they be physical or procedural that are created and supported by our laws, support that equality and recognise those equal rights in everything that we do.

Now we have a Royal Commission into the violence, abuse, exploitation and neglect of disabled people in Australia, because of the decades of campaigning by disability activists, who again and again and again spoke up and protested and advocated in relation to how we are treated. The Greens were willing to listen to the disability community, to champion our struggle through the establishment of a Senate inquiry, and that then led to the recommendation for a Royal Commission, which we'd been advocating for for the last five or so years. In this, there is a great coming together of the Greens' principles of social justice, environmental justice, peace, non-violence and participatory democracy with the disability rights movement's assertion of the rights of disabled people. And my twin journeys, as a disabled person and as a Green, also come together. There would be no Royal Commission without disabled people advocating and there would also be no Royal Commission if the Greens hadn't taken up that cause. The Royal Commission is the embodiment of the power of those things.

The victory in the Royal Commission is not the commission being established, it's the way it's implemented: it's the legislation of the Commission's recommendations. I and many other disabled people view the Royal Commission as an opportunity for justice. It's the beginning of a great moral moment in Australian history – a reckoning. An opportunity for truth and justice and storytelling, for people to come forward and to talk of the historical wrongs they or their family members have experienced. And it's not just historical cases, it's very present, happening as we speak now. Finally, after all this time, disabled people will be able to turn over every stone, get to the bottom of every story, speak our truth on our terms to a Royal Commission. And in the process, find greater strength and solidarity among ourselves. We can make it clear to the decision-makers watching that the outcome must be what we need it to be, not what they would conveniently like it to be. It's time for all the injustices to be made right.

I think some people, particularly people in power, expect us to say, 'Oh thank you very much for this investigation, we'll be grateful for anything you give us because you've spent so much money on it.' Nup. I am not impressed, nor grateful, for the money that was put into the Royal Commission. As an MP, you get to know just how fast government spends money. Five hundred million dollars is a lot of money but it's also the cost of six months tagging along behind the Americans in the Syrian bombing campaigns. It's not something our community should be grateful for. We will get louder and stronger – until these wrongs are addressed.

The way in which I've grown up and come to understand myself as a disabled person has given me the space to be proud of who I am. And as the disability movement goes forward, one of the things we've got to gift to the next generation, and to keep alight firmly in ourselves, is that sense of pride and celebration of ourselves as disabled people. The campaign for the royal commission is a good example and there are many others. Disabled people are coming into our power as a community. And part of coming into your power is coming into a radical self-love, from which you can spark joy and hope. We have struggled for a long time, and we will struggle further still. But we will get there together, in that spirit of empowerment and self-love and hope.

Nothing in my life has changed me more for the better than knowing that I am loved by my family. And that's what I hope people reading this take away. If you are a disabled kid growing up, love yourself. Or if you have just been gifted an incredible little baby that's disabled, love them. Love the hell out of them. Treasure them as the incredible thing that they are. Treasure *yourself* as the incredible thing *you* are. Know that whatever you are, you are enough. And you will be okay – you are not alone, you are wonderful. And together as a community we will make things better, smash the shit out of all the discrimination and create a wonderful bloody world to share together.

I Don't Need Them to See Through You

Jessica Knight

'Hey. How blind are you really?'

'I once ate potpourri from a bowl in a cafe because I thought it was mixed nuts.'

This amuses the young man I am talking to at 2 a.m. He has taken me home and I am trying to explain how bad my eyes are. It is my 'wearing contacts' phase. I am my own example of a post-glasses makeover. I am attempting to figure out (for the hundredth time) how to take the contact lenses out of my eyes before getting busy with this person, who has a pet rat in a cage in his bedroom. This person is cute, and I think it's quite sweet he has a pet rat. It's so difficult to remove the contacts and it causes my drunken self so much stress that I start to cry a bit at the futility of love and human connection. This lubes up my eyes so that one of the contacts finally pops out and into my hand. It works with the other one as well. Success! I put them away and turn to the young man sitting on the edge of his unmade bed. He is smiling at me. I wipe my tear-stained eyes, smudging my eyeliner. I smile back and pull my t-shirt up and off over my head.

This is being twenty-five.

*

Back to the here and now. I have sat on my glasses and now they are bent quite badly. Placing them on my nose, I find the hinges have angled the eyepieces and the lenses so that they are facing my nose instead of being in front of my eyes, their vital position in the humble mission of making me slightly less vision-impaired. There have been numerous close calls over the years, where I have been about to sit on them but realised seconds before placing all my weight on top of the unsuspecting object. This particular pair of glasses is important to me. I feel good wearing them. They make me feel intelligent and capable and a little bit sexy. *Then why were they left on the couch for the thirty thousand and fifth time*, you may ask. If you could see me right now, you would see me shrug.

It was not always like this. I have a long history of hating my glasses. They were not always considered a cool accessory, worn by intellectual posers or used as a form of fashion. Please do not wear glasses unless you need them. Pretending to be blind or visually challenged is actually really uncool. So is trying on my glasses as though it's fun to have warped vision. Your face is usually bigger than mine and you wreck the fit. This happened all through school and university. My crush in second-year uni once wore my glasses while pouring a drink of juice. They missed the glass, made a mess and left me to clean it up.

Now that I live in Melbourne and have many writer and creative friends, I am surrounded by people who need and wear glasses. It is a magical and wonderful world.

I take my mangled glasses back to the place where I got them. They fix them but say that the damage has been done to their overall sturdiness and future longevity. The end is nigh.

*

My first pair of glasses was placed on my nose when I was four. They had thin metal frames and curved over each of my ears so they didn't fall off easily.

'Coke bottle glasses!' my father exclaimed. He was not wrong. He made it clear that they were adorable. Though he and my mother referred to me as their little owl, I grew up loathing those glasses. One day I put them somewhere so safe that I forgot where they were, and for two weeks I had to go to school with nothing but my natural amount of vision. Then one morning, as I was about to go to school with my backpack on my tiny back, I looked into my mother's concerned face as she asked me one more time if I could remember this special place where I had hidden my glasses. I ran into my bedroom and opened my underwear drawer. They were there, pushed to the bottom and back of the drawer.

*

'Where are your glasses?' was a question I heard a lot while doing completely normal things like watching television or reading a book. It was so annoying. I should have been able to hold books as close as I wanted without judgement. My mother would sing-song 'Vanity, thy name is vanity' for the trillionth time as I resentfully placed my glasses on my nose and sat a bit further away from the television. It was easy for them to say it was silly and vain – they didn't wear glasses. All four of my siblings have excellent vision. My parents did not need glasses until they were in their fifties.

The bifocal years didn't help my resentment. When I was thirteen, an ophthalmologist suggested that I wear bifocals for my two-tone vision needs, so that I could read books with one part of the lens and do everything else with the other part. Old people wore bifocals. My grandparents and other uncool people wore bifocals. The word sounded crusty and decrepit to my young mind. I didn't just have Coke bottle bottom lenses to contend with anymore.

When I brought the glasses home, I stood alone in the bathroom with the door closed. I looked at myself in the smudged mirror while wearing my new bifocals. My reflection was not smiling. Because I only had a few precious moments before being found by a younger sibling, I had a quick but intense self-hating cry and went back out to continue being a big sister. A big sister who did not wear her ugly glasses.

It was at this time that I very nearly picked up a giant brown spider from the living room floor. It was hiding under a stray sock. The carpet in the room was faded floral, and while I was cleaning things up I mistook the unsuspecting spider for an abandoned toy. The worst part was that after I squealed it scuttled away under the couch, evading capture and relocation outside. Did I take this as a sign to wear my glasses more often? No.

When I did start wearing my glasses out and about, it amazed me how many dudes felt the need to come up and tell me that I would be more attractive without them. This unprompted, freely given advice enraged me every single time. These young men thought they were giving me a much-needed tip so that I might be deemed worthy of being sexed up by them. It happened a lot while

I was working as a cleaner of hotels on Hamilton Island. I took the advice of these beach-bodied douchebags with a sprinkle of sea water. No, that's not true. I felt ugly and sad.

*

Now I do wear my glasses everywhere, but my eyesight is still not great. Glasses cannot fix a total lack of peripheral vision or inoperable cataracts. I wear my glasses everywhere now because five years ago I managed to get a pair that I love. Until then I had only ever got them from the Medicare range of free frames. You had the option of about three or four different frames that ranged from super-awful to meh-not-great-but-they-will-do.

This time was different. This time I was getting my frames and lenses from a hipster eye place that served me tea and had antique-looking rugs on the floor. They even had an optometrist there who I could see for an eye test. When I got tested the optometrist sat down in her chair and gazed at me in wonder.

'How did you get here?' she asked.

I stared at her in confusion. None of my past eye doctors had asked me such philosophical questions. She must mean literally, I finally concluded.

'By tram,' I said.

'Your eyes are extremely bad. You should consider applying for a disability plan.'

This was news to me, and life-changing news at that. Perhaps my eyes were the reason I was bad at so many jobs even though I tried so hard. I did not follow her advice until three years later. It took me that long to wrestle with my ingrained ableism.

This is how I found my first true love: after seeing the kind optometrist I browsed the amazing array of glasses, the likes and variety of which I had never seen before. The chosen pair were plain black and made me look like Zooey Deschanel in *New Girl* (ha ha, okay, 'feel like') and every asshat beat-poet wannabe. When I found out how expensive they were, it was all over and the dream was dead – until a payment plan was arranged. They were expensive not just because of the frames but because my prescription was so high and unique. Thanks to my pathological desire to be special, this both pleased me and ruined me financially. The new glasses even came in a bright red case. No boring glasses house for these babies. They have got me through so much over the last five years.

*

How bad are your eyes?

Bad. Real bad. I once mistook a stranger's two-year-old child for a small adorable dog.

I go back to the same place to look at new glasses and get my eyes tested. I am nervous. What if my already legally blind eyes have got worse? What if they are going to deteriorate at the same rate as the eyes of people who get glasses in middle age? If my eyes are this bad already, surely it is just a matter of time until my eyesight goes completely? Of course I could live a happy life more blind than I am currently. I just don't really want to. I am already the kind of blind that angers cyclists as they dodge me and my lack of peripheral vision. Sunlight hurts my eyes and it takes me a little while to adjust to sudden changes in light.

On arrival I am approached by my fave assistant. She wears amazing bright-coloured glasses that match her pastel purple skirt and pastel blue blouse with white collar and bow. She makes me a cup of peppermint tea and gives me a biscuit. It is so much nicer than all those poky old windowless examination rooms of my youth in regional Victoria. Also, thanks to being an adult and having a bit of foresight, I am getting ready to replace my beloved black-framed glasses before they break completely. There is a crack forming, so I'm preparing myself. This way I can have time to pay for my new pair and not be in a blind bind, like when my last pair broke. Who can afford new and awesome glasses whenever they want without having to live off mee goreng and toast? Without getting evicted because they have spent their rent money? Not this hard-of-seeing, all-extreme-emotion-feeling babe.

Do I dare go for tortoiseshell frames? I ask myself as I am shown a multitude of this kind. There are more than thirty different types. The decision is made for me by the cost difference between getting the same frames again and my favourite pair of tortoiseshell frames. That difference is three hundred dollars. In two months I will be wearing dark-blue tortoiseshell frames.

The optometrist who greets me as I sip my tea is not the woman I remember, and my reaction proves that I'm more of a feminist now, because instead of noticing his handsomeness straight away I simply feel deflated that it's not the woman from before. It would have been nice to tell her that I finally took her advice.

Eye tests don't take so long when your eyesight only allows you to identify the large, single letter at the top of the pyramid of letters that get smaller and smaller. After the optometrist shines a weird light into each of my eyeballs, he tells me my eyes have not got any worse. I confess my fear: if my eyes are this bad now, how will they be when I'm fifty? He explains that when someone who has had perfect vision gets glasses, their eyesight has gone from 99 per cent perfect to 95 per cent. The difference is not that much but enough to need glasses. Since my eyes are barely 50 per cent working, they won't actually decline like someone with 20/20 vision will experience decline. I nod.

'So you're saying my eyes are already fucked, so I can relax and not worry.' I smile. 'Thank you for clearing that up. It was stressing me out.'

I put my glasses back on and look at him. *Oh my goodness, he is handsome*, I think, as I scoop up my tote from the floor and walk out.

December Three

C.B. Mako

December Three
International Day of People with Disability.
Shortened to an acronym, a hashtag: #IDPwD
// Coincidentally, it's also a deadline to submit this poetry //

However,
    as a carer
    with invisible disability // hard of hearing, mental health
    issues //
        we're in the lowest income bracket,
        our family plunged into poverty.
        As I type this poem, my children
                clamour for more food,
                        they're still hungry.
        We have nowhere to go, rejected by the
                migrant community,
        for carer and disabled—be both—this, us,
                they refused to see.
        For people of colour *should* be 'model minority'
        in order to remain in this colonised country.

Meanwhile,
    In the NDIS, I'm excluded.
        'You cannot be both,' they said.
        And I'm not 'disabled enough.'

—Duality.

Intersectionality.

Othered.

In the mainstream narrative,
My story is not *the* story,
Mental illness is invisible disability,
plausible deniability,
And there are already // white // people who are
telling stories of Mental Health and Disability.

Thus, I am:

Separated.
Alienated.

Excluded.
Erased.

All I see are …
Stoic stares.
Mocking glares:

But I still pursue #ownvoices
#RepresentationMatters
// And I had to ask for a loan—twelve
dollars—to enter a poetry contest //

So that my words would be heard, take hold, and

exist.

With thanks to Gemma Mahadeo, one of the founding members of Disabled QBIPOC Collective, for acting as sensitivity reader

Never Needed Fixing

Eliza Hull

I didn't grow up disabled; I grew up with a problem. A problem that those around me wanted to fix, and that I began to want to fix too.

I was raised in Wodonga, a regional town 300 kilometres north-east of Melbourne. When I was five years old, I started falling over at school. I can still vividly recall the feeling of the rocks that got caught in my knees, the warm blood that would drip down my leg, and the numb, tingling sensation. My knees grew strong and firm.

There were doctor's appointments, hospital visits, questions and confusion, but never any answers. After each surgery, I watched red blood seep through my plaster casts, the hospital fairy would blow bubbles while I lay there, and celebrity footballers visited. Medical staff constantly talked about me, not to me. At five, I also started singing, which was a form of escape.

After consulting with many specialists, my parents decided it was best for me to have several surgical procedures during my childhood. Their intention was to alleviate my symptoms and make my life easier. On reflection, as an adult, I understand that this is what every parent wants. They cared so much and tried as hard as they could. It must have been scary for them – the uncertainty of what life would be like for me – because difference is something most of us are taught to fear.

I was finally diagnosed with Charcot-Marie-Tooth, a disorder that affects the peripheral nervous system. Symptoms include progressive loss of muscle tissue and of touch sensation across my body, which causes me to walk with a different gait. During my teenage years, I would describe it to people as a problem. If a shopkeeper, stranger or new friend asked, 'What happened?'

or 'What have you done to yourself?' I would sometimes make up stories: 'I got hit by a truck' or 'I was in an accident'. But most of the time I would just reply that I had 'a leg problem'. I felt inadequate and painfully different.

When I was about to have my second round of surgery, I desperately wanted an escape, so I lied. The week before the surgery I announced with confidence to my friends that I was going to be fixed, that the surgery was going to make me walk straight. Deep down I almost believed it. I craved it so badly that my lie started to feel real. My friends created a book of well wishes, and everyone said how exciting it was going to be to finally see me run, climb stairs and walk properly. One friend wrote, 'I can't wait to be able to do sport together.'

Of course this was all innocent, we were young, and all of us, myself included, deeply wanted to be 'normal', to fit in.

After the surgery, my friends must have noticed that I hadn't been fixed, but they never mentioned it. I was grateful for their silence.

In the weeks that followed, I let all the 'cool' footy boys at school take my wheelchair at lunchtime. They raced in it down the hill. I would sit out on the oval, feeling stranded, my means of getting around suddenly gone. Strangely though, it felt good seeing the boys play with my wheelchair, like they were validating who I was.

During the recovery from the surgery, I started using crutches and splints on my legs. Mum took me shopping to buy new shoes to fit the splints. I cried. I tried to hide my tears, but they poured out like an overflowing ocean at high tide. One shoe was my standard size, and the other was three sizes bigger, and the tongue of that shoe had to be cut to fit my foot. I was fourteen and all I wanted was to be accepted. I felt like I was about to jump off a cliff – and at the bottom was a pit of schoolkids laughing at my expense.

It was the summer holidays then – during those months most days hit 40C in the shade. But on my first day back at school, I wore the oversized shoe with long pants to hide the splints. I was embarrassed to be me. Two of my closest friends also came to school wearing black pants that day in solidarity. This is one of the kindest things anyone has ever done for me.

During the long days in the sweltering heat, I didn't want to be seen. I wanted to wear a dress like all the other girls. I wanted to hide, to fix my condition, to make it disappear. I spent hours locked away in the music room, writing songs on the piano, full of angst and heart. Braces on my teeth, my hair pulled back so tight I got headaches, pimples, crooked legs, grazed knees, pain, tiredness, heavy: it all felt overwhelming. It felt endless.

In Drama class that year there were two new boys who'd transferred from another school because our Drama program was so well known and respected. They were arty and funny, and quickly fit into my school friendship group. One day one of these boys asked if I would be interested in coming to his church. It was out of town, he said, and would be full of people who could help me. 'I think if we go, there would be a real chance we could solve your leg problem,' he said, smiling. Relief swept over me. I was suddenly floating, weightless. For that whole day I believed I would finally be fixed. I asked Mum if I could go. She said it was fine, of course: it wasn't like I was asking to go to a party. I wanted to go to church. How innocent.

The boy had his drivers licence because he lived on the other side of the border, in New South Wales, where you could get your licence at seventeen. As he drove us down dusty roads under pink clouds, I sang along to the radio. I was so nervous I made pretend pictures on my knee with my fingers. We cracked jokes and I told him stories about my life. He listened attentively.

The church building was old and weathered. Inside there was a mass of people having lively conversations by candlelight. I wanted to be inconspicuous, so I stood behind a group of them in the pews. It was like any other church service I'd been to, but this time I felt jittery, my palms sweaty. I sang the hymns with the congregation, our voices blending like a choir.

'Before the service is finished, we have a special visitor who has come for us to pray for them,' the pastor said as he looked at me. 'Please can you come forward, Eliza?'

I walked anxiously to the front of the church, and a group of people quickly swarmed around me like bees, each of them chanting and praying. It got louder and louder. Hands were touching my back. I felt overwhelmed, suffocated, and overcome by nausea. Why was I here? This question kept repeating in my mind. They wanted to fix me, because I had let them believe this is what I wanted. And why did I want this? Because I lived in a world where I felt I wasn't accepted. Where difference was feared, not celebrated.

Of course the next morning I woke up and I wasn't fixed. Funny that.

Now, as I write this, I am emotional. I feel for that young, innocent version of myself. I want to tell her that she was wonderful just the way she was. That she didn't need to hide her splints under thick black pants in the heat of summer. That she didn't need to let the boys at school take her wheelchair at lunchtime, or to go to a church to be fixed.

I wish I had grown up disabled. That identity, which I feared for so long, is now one of my greatest qualities. It's who I am. As a 34-year-old woman, I am disabled and so very proud. I teach my daughter about disability, I sing about disability. I speak about disability. I advocate, and I share the stories of other disabled people. Now when a stranger asks, 'What happened?' I smile, and say, 'I have a disability.'

Having a Voice

Belinda Downes

We didn't have social media when I was growing up. I was born in 1971, and for years I couldn't even find out what my condition was called. I used a computer for the first time in my second-last year of high school, and didn't own one until my second year of university. My 1000-word essays for uni had to be stored across two files, because in popular programs like Microsoft Word, each file could only hold a maximum of 500 words.

Back then, we found information a different way, in forms that were very hard to keep current and that only spoke about able-bodied experiences. I was told things were a particular way because they had always been that way; people in authority said so. The paper encyclopedia said so. Newspapers and television – the popular culture of the time – said so.

Popular culture said – and still says today – that people like me, born with a cleft face (a rare form of cleft lip and palate) are scary. We were the villains in TV shows and movies. These representations were not true, of course, but they meant that people in authority got used to hiding people like me, and what we had to say, from public spaces. In my younger life, many people sought to speak on my behalf.

I know my own face better than anyone, but others have always had things to say about it. There was the time I was trying to get my first job, and I was instructed to register at a place that found jobs for people with disabilities. My resume was handed around without my knowledge or permission and I was ultimately compelled to take a job I knew my face couldn't handle. People still think that my disability is my facial scars. The scars itch sometimes, but my actual facial disability means I can't see properly – and for this job, working the phones in a call centre, I couldn't talk for more than a few hours a week before it seized up. I knew my face would not cope and I was right: after only a couple of weeks, I couldn't speak at all and my face became badly infected. I ended up in the mailroom for the next few months while my contract played out. The job finished painfully, with me needing to have more facial surgery to fix the damage.

Years later, my boss from the call centre told me that I had left the role, she surmised, because I was shy and didn't like the way I looked. But did you know that many people with scars on their faces actually *like* their faces – including their scars? That, anecdotally, many have better-than-average body image? I've always loved my face and its scars. I had to leave that job because the work was physically damaging. Both in my recruitment and in the reasons for my departure, I wasn't consulted. I recently learnt that my old boss had been told I was leaving their business because I lacked confidence. I was shocked that I'd been so misrepresented – more people talking behind my back and making decisions for me without my consent or knowledge, based on unfounded assumptions.

When I did have the operation to repair the damage, it solved a mystery in my life, one that was to help me develop my own voice and career.

*

I've had about twenty-five operations in my life, which actually isn't that many. As a very young child I lived in Sydney, and my mum would take me a couple of suburbs away for routine check-ups to make sure my face was going okay. Then we left Sydney and my dad bought a small business on the mid-north coast of New South Wales. I loved it there. I was even the girl school captain in my final year – because I was the only girl in that year at our tiny school.

One day, as I was preparing my books and schoolbag for high school (I was so excited to finally be going), Mum came into my room and explained to me (she didn't ask) that someone in the education department in Sydney had decided that I would have to repeat Grade 6 in another school. I had 'low self-esteem' and 'low socialisation', it had been decreed. Nobody asked me. I felt disappointed and angry. Why was no-one interested in what I felt or wanted? I've never had low self-esteem. Although many of my peers at the new school became friends that I still have to this day, that doesn't make it right that I wasn't asked.

Throughout this time I kept having operations. Much of the surgery had a 'let's see if this works' kind of approach. There was a prevailing belief that scarred faces are bad faces, and many people, including surgeons, got their ideas about scars from popular culture, not from people with scars themselves. As with the operations earlier in my childhood, again I wasn't asked; it was just decreed that I would be going to Sydney – now a whole-day trip from where we lived – and I was expected to acquiesce.

One time Mum told me, out of the blue, 'We're going to Sydney to see your surgeon. He wants to see you.' Just a check-up, I assumed. But I would remember this particular conversation with my craniofacial surgeon, when I was fifteen, forever.

'So you want to get your lip fixed?' After a six-hour-plus drive, we'd arrived in his office in Sydney, and he'd gone straight to the point.

'No!' I said quickly, not needing to think about it. It was the first I'd heard of this idea.

I have an incomplete Manchester-repaired upper lip – it looks like a little lump under my nose. I've always loved it; it's always been a part of me, part of my face, of my identity.

This was thirty-two years ago, but I can still clearly remember the puzzled look on my surgeon's face. 'But you were adamant that you wanted it done,' he said, sounding confused.

As I've said, I didn't often get a say in what happened to me – but here I had an in, and I was resolute that I was going to keep my lip the way it was. As great as my surgeon was, he wasn't going to take part of my face away from me.

'But I love my lip the way it is. I've never wanted to change it.'

I stood my ground. In the back of my mind I was conscious that it was a big deal to come to Sydney – the long drive, considerable planning, my surgeon's precious time.

'But, but,' he said, blinking, 'you were absolutely adamant that you wanted your lip fixed.' Now *both* the surgeon and I were confused, because I'd never spoken to my mum about 'fixing' my lip.

It didn't need fixing.

'Nope, never.' I stood my ground, again, knowing I was undermining the authority of my surgeon and my mum, and that all of this could come crashing down on me at any moment if Mum signed the paperwork, because I was still a minor.

Then my surgeon said something that to this day reminds me to always speak up for myself. I didn't realise it then, but it was a very important piece of a bigger puzzle.

'But your mum said you were adamant you wanted your lip fixed.'

We looked at Mum. She didn't say anything, but both my surgeon and I knew something wasn't right.

A victory had occurred. The surgeon had heard me – he'd heard my voice and my wishes. I still have the incomplete Manchester lip repair to this day, and I still love it.

As we left the surgeon's rooms and headed home, I wondered why she'd done that, my mother, but I wasn't game to ask.

*

Over the ensuing years, Mum unfortunately developed a poker-machine gambling addiction – partly because she was in pain from not being able to use her own voice as a child. I only knew about this from small, occasional comments; she'd get angry if we asked anything else about it. She mentioned that as a child she'd be hit if she 'backtalked' (I read that as speaking up appropriately), and that she was not listened to. Gambling addictions cost not only a lot of money. Our mother lost a lot of time from her life and relationships.

It was tough for me too. I couldn't help her, and increasingly she ignored me, just as my own voice was becoming stronger. The day I turned eighteen, she took me to the pokies, hoping that I might join her, and validate the addiction. Poker-machine rooms are designed to numb people's minds and personalities. There's dim lighting, no view to the outside world, the club serves you drinks and there are no clocks to tell you how much time you're wasting. I went because Mum invited me but I complained incessantly, so she never invited me again, although I often had to go in there to remind her to come home in the evenings after school.

We lost our house.

As I grew up, other older people helped me in different ways. I still appreciate those people.

I left school in the late 1980s, and I'm happy to say that apart from a bit of teasing when I repeated Grade 6, I wasn't bullied in high school.

*

It came as a huge, confusing surprise many years later, while I was planning the operation to fix the damage caused by the unsuitable call-centre work, that Mum contacted me. She wanted to help. I was living on my own in Newcastle at the time, and she offered a place for me to recover on the mid-north coast; and even though I was now twenty-nine, she would come to Sydney to look after me straight after the operation. I was having surgery to fix my bottom eyelids. I did need help, so although I hadn't seen her in a few years, I said yes.

The day of the operation came. Mum was near, but not quite with me, hovering around the staff, doing the paperwork; she hadn't really asked me anything, just busied herself doing 'things'. As far as she was concerned, it seems, I still had no voice. But this was the year 2000 and I was twenty-nine. Things had shifted.

The first indication something was up came when the nurse asked me to sign a consent form. I was an adult, after all. She ran through the procedure and its risks, asking me if I understood or had any questions.

No questions from me – it was a clear procedure that I'd discussed with my surgeon. It needed to be done. It was the reversal of a an operation I'd had, aged seventeen, which Mum had manipulated the surgeon and I into.

But the nurse had a question: Mum had been lingering outside my hospital room, and all the nurses on the ward knew who she was, but now she was nowhere to be seen. Where was she? She was meant to take me to her place afterwards to recover. Was she okay?

After a frantic search over a few hours (we didn't have mobile phones at that time), they eventually found her. She was at home, up the coast, a six-hour drive from the hospital in Sydney where I was about to have surgery.

Sitting there on the ward, waiting to be taken to theatre, an enormous realisation struck me; various pieces of a lifelong puzzle finally began fitting together. My mother had been hanging around the ward to get a copy of the medical insurance invoice. She had been unable to, and now she was gone.

Before medical administration was fully digitalised, we would take my surgical paperwork to the insurer to get cash for the hospital bill. But now not only was the consent form signed by me (not Mum), but also the form went directly to the insurer to pay the bill, online.

Mum had taken hospital invoices and leant on friends and relatives for financial support. For many years she had used my surgeries to bankroll her gambling addiction. Why did my mother run away? There was no invoice, no paper bill, for her to take with her.

Later, my relatives told me of the funds they had given her upon seeing my medical bills. She had been lying to everyone about me, talking behind my back, not allowing me to talk to them. Because she had no sense of herself as a person, she saw me as just a means to earn money. Friends and relatives were manipulated by her stories: 'If you loved me, you'd help me help my daughter.' Every operation, necessary or not, was used for this purpose. Complicating the situation was that not even the surgeons knew what was necessary, my condition is so rare. But I loved my face then, and I still love it. It's my mother's betrayal that has had the biggest impact on my life, not my scars.

*

Fortunately, Dad came to get me from the hospital and gave me a place to recover. He even got mashed prawns, my favourite recovery food.

Mum died in 2009, after a short illness. The very last thing she did was apologise to me on the phone from her hospital bed in central New South Wales. We hadn't spoken to one another since just before the operation, nine years earlier. While we talked, she asked what I did for a living.

'I'm a linguist, Mum . . . I teach teachers how to help kids find their voice.'

Chlorophyll Like Pink

Patrick Gunasekera

Me five or six. Suburban backyard big, grapevines boiling brown in the sun. Dad outside gardening busy chicken-like. Broad-brimmed hats many enough for all us by the front door. Purple evenings jelly and ice-cream, do your spelling at the kitchen table I'll watch. Don't be silly with me. Stop crying. Echo anything from my ears, my voice can be whole world wide yes. Little throat reverberate and don't be scared. He's Dad. Nothing bad. Banging hands on the table so happy to be alive. Always sing when I nervous, he won't hit so hard for bit then. Or just be quiet he'll go away. Except he thrown the bowl of milk in my face I tried so hard to disappear. I'd eaten all the oranges that day why.

Getting taller. Taller than my teachers some. Best at class clever boy. Do it like Patrick. Well done. Knew not to stim at school, even but getting in trouble the worst feeling, please don't hit me too make me unseen don't look at me with those bloodshot eyes. Don't. Do it. Again. Shaking in my shirt rest of the day until bed. Get out our hats and run run to our schoolbags, key rings bright and silicone in the shade. Share food on the grass at lunch not supposed to but it make amity us. Joke of naked bananas, Tiny Teddys being silly sexual. Rougher boys talk about the teachers that way too. Never felt good to me. Too much shame already at home. Found out exploring with a friend down the road and we in deep water. I didn't know it was bad until then, Amma ask me what the worst thing we did I don't know just be doctors like touching and pretend.

Thirteen me panic body don't go outside go home go to bed. Every time cross the road speak in class. Heart racing no breath. Everyone see me too much stop stop. Year 8 and new marks down

10 per cent again from last year. Not enough yet to B grade no one say I'm struggling then so. Sir can you explain again please. Sir I don't get it. Sir still no please. They all see me. Stumbling. Not good enough. Stupid stupid. I couldn't finish this assignment no sorry. Sorry no. Shower in the morning steamy slow too long every day can't use body efficient. Dad point the garden hose to my face for that. Dead weight me like a nobody. Better off dead me. School too big go home stay home year or so. No one wants me. No more smart student me. Nobody. Dad learn to hit less with hands. Learn new ways to squeeze my numb body. You are not allowed to be artist no. Not that kind of queer too much no. Well then we won't let you. You. Can't. Live. Like. That. Psychologist not helpful me for, Dad being intrusive there too. Come into the room him say I never belonged anywhere in my life, choosing to be gay to belong somewhere. He's not really gay though. That therapist's a *bitch*. Why don't they talk the deeper issues. Nowhere now floating lost. Too much for school. Too gagged for support. All along Dad the reason why I sick he no one talk of, no one look he's here can't say.

Hospital at fifteen now scared surrounded. Monster man out for me. Eucalypts on the street watch me report back he's here we get him soon. My friend no name they care understand like no other, just for me and angels come stay here. I have crossed the Atlantic Ocean twenty times in the last year. The nurses do best they can. Young and gentle hostile. Patrick what's going on. Talk to me. Would you like a Milo would that help would? Nothing speaks too colours red in the room they here to get. Me. Patrick you're not psychotic. And you're delusional where sexual orientation. Not seeing reality wearing makeup like a woman. Me discharge then back again got worse they didn't believe me. Different hospital. Medication makes me sleep good and I heard thumping they here no. But they poison didn't they. Patrick you're talking to yourself. No I'm not! Yes you are. Nurse I'm scared meds been infiltrated, they'll get me I won't take them. Wide rooms tables flipped security guards. Plastic cups I gave to a girl squeeze like a stress ball you'll feel better. I just sat and collaged every day. Patrick you'll need to leave if you don't want to be treated. You need to take your meds. Not ready to leave still, back out stuck, better but cut my arm deep angels helped me to. No control but over my own bloodshed. I tried to tell them. No one listen again.

Back at school next year February hopeful new. Navy carpets black shoes and noticeboards full up. Paper planes, salt and pepper cafeteria sit outside the library friends. Running the oval wrestling a boy I like, laughing big kids we. Still takes me long to write but better they understanding you do what you can Patrick you won't get in trouble today. Less subjects thank you. Together free periods Ben and I across the table. Comic books and stimming like safe us. Never look down on a neurotype us. Visual Art my favourite homework. One day I change the world like them I learn. Painting the prime minister Tony Abbott, like ego bird and danger good marks. Exams all big I take long writing still. Unfinished pages and tumble down I can't. Miss I can't do Year 12. Not in one year no. Try no beating heart please I want to finish school I can't. Patrick it's not about learning it's about achieving. No.

*

Sixteen me first day at TAFE. Concrete walls graduate art hanging from high or hidden in plain sight different like. Orange logos glass and happy warm. Breathing free take your time Patrick do it how you can. Your makeup is nice today. And your coat pink like. Learn Bauhaus postmodernism gaze and voice. World bigger than I was told. Bigger grow I standing sure. Makes me dream. Green and blue pulling out marks and touch the paper steady. Thick paint gloopy dirty pants tell truths howl on white primer too. Washing we palettes crashing sinks sudsy I love how you work. Me too. Show you later. More possible me make sex and masculinity no one says stop too much queer. Blush cheeks smile go home Amma I'm happy. Flapping dance around the room loud loud glee don't stop.

Eighteen me Dad still funny me gay and slow. Tell me again wrong am I no job no nothing. A man your age shouldn't be like you. Apartment in the city Amma will pay but doesn't feel scary me. Tall old place like a lighthouse safest home I ever lived. Thank you Amma I make you proud most soon. On alone remember me belongings all here together safe. Deep come back sorrow cry. Remember I nobody must be change or nobody. Grieving little boy he hit me like a rag doll. My little boy I'm sorry. Child bad no free until now. I say strong. NO. MORE. He gone now. No more. Never beat me hands or words again I won't let him. Go away we never speak again. I morning star glow radiant golden every day brighter with my life. Light of body new caring gentle. Giving light in my lighthouse no dark again him or anyone ever I won't let.

But muscle body then. Stop. Lie down don't no pain what's happening. Walk stop no can't. Stay home all day can't walk up and down the stairs this one no. If you exercise better yes try why don't you. Fifteen-minute workout can't do nothing three days. Lie down stim too loud the many people here too much too much. No parties more any, no gigs see my friends no nothing but late night knocks me out too busy for take rest recovery can't sorry no, maybe another time if it's morning afternoon or so? Ben tells me stimming and sensory, disability politics. Dinner home thank you. Nothing wrong I'm here I love you. Take time be still don't need dishes clean no it's okay today. Okay. Amma doesn't believe I'm disabled still not then or this one too. I taking weeks to get better five day workshop or painting sit there back hurting. Can't leave the house. Calling calling friends no one around help who am I. Do I matter? Sit down at the back where the seats they all around other side of the room. Again alone. Spoons too low for language mustn't be interested. No I'm listening to everything please I'm here. Again twice theatre universities told me not to apply. No place for crips. Same white educated rich through and through always we here theatre. Oh sorry yes but you can use the lift of course oh sorry yes. No we don't have the budget for an interpreter. No I don't know of many disabled artists here working. I know why. Captions performance me accessible is political but no one care for me reciprocate no. Patrick you were asking for too much. You are not allowed to need no those okay look no. Every day fighting back. Every day being own hero I no one else doing this work no crip consciousness here tokenism and tickboxes Perth arts.

Alone and Stella Young writing read alone in bed on smartphone me. Digging digging strength and meaning her words. Nothing bad my body no not my fault your responsibility yes you. Social model. Changes everything this me. Social value me, systemic struggle me, not my fault. She write one day sixteen-year-old self yes you will have sex a lot stop worrying. I cry hear yes I will too somebody one day and many true don't worry. Doesn't matter great but still. Everyone talking like it's so easy to access now. Even masturbating makes me tired. Hopeful now cry okay it's okay. Leah Lakshmi Piepzna-Samarasinha hear your voice podcast isolated but you there here talking to me. Your great stories care work and no one left behind everyone matters that's me too me too. Lie on my floor seek relief but know this here politics my body mine power here. Dream here community crips lie on the floor yes crip body good. One day sex too. Today honour this body mine great like a pine tree. No one take what my elders gave me now. They would not forget me no. I matter.

*

Joel sits beside me lying down again on the floor. Sitting on my bed tea come over laugh together, me lying down again he loves me still. Ben dinner again thank you I'll pay next time, cuddle like lover friends he echolalia my vocal stims. Danyon and me I'm late sorry slow morning again. So many leave the house too much late again. But. He hug and sit down me no worries, talk video art exhibition lots to say. Mouth no articulate less I slur lisp soft consonants he okay love me still. Hey Aisyah how are you for spoons are you up now talking or no? No. Cool. Steven teach me learn together me too, why don't they no there's need access plan for footpath closed, should be regulation there's steps other side there. Ugh. Art centre we photograph broken lift theirs on workshop day we. One day we artists our own spaces here strong. Indigenous sovereignty, unlearning masculinity, crips and poor angry we dreaming together futures our own.

Body mine brick house beautiful and resilient. Body he cook and paint, use camera nothing bad no ever never say again. Body creeping passion loud fingers and toes onstage. Body flap rock sit down loved too. Body ask for chair, will not move no I no get me a chair this is my access need I'm allowed I matter. Body mine faggot lively colourful, eyeliner earrings kinky and confronting power yes mine. Laugh their stares in fear, ha, they stare how my beautiful fag. Body he wobble legs no can't stand. Can't leave home no today not that's okay. Okay. Okay. Rest an act defiance of yes.

Admire him crip body. Adore him take the lift yes. Desire him life his own way now. Love him no one hurt again him no. Dream him future bright and alone no one care all each love. Dream him big and bright here now.

Et Lux (also, light)

Robin M. Eames

I was the eldest of four. Now I am the eldest of three. My sister Lucy was born with spinal muscular atrophy, a genetic disorder that causes muscle wasting. There are four main types of SMA, one of which is usually fatal in infancy, and others in which life expectancy is normal or near normal. When Lucy was diagnosed, my parents were told that the only way to identify which type she had was to wait and see if she survived. She did not.

For the entirety of my formative years, I associated the idea of disability with Lucy and death. I didn't realise that I was disabled as well; that I too was born with a systemic genetic disorder, but one that affects my connective tissues rather than my muscles. I didn't know that I was autistic, or that I would grow up to manifest a number of mental and chronic illnesses. I knew that I was weird, and I knew that I was different. But as a child I never understood myself to be 'disabled'.

I rarely talk about Lucy, but her life and death shaped me profoundly, in ways that I struggle to articulate. I grew up with her ghost. When I was contemplating what to write about for this anthology, I kept returning to her. Lucy's story isn't mine to tell, but I can't separate it from my own. So this is an essay about the two of us.

Lucy was four years younger than me. She had dark hair and blue eyes, like our dad, but I was convinced that her eyes would eventually turn hazel, like my own. In most of the photos of her she is grimacing or vaguely quizzical. She spent a great deal of her life in my arms, and I was the first person to make her smile. I try to remember these things about her, and not what she looked like after she died. I don't always succeed. The functions of memory are cruel.

This is the oldest trauma of my life. The process of stitching together this essay was clumsy because I kept dissociating while writing it. I'd think of her name and be flung out of my body. I'd picture her face and go somewhere else, somewhere pale and unreal, all fog and fugue.

Mourning someone who died so young is a strange, oblique kind of grief. Sometimes I feel like we're all mourning who she wasn't, rather than who she was. We wonder about the person she might have become. She left such an imprint on our lives, but it's an empty space, the presence of an absence rather than the absence of a presence. A shadow, or an outline.

Lucy never got the chance to grow up disabled in Australia. Mum often used to say that if Lucy had lived, she would have been in terrible pain, and she would have had to use a wheelchair, as if that softened the blow of her death. When I started needing to use a wheelchair a few years ago, I thought about that a lot, and for a long time it brought me heartache and shame. We are given so many societal narratives framing disability as a fate worse than death. I understand my mother's reasoning – she viewed disability in terms of suffering and limitation, because that was all she knew. She thought only of loss. To her, a wheelchair was a symbol of confinement, rather than of mobility and freedom. She had no other frame of reference, and neither did I. It's been a steep learning curve. I don't know how different things would have been if I'd grown up with a sister who used a wheelchair. If we'd grown up disabled together.

We moved around a lot when I was younger. I was born in the UK but all of my siblings were born in Perth, on Whadjuk Noongar country. If Lucy had lived for longer we might have stayed there. The map of our lives would have changed drastically. She would have needed occupational therapy, physiotherapy, assistive equipment, and consistent medical and disability support – the kind that I need now. I often wonder what our childhoods would have been like if she'd lived. If we'd be close, or estranged; if we'd have interests in common; if she'd be cheerful, or quiet, or sarcastic; queer, like me; trans, like me – or not, like our siblings. I wonder what kinds of music she would have liked, whether her sense of humour would have been as macabre as mine. If she would have been placed in mainstream schooling, or separated from the rest of us.

Only one of my schools had a disability unit. I went to some of the Special Ed classes there and had counselling during Tuesday lunchtimes. I was seven. To my knowledge there was no documentation then about my disability, but looking back those factors of my education seem like a plot device, the kind of clumsy foreshadowing you can't help but notice because of its inconsistencies.

My memories of my childhood are murky, which I don't resent, since most of it was thoroughly miserable. I had trouble making friends, and my home life was difficult. I was desperate to connect with other people, but terrifically bad at doing so. I was always too much or too little, too withdrawn or too intense. When I felt overwhelmed, I stopped talking altogether.

Now that I know I'm autistic, my childhood makes a lot more sense, but at the time all I knew was that I was different. Being different is a beautiful thing, but it felt bad. I was not always capable of what was expected of me, and what I was capable of was often unexpected. My vocabulary and interests were out of step with my peers in a way that I couldn't make sense of. Changes to routines and structures were extraordinarily distressing, for reasons I couldn't vocalise. Certain environments were painful, and I didn't know why. I couldn't handle spaces that were too bright, or too loud, or too crowded. Everyone wanted me to be someone I wasn't.

I spent much of my youth reading, climbing trees, and reading in trees. It was a struggle to get me to wear shoes. I remember sunlight filtered through eucalypt leaves, dappling shadow underneath, like the way light appears underwater. The air felt clear and sweet. When the wind rushed through the leaves, it made a kind of wonderful, unfamiliar music. I was terribly lonely, but up there in the branches my loneliness somehow felt peaceful. I used to scribble little notes onto fallen scraps of paperbark, and then tuck them back into the boughs.

Trees were easier than people. At a certain height, letting the wind flow over me, I felt like I could finally breathe properly. I loved the way the sun threw fragments of light over everything, the leaves shot through with gold. Later, when we lived by the coast, I used to go down to the water's edge very early in the morning to watch the light glancing over the waves. Later still and somewhere else, I found that I loved the dawn even more than the dusk. The sunsets were spectacular but the sunrises were even more so: cold and quiet, the whole world made soft, and the sounds of birds and the wind rising up over everything.

Sometimes the light was painful. When there was too much of it, when the sky was too bright and too wide, I found it unbearable. I was undone by the heat. My body was not built for warm climates, and every summer felt harsher than the last.

There were other forms of pain. I bruised too easily and healed too slowly. I was always tired. I had a bizarre constellation of seemingly unrelated symptoms and injuries. I would get awful shooting pains around my joints that were dismissed as 'growing pains'. In fact, they were early signs of the connective tissue disorder I didn't know I had, which remained mostly dormant throughout my childhood but worsened as I got older. I think now that I have been in pain for nearly all my life, but I didn't realise because I didn't know what *not* being in pain felt like. I thought it was normal, and that I was the abnormal one for struggling with it.

For the most part I don't like framing my disability in medical terms. Many disabled writers and activists have spoken about the differences between the medical model of disability, which frames disabled embodiment as the problem, and the social model of disability, which frames society as the problem for failing to support disabled embodiment. (Alternatively: in capitalist Australia, society disables you . . .) Under the medical model I am considered disabled because I require a wheelchair for mobility; under the social model I am disabled because so few spaces are wheelchair accessible. I am quite fond of Alison Kafer's political/relational model of disability, which acknowledges the ways in which disability is constructed in political and interpersonal terms. Disability isn't located only in the body, but in the way our bodies interact with the world and with the people around us.

The boundary between illness and disability is sometimes blurry, and in my life I am often unable to distinguish where one ends and the other begins. The process of diagnosis was exhausting, and hideously expensive, and it took years. Doctors in Australia aren't taught much about connective tissue disorders, so nobody knew what to do with me. Without a diagnosis, I couldn't access support or treatment. Without support and treatment, my disability degenerated to a point of crisis. I lacked coping strategies. I didn't connect with the disabled community because I didn't know that the disabled community existed. I didn't think of disability as an identity category or an axis of marginalisation. I couldn't even begin to fathom the idea of disability pride, because I was still thinking about disability in terms of pain and suffering, rather than community, resistance and radical survival. I still thought of Lucy and death.

By the time I was diagnosed, my prognosis was grim. If I left the house at all, often it was only to end up in the emergency ward or the acute spinal ward. I was having episodes of respiratory arrest not unlike what Lucy ultimately died from. Most of the body is made up of connective tissue, or held together with it: blood, bone, cartilage, cardiac valves. When I learned that I had been born with a broken heart, it felt like some kind of horrible prophecy; in an awful, illogical way it made sense of how unhappy I'd always been. I felt like my life was over.

And then it wasn't. I muddled along, trying not to die, and maybe at some point I got the knack of it. I made disabled friends and lovers. I finished my undergraduate degree. I started seeing new doctors, gained access to new treatments and better structural supports. I started a hydrotherapy program, and things improved to an extent I'd thought impossible. My lifespan is still markedly reduced, but that's not as scary as it once was. With luck I will be able to put off heart surgery for many years yet, and preparing for it feels like an ordinary necessity rather an unspeakable doom hanging over my head.

Survival is terrifying and wonderful. I am planning for my future again, for the first time in a long time. Last year I started a PhD. I have been reading books, writing poems, making friends, finding community, falling in love, fighting for change, wheeling really fast down hills. I have been living a life.

Over the last few years I've formed deep and loving connections within disabled communities, including with a number of ferocious, funny, vibrant crips with SMA. Many of them were told that they were unlikely to survive their childhoods, and yet they did. This may be partly ascribed to improvements in medical technology and social infrastructures, as well as pure luck (and socioeconomic background). I am also sure that sheer grit and will played a role. It takes a lot to persist in a world in which you are told you don't belong, and disabled people have some of the most steely, steadfast instincts for survival that I've ever encountered. We must, if we are going to live in a world that doesn't want us. Do not interpret this as inspirational. If anything it should be a call to action against injustice.

My disabilities may limit the length of my life but not its value or its fullness. All lives are marked by grief and joy in equal measure. Nobody loves without suffering, and nobody knows gladness without pain. My life is not unique for that, and no more tragic than anyone else's (at worst I will accept that it is something of a tragicomedy). There are forms of happiness available to me that I would never have known about if I wasn't disabled. And I am happier now than ever before. I am living deeply, and fiercely, and without reservation.

If you're reading this and you're in a rough place, I don't have all the answers and I can't promise that things will get better. But I can say that you're not alone. We're out here and we're fighting for you. There is a vast world of disabled people who have so much love to give and so much to live for.

The name Lucy comes from *lux*, meaning light. It used to be a name given to girls born at dawn. Lately I've been trying to wake early to catch the sunrise, to watch the bloom of light over tin roofs and eucalypts. I think of my sister often, but I'm going to take my time before I meet her again. I want to make the most of the time that I have. Before I die, I want to live.

Don't Have a Bird

Sandi Parsons

There are so many rites of passage you've already missed out on, and the school ball is destined to become another item on that ever-growing list. You try to delay the inevitable until every breath from your lungs sounds as if cystic fibrosis is cackling through you. So, with a resigned air, off to hospital you go.

Although you've been denied the opportunity to attend the ball, no one is prepared to give up the ritual altogether. Instead, your sister Mel, your mum and I, arm ourselves with my ball dress, a curling wand and a bag of makeup. Together we crowd into your hospital room.

We giggle while we do your makeup and curl your hair, then, when you're finally dressed, we start our photoshoot. You shine with happiness. As the chief photographer I have a most important task: to make sure your bare feet never appear in any of the photos to spoil our carefully crafted illusion.

*

There is a sense of belonging, that someone understands you when they bestow a nickname upon you. But I don't get mine.

'Why Bird?' I ask. 'I'm no bird, I'm all woman.'

You roll your eyes and explain it again. 'Bird as in "Flip the bird" or "Don't have a bird".'

'I'm pretty sure that's "Don't have a cow", and it's from *The Simpsons*.'

Your reply is swift: 'In the olden days, before Bart turned it into a cow, it was a bird. Besides, you can't argue that you're kind of grumpy.'

Your expression is smug, unmoveable. You are utterly convinced of your righteousness and you laugh as I stomp off.

*

Journal writing holds no appeal for me. Instead, I write extraordinarily long letters in exercise books to you. I add badly drawn illustrations, jokes and the occasional piece of trivia – anything to fill the pages, because your golden rule as my reader is that we can't discuss anything written until the exercise book has been filled, presented and read. A bonus feature of this rule is that it encourages writing frenzies that carry on long into the night.

You are the perfect reader because I get to watch and judge your reactions as you read. One night, as page after page sees you dramatically perform an exaggerated eye-roll, you finally look up, throw your hands into the air and exclaim, 'Six pages! For six pages you went on about how I rejected the bread.'

I give my best deadpan expression in return, and take a deep breath before informing you, 'I stand by my statements. It's a terrible thing to have one sole purpose in life. For those poor lost slices of bread, all they wanted was to be eaten and instead they were faced with rejection.'

I flounce from the room before I lose my composure.

*

The evening is punctuated by giggles and coughing as we paint our faces. We complete our look with skin-tight jeans and t-shirts. I'm a dashing Paul Stanley, my curls allowed to swing loose, while you are the skinniest Gene Simmons I have ever seen.

When I phone ahead to order pizza, I grandly announce that KISS will collect this order. We're used to people staring when we're out in public. Usually, it only takes one little cough to start the ball rolling and from that moment onwards you collect looks of disgust that suggest, without subtlety, that you are a walking health hazard.

Tonight the looks are different. People stare and laugh in delight at our antics.

When we arrive at the pizza shop, we discover our food is not ready yet. Instead, poor Ross not only has to make our pizza post-haste, but he's also lost five dollars for betting the call was a prank.

*

I feel my eyelids start to close and know that my bed is calling me. The party is no longer raging, and I feel confident that you can take charge. After all, if there's any trouble you can always wake me.

In the morning, the house isn't a shambles, and I am reasonably happy.

Until I venture outside.

There, on the roof, is our garden furniture. The table, chairs, even a resealed carton of beer. Everything arranged neatly, as if for a private party. I wake you, needing an explanation, but you have none. I make a mental note never to go to sleep and leave you in charge of a party again.

I don't heed my own mental note.

The following week, as I try to sleep, a procession of people enter my room to get 'just one more coat hanger', and I know that, once again, you're up to no good.

*

'I'm having a bleed,' you say, announcing the obvious as you gracefully lean over the sink and spit out a mouthful of blood. You look calm and collected as you lean and spit at regular intervals.

'Do you ever resent it? That I'm so well and you . . .' I wave my hand towards the bloody sink instead of saying the words out loud.

You shake your head as you spit. 'I don't resent you, Bird. I feel sorry for you.'

I'm so stunned for a moment I don't say anything, then an awkward 'Huh?' bursts out.

'Everyone's going to die. You'll end up all alone. I don't want to be the last one standing.'

*

You fail to provide me with coherent directions, so I drive around the roundabout in a continuous loop. You say nothing, but even in the darkness, I feel you frowning at me. I take potluck and exit the roundabout randomly, only to find it's a cul-de-sac.

As I turn, I spy a guy through his lounge-room window. He's naked, fresh from the shower. I presume he's about to get dressed. A glance in your direction suggests you haven't seen him yet.

Subtlety has never been my strong point, but you take notice as I drive up onto the lawn and flash my high beams on the naked guy. You burst out laughing as he drops to the floor.

*

I plonk myself onto the couch and force my face into a blank expression. I look you dead in the eye before I speak. 'I'm not inviting you to my wedding.'

Your arms fold defensively across your chest as you glare at me. 'That's not very nice. Why not?' You are so indignant it's a struggle not to laugh.

'Because bridesmaids do not get invited. They are expected to be there.'

You squeal with delight.

*

I stand in your lounge room, my enormous belly preceding me. Mel drops to my side, cups her hands and bellows, 'Hello, baby!' directly into my stomach.

My belly lurches violently as my baby scoots as far away from the bellowing as possible, right into your hands.

You murmur soothing words and stroke my tummy's lumps and bumps, wondering if a little elbow or foot is prodding back at you.

With you getting all the attention, Mel demands to change sides, but once again she cannot contain herself and bellows into my belly. I feel my centre of gravity shift as my baby moves to avoid the noise.

You stick your tongue out at Mel. 'He likes me best.'

*

You raise one brow when I ask if you remember that episode of *Roseanne* where her sister gets married, and the baby cries and her milk comes in.

'It wasn't that unrealistic,' I add.

As if on cue, Jarryn cries, and wet spots appear on my t-shirt.

We both start to giggle, causing Jarryn to cry louder, which in turn makes the wet spots on my shirt grow.

It's a never-ending cycle of mirth.

*

You settle yourself at the dining table, skipping any pleasantries. 'I've decided,' you announce, 'that it's time to go to Melbourne. To go on the transplant list. If I wait much longer . . .' Your words trail off, and you shrug your shoulders.

I should have seen it coming. I should have noticed. But as a new mother, I was distracted.

I don't trust my voice, so a nod is my only response.

*

I research 'Flip the bird', finding what I believe to be an urban legend that contains gruesome details about two warring parties, and the subsequent removal of index fingers. The resulting attribute involves the wronged party flipping their middle finger to indicate they could still shoot arrows or 'pluck yew'.

I print this off and paste it in the latest exercise book I have written for you, along with commentary concluding that I remain unconvinced that 'Don't have a bird' is a real saying and that you must have it confused with 'Flip the bird'.

I pack the exercise book, along with a stuffed Big Bird, for you to take to Melbourne.

*

A phone call in the middle of the night usually means bad news, but I instinctively know this one does not herald doom.

On the other end of the phone, Mel confirms my instinct was right – you've been offered lungs and are off to surgery.

*

I watch you battle with Jarryn. Up and down the hall you both race, lightsabers clashing. I think the last time I saw you run was in 1986. How perverse is it that you can finally run just as I start to struggle?

*

'Chronic rejection.'

I don't hear the rest of the sentence; it is a blur of sounds. I don't need to hear it though, to understand the complications and consequences.

After a while, you speak again. 'I was offered a second transplant if I want.'

My head snaps up, and we lock eyes. I know what you're about to say, even before you say it.

'I said no. I figure I had my shot, and it didn't work out. It's not fair for me to take that chance away from someone else.'

I could argue, plead, even beg, but I know it would be wasted breath. I might be an angry bird, but when it comes to having a stubborn streak, yours trumps mine.

I know you have wrestled with this choice; I need to respect it.

*

'Bird's the word!' you chirp as I walk into your room.

Before Jarryn can ask, you hand him the control to your bed. He zooms you up to the ceiling, then tilts both the head and foot of the bed until you are nearly folded in half. He brings you down and jumps up beside you to repeat the process.

'You have Aunty Julie wrapped around your little finger,' I say.

Jarryn holds up his hand, carefully inspecting his finger.

'No, I don't,' he says.

We laugh, and Jarryn joins in, although he doesn't understand why he's laughing.

A nurse stops by to give us a noise warning.

*

I drop Jarryn at school and head to the tattoo parlour. I stand there for ages, gazing, until finally my eyes settle on a ladybird.

Something inside clicks. I've found a 'bird' I can live with.

The moment the tattoo is complete, I go straight to the hospital to show you.

*

Every time I stop by, your hair seems shorter. Your new buzz cut is extreme, and I don't understand.

You wave your arm breezily, dismissing the loss of your hair as a matter of no importance.

'I got sick of having bed hair,' you say, as if that is all the explanation I need.

*

I run my fingers through your wispy hair while I hold your water cup. Jarryn plays at my feet. Today is not a good day. Today you drift in and out of consciousness.

Aware that something is different, Jarryn looks up and asks me if Aunty Julie is going to die.

'Yes,' I say. 'But not today.'

He accepts this and continues to play.

*

Even when you're dying, you are stubborn, clinging to life one breath at a time. It's been twenty-four hours since I dropped everything and dashed to be here.

In these last weeks, you said you wanted everyone to get along. As we talk and remember something silly you once did, we share a laugh, and it's in that moment that you die.

You chose the perfect moment to stop breathing.

*

I speak of Aunty Julie to Jarryn, and he frowns. I show him a photo, and he nods. I don't think he can remember you, but I do, so I tell him stories of how he'd sit on your bed and zoom it up to the sky.

*

Jarryn walks too fast. I need him to slow down, but I no longer have the breath to tell him. I sit on a wooden bench, watching as he scoots down the shopping centre, not noticing I've stopped.

Once, it was me who was young and impatient, while you sat, gasping to fill your lungs. I wish I could tell you I'm sorry, that I didn't understand then, that I do now.

*

As I surface from my dream, I'm convinced someone is squirting the back of my throat with a water pistol. I cough, trying to clear my mouth, but it continues to fill with liquid. I spit into tissue after tissue, and it's only as I wake properly that I realise I'm having a massive bleed.

My heart beats faster as my mouth fills with blood, again and again.

When it finally stops, it takes a few minutes for my heart to stop pounding. I look a fright – there's blood throughout my hair and I'm surrounded by crimson tissues.

I think of you, and of how calm you appeared, casually spitting blood into the sink, giving grace to this act of betrayal by your body.

I wonder if this is another 'thing' that I will have to get used to.

*

Hospital in the Home is no longer an option, and I'm forced to spend time in the hospital. Worse, now I need supplemental oxygen.

At the end of two weeks, 'Uncle' Gerry pops in to have a word with me. It is, he says, a conversation he didn't think he'd have to have with me.

My heart stops beating for a moment because I know what's coming next. It's the chat you never want to have with your specialist.

You know the one I mean.

The one where he tells you there is nothing more he can do for you, that it's time to start thinking about a transplant.

*

Every step I take in your footsteps increases my anger. You didn't tell me that not being able to breathe *hurts*. I think of all the times I pushed you to do things, made you participate. How often did I tap my feet as you tried to catch your breath?

All you ever wanted to do was sit. I couldn't figure it out – sure, you got a little out of breath, so what? You'd catch your breath next time you sat down. It was no big deal.

But this task of continuing to breathe *is* a big deal.

My ribs ache. My back cramps. My head pounds.

Trying to catch my breath is terrifying. As I pant, struggling to inhale, my heart hammers and silent fright shudders through me.

What if I can't catch my breath again?

What if this is it?

Breathing is such damn hard work.

A quiet voice in my head reminds me I'm not actually mad at you. I'm mad at myself. I'm frustrated, thinking of the times I made you go out when I should have stayed home and rubbed your back or brushed your hair.

I'm horrified by my stupidity. I always thought cystic fibrosis picked you off because you were weak.

I couldn't have been more wrong.

This dying business is far from easy. Yet you died as you lived, quietly and with dignity.

Me?

I'm busy whinging and whingeing to anyone who will listen.

*

I gasp for breath, and all I've done is walk, ever so slowly, to the bathroom. I have the oxygen cranked up on the highest setting, sending a hurricane whirling up my nose.

I can't catch my breath.

I sit on the edge of the bathtub gasping. I still have to shower and wash my hair. It dawns on me that life would be easier with shorter hair, so I vow to cut it. An image of your buzz cut flashes in my mind and, finally, I get it.

There's nothing glamorous about dying; glamour has no place here.

All that exists is trying to be comfortable, trying to survive a little longer.

*

I don't know how you coped while you were waiting. I didn't ask. I didn't think that question would ever apply to me. I was supposed to be bulletproof. To overcome the odds.

I refuse to believe that I am waiting for someone to die. Instead, I wait for a family to say yes.

It's not like waiting for Christmas.

I'm scared I might not make it.

*

I wake in ICU, the pain pulsating through my body in unrelenting waves. For the first forty-eight hours I tell myself: *Julie survived this, and so can I.*

My mantra repeats inside my head. The words looping, rolling and colliding with the hallucinations the pain medication creates.

No wonder you only wanted to do this once.

*

I have so many more questions now. Questions I didn't ask you when I had the chance. Too stubborn to believe they would ever apply to me.

I want to sit with my best friend and ask about bras, scars, tingling sensations and numb nipples.

Instead, I'm stuck having clinical conversations.

*

The realisation dawns on me as people walk into Tom's memorial. There are too many faces missing from my childhood. I am not truly alone: I still have friends with cystic fibrosis. But when it comes to the group of tightly bound friends whose lives intermingled outside their hospital stays, the future you visualised for me when you were seventeen has now come to pass.

I am the last one standing.

I always saw each year I survived as a badge of honour for beating the odds. I never considered the cost.

I mourn, not just for Tom but for everyone I have lost.

*

As I walk past an Angry Birds display, the wording on a lunchbox stands out: 'Bird is the Word'.

With crystal clarity, I hear your voice inside my head chirp 'Bird's the word!'

I pause. You would have had *way* too much enjoyment presenting me with an Angry Bird, but I don't need a lunchbox.

Procrastinating, I look at my phone and realise it's your fortieth birthday, so I buy it anyway.

*

We shared a love of Stephen King novels, and with the new movie version of *It* showing in cinemas I figure it's the perfect time to revisit this old favourite. Besides, I haven't read it since we were housemates. After so many years, it will be like reading a whole new book.

I listen to the audiobook while driving home from work. As clear as day, the narrator says, 'Don't have a bird.'

I pull to the side of the road. My shaking hand presses rewind to check I haven't misheard.

I find myself laughing and crying at the same time.

Laughing, because 'Don't have a bird' *did* originate in the olden days, just like you said. More precisely, it came from the 1950s in the town of Derry, as created by Stephen King.

Crying, because the knowledge arrived eighteen years too late.

A Body's Civil War

Tim Slade

In my home
I fall – a tripwire
invented by me –
my left femur broken
to smithereens, where
it ought to connect to the hip.

Four weeks I lay in the bunker
of the Launceston General . . .

I stand to the white flag
of a doctor . . . ***Diagnosis*** –
AUTO-IMMUNE & ASSOCIATED
DISORDERS (a body's civil war):

osteoporosis (one brittle soldier);
type 1 diabetes (insert a low G.I.
joke HERE) – *late onset;*
generalised anxiety; one blown inner-
ear – this shell shall serve, as warning:
the eternal siren of tinnitus –
meniere's syndrome – dizzy,
and no hearing to speak of
there now . . . 'Remind me again –
which one is shot?'

He lives
by a disability pension,
due (not at all like reading in the dark
depression
of war, a letter from your waiting
lover) *to:*

chronic fatigue syndrome (synchronise watches)
& rheumatoid arthritis (stand-up straight, quick-march) &
(bullet) *powders, trigger-foods,* (the gun of)
perfumes (safe for humans) – *all falling under*
multiple chemical hyper-sensitivity &

I remember him saying something about that . . .

Auto-immune syndromes
(friendly-fire, the enemy) . . .

'Mmmmm . . .' *wiggle nose*

Could it be this man is not a hypochondriac?

In future wars
I hope for a doctor
who is less rifle-straight
when I make the merest
movement in the daylight,
or should I whisper
of the battleground . . .

A body's civil war –
my young life.

Luck and Anger

Todd Winther

My diagnosis of cerebral palsy means I am a person with a disability. At the same time, a desire to distance myself from my disability has been the driving force of my life until now. The world of my disability is tiring. The physical challenges I face are obvious, but the psychological scars of confronting these challenges on a daily basis are a greater burden.

This thought didn't occurr to me until shortly after my twenty-seventh birthday, when my world came crashing down around me and I had to rebuild it from the ground up.

Prior to this, I had considered myself 'lucky'. After I was diagnosed with cerebral palsy at eight months, my parents helped me fight the initially grim prognosis. Against medical expectations, I began to talk, feed myself and interact with the world around me well before my tenth birthday. This was achieved through equal parts luck and tenacity.

Growing up in South Australia in the 1980s and '90s, I was in the right place at exactly the right time. I was able to access both a wonderful education and top-class therapies catering to my disability. Thanks to the work of the Regency Park Centre in Adelaide and my family's determination, I progressed at a rate nobody, not even me, had expected.

I knew even as a child that I was in a privileged position compared to many others with disabilities. I learnt how to communicate my wants and needs. I had a family who fought (and continue to fight) with every fibre of their being to ensure I could make the most of the abilities I had. Many of my contemporaries didn't have these twin advantages.

After finishing primary then high school in a mainstream educational environment with reasonable results, two thoughts came to dominate my mind: I must not waste what I have; and I must carry on and set an example for those who can't, so the community can see that people with disabilities can achieve things, against the odds. When anybody raised the topic of my disability, I would always mention luck. I would say I was 'lucky' not to have become as disabled as I thought I was going to be. 'Lucky' that I was able to make the most of my opportunities. 'Lucky' that, as I'd hoped, I was able to shed the stereotype of helplessness and accomplish things in the able-bodied world.

I completed two university degrees and became consumed by aspirations of a political career: first as a candidate; then, perhaps more pragmatically, as an operative behind the scenes. But as I was dreaming of this career, a glaring deficiency became obvious, and it was not the cerebral palsy.

I was so focused on my intellectual interests that I had developed almost no life beyond this. Aside from other people with disabilities who I grew up with, I hadn't forged many long-term friendships. I viewed any connection I did foster largely through the prism of intellectual symbiosis, mostly because I was arrogant, absorbed in my own ambitions. I was far too busy to go to parties, experiment and get into trouble like most people in their teens and early twenties. I was going to change the world! I was on a mission.

I did try to explore my adolescent sexual urges. But I was unsuccessful because I had no idea how to meaningfully connect with my peers, much less the girls I was attracted to. Every rejection was more painful than the last. At the time, I assumed the reason for these constant rejections was my disability. I thought I was being punished for things I could not control.

By my mid-twenties I'd become desperate, searching for validation anywhere I could find it. When I entered my first relationship it was for all the wrong reasons. I made the sort of mistakes that other people my age had made a decade earlier (and which at the time I'd scorned them for). The relationship was doomed to become a spectacular failure.

When we broke up, the month after I turned twenty-seven, everything changed. I was facing my first heartbreak, the end of my first intimate relationship. I felt it had been my only chance to explore the world on my own terms, but it had all blown up in my face. I wasn't satisfied with the life I had once lived, but I was forced to return to it. I would have preferred anything else.

At their wits' end, my parents insisted I see a psychologist. I spent the first two sessions sobbing uncontrollably while trying to explain that I had lost my only chance at connection. The therapist listened sympathetically, saying I had every right to be sad.

About halfway through the next session he asked me a question, with an intensity I had not heard before. 'Why are you so angry?'

'I'm not angry. I'm sad,' I insisted.

'I know that. But think about it. Why do you think you'll never experience a connection again?' he prodded further.

'Because I'm disabled. Nobody wants to be in a relationship with someone with a disability.'

'How does that make you feel, Todd?'

The answer hung in the air as he said my name.

'Angry!'

'Have you ever been angry about your disability before?'

That question changed my life, and how I understood it. I had never thought about my disability in that way before. Being disabled was a monumental inconvenience, yes, but it hadn't occurred to me that I might be angry about it. I was 'lucky' after all. I'd beaten the odds of my diagnosis. I'd finished school and achieved everything I wanted to academically. To be angry about my disability would be selfish, I thought. How could I be, when I'd had such good fortune when many others with disabilities had not?

This was the most profound moment of my life to date. Anger had always lurked beneath the surface. I had been in denial without ever realising it.

I am angry because I don't have control over my life, and I never will have control over it.

I am angry that I need help with the most basic things every day.

I am angry that, because of these facts, I have never had true privacy, and I never will.

I am angry that I will never be able to go somewhere without planning contingencies in case I need to go to the toilet.

I am angry I will never be able to play AFL football.

I am angry I will never be able to hit a cricket ball the way I want to be able to.

I am angry that I will never be able to run to avoid the rain, to sprint through wide open spaces.

I will always be angry about my disability.

And now I realise that holding on to that anger, and expressing it, is both healthy and necessary. Anger has allowed me to understand my disability and my relationship to it, in ways I never thought possible. Since that therapy session, and this acknowledgement of my true feelings, I have become more honest with myself, with those I care about and those around me.

Anger is a powerful emotion. Sometimes it makes people feel uncomfortable. It can alienate people if they do not understand the motivation behind it; it can shut down communication. But it can also compel people to examine their feelings and assess their responses.

Of course, anger is not the only emotion I have about my experience of disability. However, recognising that anger has unlocked other things inside of me. I have a deeper understanding of my behaviour, and the things that drive me. Harnessing that anger in a productive way has been central to my successes; without a determination to prove the doubters – and myself – wrong, I would not have done so well at school or at university.

On the other hand, the anger I've felt towards my disability, and my inability to control that anger on occasions has led to some of my greatest mistakes. In hindsight, I can see that I didn't develop the social skills and relationships I craved when I was younger because I was angry at the world for perceiving me differently. I will never know if that perception was true or not because I was too angry to test it out.

It's no coincidence that since I have acknowledged my anger, I have become a more well-rounded person. While much of my brain still resides in the realm of the analytical, I have established relationships that are healthier and more consistent than before. I have developed empathy, not just for those who I can relate to, but for those who I can't. Anger has allowed me to better articulate my thoughts in a coherent and logical manner, which is why you are reading this now.

I now believe that I can be both angry and lucky at the same time, and that they are equally important. I'm angry that I can never have all the things I want, but I'm lucky because of all the things I do.

How I Learnt to Stop Worrying and Sing 'The Robot Song'

Tom Middleditch

I am diagnosed with ADHD and autism, formerly known as Asperger's syndrome. I do not consider myself disabled, and have not faced many obstacles in life due to my conditions. However, the majority of those who are diagnosed with autism are disabled by it, and our society is structured in such a way that a lot of things are much harder for neurodivergent folks like myself. The notion that one is expected to get over one's impediments, without any training in how to do so, is something that everyone living with disability experiences – as have I.

One thing I value, both as a personal trait and as something others expect of autistic people, is that I can be very honest. This forms a large part of my identity – or at least that is what the ego-driven part of me would like to think.

I work as a consultant on autistic representation in the theatre. When I go to a show, people often ask me for my feedback afterwords. I try to be courteous and to frame things in a positive manner: a process I refer to as Hot Gives (because I intend to give ways to enjoy, rather than just Hot Taking away reasons to feel good). But I'm not afraid to say something if a piece has angered or confused me needlessly, or just straight-up bored me. I know hearing my personal reaction can be hard if you're not ready for it.

In 2019 I attended Arena Theatre Company's *Robot Song*, a family show about an autistic child. Jolyon James, the writer and director, came into my world through the show's assistant director, Sarah Branton, with whom I had worked on earlier projects. Jolyon is a BFG of a man, with a grand cheeky smile and a comforting demeanour. And he is also interested in autism, so we became fast friends. Before the show opened we discussed autistic representations on stage, and Jolyon had talked with me about specific inspirations for the piece, such as the true story of an autistic child who had received a letter saying he was hated, signed by all the children in the class, but which was later revealed to be the work of only two children.

Robot Song was praised across the board. It premiered in Melbourne in early 2019 at Theatre Works, before setting off on a tour of regional Victoria. When I went to see it myself, I brought along my partner, Lizzie, the smart one in our relationship, because I was certain we would both enjoy it.

As I sat down to watch it, nestled among an audience of families, peers and general robot enthusiasts, I anticipated a lovely romp for children and their parents about an autistic girl and her robot.

When it finished, I had never wanted to leave a theatre faster.

I hated it.

Through and through.

I talked Lizzie's ear off all the way home, angry and confused that a show for children could have so upset me. We both agreed it was a remarkable piece of craft; you couldn't fault it there. But the content, the story, the characters: they all struck me as wrong, deeply wrong. Even writing this now, I remember the intensity of that frustration. It sat hot and heavy behind my navel, and a thin film of it coated the front of my skull, under my skin.

*

After simmering for a few days, I managed to crystallise my anger with the piece down to three critical points.

1. A major song, sung by the father character, was about the lead character, Juniper, doing a shit on the carpet and her father picking it up. The use of embarrassing moments in autistic children's lives to demonstrate how frustrated their parents are is a breach of autistic children's rights. These incidents should be reserved for private discussion between parents and children unless the child gives consent. To sing about it so jovially felt like the worst possible way to define the relationship.

2. Juniper was suspended from school because she had pushed a child over, breaking her arm. She was subsequently confused about why people didn't like her. It struck me as obviously demeaning of her character that she could not put two and two together: she had broken a child's arm, and children would rightly be scared of someone who was that violent.

3. The core tension of the show emerged from an incident when Juniper received a note from her classmates that said they all hated her. The show's climax was the robot telling her that the letter meant the exact opposite of the literal meaning of the words. This was, to me, gaslighting of the highest form. Encouraging Juniper to read all criticism, whether made in good faith or bad, as compliments, she was being set up for a very hard time in high school.

The play ended with the main character asking the audience to stand up and clap along. In a show that encourages the idea that being different is okay, the end reinforced the notion that everyone in the audience should follow instructions and be identical, standing up and validating the world of this impertinent girl.

The fact that something I found so awful could garner such praise, such love, made me want to stop making theatre. If this was the kind of story that people found uplifting, fulfilling, worthy of rewarding with full houses night after night, then there was nothing I could make that would ever please anyone, without having first to deeply upset myself.

And then Jolyon asked for a coffee and a chat, because he wanted to know what I thought.

We sat down at a table a week or so later. I opened the conversation by saying that craft-wise the piece was wonderful, and that all my opinions were being shared in the interest of autistic representation. He told me he was a big boy and not to censor myself for the benefit of some squishy emotional thing in him.

So I didn't.

I laid it all out: everything that had frustrated me. I think I spoke calmly, but the earnestness of my tone must have given him an indication that this piece had hurt me.

But Jolyon wasn't fazed at all. He was smiling. In response, he said that they had considered all these points and addressed them in the text of the show.

What?

He showed me the script and asked me to look again. And I was faced with the reality that I simply hadn't heard the dialogue.

1.

Juniper: Dad! Let's do 'The Poo Song'.

Dad: Ohh, I don't think we should do that one, Juniper, that's just a silly thing we do at home.

Juniper: It's good for the show, it gives the audience valuable background information. It's a true story about Dad accidentally picking up one of my poos in his actual hand. I mean, gold.

Dad: Well, it's your show.

'The Poo Song' happened because Juniper repeatedly requested it. She was fully aware of the nature of the story, comprehended the social stakes, and insisted it be sung anyway. She saw it as important that people understood how much her father loved her.

2.

When Juniper pushed the other girl and broke her arm: she hadn't meant to hurt her, so she couldn't see how she was at fault. But there was a reason why Juniper had done this: the other girl had wrecked a VHS that belonged to Juniper's dad. Worse, it was the original source of Battletac, the robot. Of course Juniper was angry and didn't want to go back to school: that is a perfectly reasonable reaction from a child.

3.

Battletac: Why would you want it to disappear? This letter is proof.

JUNIPER: Proof of what?

BATTLETAC: Juniper, there will always be letters. If you weren't smart, kind, strong, creative – different, this letter would never exist. Life is full of letters but you get to decide what colour they are.

It was about how she would always have, in her life, people who would say bad things. It was up to her to decide which words mattered and which didn't, which ones she would let drag her down, and which she would let be other people's problems.

The only criticism that Jolyon had no textual response to was my final point. He conceded that on a night when the audience included wheelchair users, they had made an exception. The resolution to this problem was to make the request more inclusive: people didn't have to stand if they chose not to, whaterver their reason.

I left the meeting stunned.

My frustration was still there, but it could no longer be called anger. Calling it anger had clouded my capacity to see the show that was happening in front of me.

How could I have missed such clearly stated text? The play was designed for children. It wasn't a matter of interpretation or subtext: it was so obvious that all I needed to do was read the script.

How had I got it so wrong?

As I mulled it over, I realised that *Robot Song* had led me to a place that was all too familiar.

A cupboard.

*

I've often asked my friends what they consider to be non-toxic expressions of masculinity. I've received many wonderful answers, such as sing-shouting in a circle or jumping up and down with arms wrapped around your friends. Effortlessly carrying a child. That hug where you give the other person two or three moderate thumps with an open hand and then settle in.

Above all, though, the most common thing touted as wholesome masculinity is being vulnerable with your emotions. If I want to be a good feminist, a new kind of man must be validated. So. Here goes.

As a child I was on ADHD medication. I needed that medication – it got me into university – and I wouldn't change it for the world. But it had drawbacks. The most notable was that I didn't really eat much, because food didn't taste of anything.

Watching videos of me at twelve years old, Lizzie said I looked like Mr Burns in that episode of *The Simpsons* where everyone thought he was an alien. Gacked out of my mind and, above all, sullen. A white, freckled child with curly ginger hair, skinny as a rake and with a mouth full of teeth more appropriate for a puppy than a boy, which he did everything to hide.

This boy was with me in the cupboard. He was face down on his knees, which were sodden with tears.

He'd had a bad day at school.

*

I wanted to start this sentence with 'unsurprising'. That it was unsurprising he was a weird kid, that he was friendless until high school because he didn't understand how to be friendly on other people's terms and no one could explain why.

I wanted to start the sentence with 'unsurprising' because it's unsurprising this kid was bullied.

I was beaten up several times, in front of others who could have done something to stop it. Once, a bored group of children followed me home and chanted outside my house for me to come out. My father chased them away with a car.

But 'unsurprising' is a villainous word, because it implies this is inevitable: that my treatment was justified, that I learnt lessons from it that did me good. I didn't. All I learnt was that I was a pasty, specky, awkward creep who deserved nothing but scorn and rejection.

This particular day, the day in the cupboard, was a week after I had been told about my diagnosis of Asperger's. Somehow that news made it to the school. It made it to the ears of the worst bully, a bully whose own life was more full of chaos and anger than mine, and who – maybe for power, maybe for attention, maybe just because he could – decided to reveal that fact to me. He would remain my taunter, my haunter. And now he had a medical reason for his actions.

Worst, he let me know he knew about my diagnosis through a terrible joke. Something about burgers made of ass.

The rest of that day was unsurprising.

I ran home and locked myself in that cupboard. I ignored everyone.

I don't know what my parents thought. I've never asked them. I don't know what my brothers thought. I've never asked them either. All I did was hide in that cupboard, crying and beating my head and barking, then whining, then whimpering: 'Go away, Asperger's. Go away.'

As I look at this child now, I know the word that describes my feeling, but I can't say it. Is this ...?

I am asking that question seriously for what feels like the first time. Maybe it's happened in the past, but it didn't lead to any therapy. So I shall call it what it is. Trauma. But is it? Do I have the right to name my own experiences like that? Do I really think I could use that to get therapy for free? No. Never. I've never been diagnosed with trauma.

I mean, this is such a common experience. A child is bullied at school for being weird. It wasn't sexism, racism, classism, hell it wasn't even ableism. I was just weird. Could I really justify being so upset over the plot of a John Hughes movie that never got made because it was too boring? Never. This cannot be legitimate, everyone is bullied, and I am no different.

And yet I was angry at a children's show, and back in this cupboard, with its pale carpet and pale walls and a pale, pale boy, who no one is checking in on.

Guess checking in is up to me.

So even if I cannot diagnose it as trauma with the authority of a psychiatrist, what I *can* do is call it traumatic. I can give myself permission to say that this memory still hurts. That the kid is still in that cupboard, asking for his mind to go away, because maybe then he will be acceptable.

In calling it trauma, I give myself permission to care for this hurt, with the tools I have at my disposal. Just as I have with autism through my arts practice. And guess what: I have just seen a show that has given me the tools I need.

I kneel down to face that kid.

Hey.
Here's the thing.
They are wrong.
And this is why.

*

That 'Poo Song' reminded you of the story that your parents told you, from before your memory started taking notes. When your family stayed at that motel, and you were so hungry you ate eight gourmet sausages, and then, later in the bedroom, explosively vomited them back up. Your parents were so shocked and embarrassed that they fled with you and your brothers. Years later, they laughed about it. You always thought that they were ashamed, but there's another way to see this. That your parents were willing to shield you from the consequences shows how much they love you.

The story about Juniper recalled those bullies who beat you, of how no one defended you. It will take you a long time to learn this, but the ways you were trying to be friendly to other people were not familiar to them. And that is okay.

There was no way you could know that, and no one explained it to you properly. Those beatings were never justified. Beatings never are. You don't have to pretend to know karate in high school, or say some nonsense about being proficient with a sword: those lies don't work. You can't be critical of mistakes you made as a child, when the knowledge of how to navigate the world was invisible to you and no one understood you as you understand yourself now. Everyone was trying to look out for themselves, like you were.

The letter that Juniper received reminded you of the end of that year, where everyone wrote compliments on the back of each other's photos. On your photos, everyone only wrote 'funny' and 'tall'. Those weren't the only valid things about you: you just didn't know how to make others comfortable, and they didn't know how to make you understand that. You don't need to defend yourself from that.

One day, you will meet a friend from high school. (Yes, you will have many.) And you will catch up and laugh and have coffee. And you will talk about high school, and how it had been much better for you but you still felt it must have been a challenge to be around you, and she will say it wasn't, people just didn't know how to interact with you. But they wanted to.

And right now, this wishing away Asperger's. Don't. It isn't what separates you: what separates you is their ignorance and your naivety. You were young and in a world that didn't know how to teach you and be with you. But you aren't in that world anymore. Now you get to be the person you needed back then, you get to be that person for other children who might be at risk of having a similar sadness, and thinking it is justified. If you are going to work to defend them, you owe it to yourself to give yourself what you need. *Robot Song* gave me that, and now I give it to you.

As I stand, I realise that, until now, I have been outside that cupboard, defending that child. Defending that misery. Defending it from anything that validated that trauma, any representation that suggested, even indirectly, that what happened to me was expected, deserved and fair. And this has extended into my art, into the way I create stories that explore autism, and into my arts criticism.

Whenever I saw a story being attacked for bad representation, I would jump in and participate in the argument. While I stand by why I've written about other pieces, I can't deny that my impulse to do this was partly fuelled by a need to protect that kid in the cupboard. And then along came *Robot Song*: in that case, my impulse to criticise was *completely* fuelled by that need to defend myself.

But I didn't need to.

So I stop.

And that boy looks up.

And he smiles his puppy dog smile.

*

It is here that I ask the toughest question of that show. *Robot Song* was, for me, a re-traumatisation. It helped me understand that my childhood experience, even though not one of war or assault or a terrible accident, could be thought of as trauma. It also gave me some tools to deal with that trauma. But is that a morally acceptable thing for theatre to do?

I can't answer this question for anyone else. I can only answer it for myself, as an incomplete, doing-his-best, all-too-human puppy of a man.

I don't believe I was owed a warning. A general content warning about bullying and autistic representation would not have given me the information I needed to decide whether to attend, and the amount of detail I would have needed to understand is not a standard I would imagine ever extending to other arts. That would be tantamount to validating the reasons people avoid certain content, and in my case not validating it made it easier to absorb. Indeed, going in with the assumptions I held removed barriers that I had erected to protect myself from effectively engaging in other stories. Stories that had conditioned me to believe that bad representation was representation that made me feel bad when I watched it.

But in this instance, what I learnt – and the point I hope readers take away – is that sometimes Hard Representation – not even intense, but the kind of representation that asks the hard questions – can feel like bad representation. It is hard because it is real. But it isn't always bad. Sometimes it makes the best stories. These are the stories that point to the places that are cold and unloved and say with a knowing smile: 'I think you deserve to do something lovely about that.'

*

Robot Song has been nominated for a Helpmann Award.* Of course, this news is fantastic, both for the *Robot Song* team and autistic stories in general. But it's terrible for the part of my ego that thinks only I can and should tell autistic stories and that is frustrated when others' efforts are validated.

That part of me gets chipped away more and more, as I realise that it was only there to protect me. Now I have the tools for self-care, so I don't need to look after that part of myself so vigorously and am able to open myself up more to stories that hold harder lessons.

That's not to say I'm going to suddenly love all autism stories. Far from it. This critical eye of mine still knows what it's doing. If anything, I expect I will become more withering in my critiques, and more supportive of the genuine heart in the works of others.

Here is one.

I've insisted Juniper is autistic, but that label is not applied to her in the show. I think this is a mistake. If she isn't called autistic, people will continue to believe that you can't empathise with an autistic child if they are called autistic; that it's more important to have a precocious child, a unique child, a special child. Any label other than what she actually and obviously is: autistic. Let them empathise with an openly autistic character, and they will empathise with an openly autistic child.

What this does mean, right here and now, is that I can stop worrying, and love the *Robot Song*.

Just don't ask me to sing it. It isn't my song to sing.

* *Robot Song* went on to win that award. My ego is doing fine.

A special thanks to Lizzie Lamb, who was the source of many of the good ideas in this piece. The best one came months later and couldn't be put in elsewhere, so here it is: 'Everything can traumatise you: you just have to pick which ones you will let define you.'

This piece was originally commissioned by Alison Croggon on Witness Performance.

Free as a Bird

Jane Rosengrave

This chapter is the result of an interview between Jane Rosengrave and Carly Findlay.

My name's Jane Rosengrave.

I've got an intellectual disability and I'm a strong, powerful self-advocate. I'm fifty-six, but I don't look it.

I was put into an institution from day one, when I was born. I was in two different babies' orphanages, for six months, then I went to an orphanage in Sebastopol. I was in orphanages until I was five years old, and then I was moved to another institution. I lived in institutions until I was twenty-one. It was meant to be sixteen, but in 1979 they put the age up to twenty-one so we could stay there a lot longer. It was good in one way, but in another way it wasn't – because us people never had families to go back to.

I was put into an institution because I had epileptic fits and because I was Aboriginal, which I didn't know then. Me and my sister were always kept separate from my family, but our older sister and our brother, they were always with the family. This was because me and my older sister have got different dads.

I was born in Melbourne – my mum was in Fitzroy in the '60s. I've got three siblings, I have, and I'm the youngest. And then after that, that's when wewere taken from the family because we were kept dirty, unfed, smelly, not looked after properly, and we were taken into care. And then I went from Allambie to Tarana, in the babies' area – under six months, and later on I was transferred to Ballarat, to Nazareth House Boys' Home Sebastopol, in St Joseph's Home for the babies.

I wasn't sexually abused in the orphanage but I was physically abused a lot there. The beds were in a row, each ward, and of a morning the nuns would say, 'Right, everybody, out of bed, stand beside your beds!' and they would throw the blanket back on every bed, and they would feel to see if you'd wet it. And if you had wet it, you'd be staying standing, but the ones who hadn't wet their bed were allowed to get dressed and go to brekkie. We had to lie back in the bed, in the urine, and we had to have the sheets pinned over us, pinned to the pillow with the big, huge safety pins that they had in those days.

I was a problem child at the orphanage, because of my epileptic fits, and the nuns used to call me 'monkey'. I don't like that word but now I know why [they called me that]. I've got photos of myself so young, very dark brown. So that's why they used to call me 'monkey', because I was a problem child and because I was Aboriginal. It's awful.

Some good things happened in the institutions. We used to go on the tram of a night-time – just once a week, on a Friday night. We were allowed to go on the tram to the lake near the orphanage in Ballarat. And the ones who wouldn't eat their tea that night – I was one of them – the nuns would say, 'Right, by the time this tram comes back for you, if you don't eat your tea up, you won't go for a ride in that tram.' Sometimes I didn't eat my tea by the time the tram came, me being very slow at eating, and the nuns would say, 'Right, you're not going for a ride in that tram, you're going to go to bed.' Other days I ate, and I got a ride on the tram.

Sister Paul (she's passed away) was my favourite nun. She used to spoil us, she'd buy us new clothes from Myers. *Myers*, you know! And there was a David Jones too. Mainly they were new clothes for when people asked us to go for a holiday. I mean, they had to ask the nuns. I used to go for a holiday with the Browns – people that lived in a house in Sebastopol, and out at Dunkeld, on a farm. I used to enjoy myself on the farm because it was very wide open, not like the orphanage. I would help out milking the cows. There was one of the brothers always there with me, and they used to put those seats down near the cow because the cow was tied up. I can remember me sitting down next to him, he would do two and he'd let me help with the other two – milking the cows in the bucket.

I used to drink the milk afterwards. Ooh yeah! And it was full – it had cream on top. And another thing I loved was playing around with the sheepdogs, they had three sheepdogs then. I used to chase the sheepdogs when I was little, and even round up the sheep. When they used to shear the sheep, I would hug the wool. The lambs' wool was my hug, because I didn't get many hugs.

I always played in mud and all that. I reckon the reason I played in mud a lot when I was on the farm is because I was Aboriginal. That's why – and water. It was getting back to the earth, back to the water, I reckon. See, I've got some photos of me in a mess, and one in the kitchen. And then with the sheep and that, I've got a photo of me carrying a little lamb.

After I was in the orphanage, I went to a bigger institution which was called Pleasant Creek Training Centre in Stawell, which was not so pleasant.

My real mum passed away when I was in the institution, when I was eight years old. They got this information from the front office and they said, 'Jane, do you know that we just found out some information from the front office that your mum's dead, do you know that?' And they didn't really care. I didn't know, before that, that I had a family. But after that, once they said that, that's when I – I was only eight years old, and it was in the dining room and I wouldn't eat my tea, and the staff member took me away from the dining room, and [took] my tea, took me to the ward and I just wouldn't eat it. And she said, 'Shut up, just eat your tea.'

I was at Pleasant Creek until I was twenty-one, and this is where the sexual abuse happened, and physical abuse. I was sexually abused by a man at Marlborough House, which was a government place for people from institutions who never had families to go to, a break away from the institution. After it happened the man said to me, 'Don't you ever tell anybody this because if you do, you are not going to see the Browns again,' because he knew that I was getting spoilt by the Browns.

The second sexual abuse was when I was thirteen, on a Sunday, or a Saturday. It was when everyone went swimming, and we weren't allowed to go swimming. The boss would not let senior girls go for a swim, and we wanted to. So I said to the senior girls, 'I'm going to go down to the front office', because he's in charge, higher than our staff members. I went down there and I said, 'Excuse me, our ward's not going swimming and all the other wards have gone swimming.' And he goes, 'Well, first, you could do me a big favour ...' After he abused me, he said, 'I'll ring up the warden and make sure that you go swimming, but you do not mention this to anyone, or you'll not go swimming again when I'm on a weekend.' That was the second one.

And then the third one was on a Sunday with the bus driver, taking us to church. He got attached to me. I went back with him to the bus company – when I was sixteen. And that's when I was raped. Which I didn't know then. I asked him, 'Why am I bleeding?' And he goes, 'Because you've got your period.' That went on for three years, that did. On a Sunday, because I was allowed to go out with them, but as long as I don't say anything, they let me come out, you know. Because in those days they didn't do records, they didn't see if you've got a good record, like a Working with Children Check. The bus driver asked me would I like to work up in his milk bar on a Friday night and Saturday morning. And I said yeah, so I worked up there for three years, but each Friday night – it was from 5 until 9 – he was always the last one to stay at the shop and the family would go home. And it's only him and me there. The abuse went on for three years.

Some days I went back to the hostel upset, crying and all this, and the nurses would say, 'What's the matter?' and I would say, 'Nothing, I'm just a bit tired, you know, had a hard day.' I wouldn't say what was going on. Yeah. And that went on for three years.

It wasn't my fault. Never.

I never felt that I could talk about the abuse to anyone, because in the institution there were no favours, we were just treated like a bunch of sheep, from one paddock to another paddock.

After I was in the institution, I went out into the CRUs – community residential units – and I never talked about the abuse. But when I met my ex-partner I talked about it.

There were round 300 people at Pleasant Creek. I always hung around these Indigenous children. They knew I was Aboriginal. I had a sense, but I wasn't too sure. I found out I was Aboriginal when I was at a conference in New Zealand in 2009. I told my story at that conference.

Once they heard it, they said to me, 'Jane, that story was great, that was brilliant what you said.' And then they said, 'Do you know that you've actually got Aboriginal in you?' and I go, 'What are you talking about?' They go, 'You have actually got Aboriginal in you.' And they even said, 'We can see it, and we can even hear it, in the voice.' So I just kept it to myself, and then when the conference was done and when the holiday was finished, I went home, and then I looked in the mirror and I just stood there. 'Oh yeah I can see it actually,' I said.

That's when I started asking people here in Victoria. They said, 'You are Aboriginal, definitely.' But they wouldn't tell me who I belonged to. I was at the opening of Open Place (an organisation for children who are put into institutions), and someone said, 'Who's that woman, she looks familiar, she looks like one of the Bambletts.'

I found out later on who my father was, which I'm proud of. I never got to meet my dad, but one day I would love to go up to and stay there for a while and talk to him in spirit. His grave is up in Moama, up in Shep way, at the Aboriginal area. I'd love to do that one day.

I went to a special school in the institution. It had a stupid name – Pleasant Creek Special School. It was not so pleasant. And not so special.

I was in a sheltered workshop, in the special school. I was so young then, I was about twelve, eleven, ten. We used to make pegs and baskets. We didn't get anything. We used to make moccasins as well, in the boys' area, and it used to be like slaves there. They used to put the moccasins in a box and send them to Melbourne. And little beanbags as well. And pegs and baskets, wooden baskets that you hang.

I used to go grape-picking too, in Stawell and in Great Western. I would have been about eighteen or seventeen. In those days it was a dollar a bucket. We used to do it once a week or once a month, and we used to try and get a hundred buckets done a day, so we could get a hundred dollars. In those days a dollar a bucket was like slaves, like those sheltered workshops.

I feel bad that sheltered workshops still exist, because people should be paid properly.

Definitely I'm a leader! I'm a strong, powerful self-advocacy person and I've a voice to be heard. I've been through the rigmaroles in the institution, from the bad to the good, and I'm an elder of my family as well. And I get other people to follow their leaders on telling their stories to be a self-advocacy person, and to have people hear their stories as well and to be accepted out in the community.

I'm a member of the Reinforce self-advocacy group. Reinforce is an organisation for people with intellectual disability, which has been running since [the] 1980s and they have had that support beside them. In the earlier days (I wasn't a member because I was still in the home then) but in the '80s they were demanding the government close these institutions because it's not right for us to be there.

And I'm even in the First Peoples Disability Network as well, in Sydney. I'm a board member. I listen on their committee and I bring up ideas for them. I'll be on another board too, travelling around with Indigenous people with disabilities. It's to do with the First People's Nations, and it's about being accepted in the community and about what people with a disability know about their rights.

I won a Human Rights Award. Ooh, that means a lot to me. That was in 2016. The award was for my advocacy around the royal commission [into institutional abuse]. I travelled around with People with Disability Australia to get other Indigenous people and people with an intellectual disability who are not Indigenous to come forward and tell their stories, and to know that they will be believed, not ignored. I'm very proud.

People with Disability Australia asked me would I like to travel around with them, with this royal commission, and tell people about my story for other people to come forward, and they said it would be paid work and that. And I said yes, definitely.

I felt powerful telling my story. But I was scared, still. We went up to Pleasant Creek. I had a couple of panic attacks.

Since telling my story of abuse in institutions, I've heard some other people's stories. I've empowered people to speak out. I am very proud of that. To me, disability pride means powerful, strong, you've got a voice to be heard, you are not to be denied, you are to be accepted in the community.

My Aboriginal culture also means a hell of a lot to me – very, very important – and my tribe Yorta Yorta, which I found out that that's where my tribe is from. And I love saying the Welcome to Country as well. I do Welcome to Countries now, because I'm the elder of my dad's side. And I do painting as well, dot painting.

The advice that I would give to my young Aboriginal sisters and brothers is that if they want to tell their stories and if they want people to listen to their stories, they will be believed. They will be listened to, they will be taken seriously. And they will be listened to and made sure that their story is told when something is done, you know what I mean?

I've definitely found happiness now. I live in a safe home. I wanted to be in a place where you've got to get a key to open it up, open the door, you can't just barge in, where I'd have my safety and my privacy. I love it there, I do yeah! I feel safe. I have lots of friends in the home. I am just as free as a bird and I'm going to be single – stay free as a bird and single for the rest of my life! And that's the way it's going to be for when I go into the ashes. I'm not talking about the cricket ashes! You only live once on this earth. You're dead under the ground a lot longer than what you are alive, so while you've got your legs still kicking and while your heart is still pumping, get up and make the most of it.

The Boy Who Ached [Fibromyalgia]

Marla Bishop

Here is the story of the boy who ached,
whose world quaked
beneath his
unsteady feet
in search of the truth
amidst a system
filled with
uncertainty
to feel
free,
who fell to his
knees
in agony
from misdiagnoses,
who saw friendships dwindle
one
by
one;
for who could understand
the incomprehensible
'fake'
symptoms
of a boy
who aches
&
shakes
invisibly

a boy who was
unemployable,
&
lost
in a painless world
counting spoons
on the table
as if they were breaths
the depths of this
suffering
bruised his insides
until they bled
so he hid
beneath the covers
&
wept;
they gave him
pill
after
pill
but still …
he ached.
He quaked
amidst
medical mistakes
but he tried
to stand
anyway,
even if his
bones
would
groan
he was determined
to live,
to survive,
so he tried
&
would fall

sometimes
but the doctors
finally
got it right;
friendships grew in
abundance;
he studied in doses;
&
while there were petals
hanging by a thread,
he blossomed again.
Here is the story of the boy who ached,
who still aches,
&
wouldn't have it
any other way.

Red Dust, Jet Streams and Chanel No. 5

Gayle Kennedy

Among my earliest memories is one of standing on a table, surrounded by smiles as I sang the old country song 'I Want a Pardon for Daddy'. The faces are beaming, encouraging. The faces are black.

My next memory is being trapped inside an iron lung; this segues into a leafy garden and a boy called Brian. Both of us are victims of polio. We cannot walk.

At the rehab hospital, we have created our own little world, Brian and me. We call each other 'Mummy' and 'Daddy' and have tea parties with teddy bears and dolls. The nurses indulge us with cups, saucers, cake and a teapot filled with chocolate milk. We ask for extra cake or biscuits for our toys. We hide those extras for secret picnics. It makes us giggle to think we have fooled them.

Each day we swim in a hydrotherapy pool filled with soothing emollients, along with a little girl who has been burnt from head to toe. The girl is allowed into our imaginative domain during those sessions. We are three children who have no idea there are others in the world who are strong and able, with smooth, undamaged skin and limbs that obey commands.

When we emerge from the pool, we are spoilt and cosseted by the nurses, the orderlies and the cook, Linda. The hospital is our castle, and we, its rulers, are already unknowingly acquiring the mental skills we will need to survive what life has in store for us, the different, the damaged. We pay no heed to how others see us. All that matters is how we view ourselves.

I see no other black faces during the three years I am in the rehab hospital. Everyone is white. There are no mirrors; I am reflected solely in the faces of those around me. I never take the time to observe the colour of my skin. It is of no consequence in my world. I am, for all intents and purposes, the same colour as everyone else in the hospital.

I sleep very little in the ward. My overactive imagination turns the shadows into monsters, and the children's breathing around me is loud and threatening. I always end up whimpering and being gathered into the arms of a nurse who dries my tears and carries me to the nurses' station. I am fed buttered arrowroot biscuits and cold milk and entertain them with childish stories and remembered songs. I feel loved and safe.

After countless hours of physiotherapy, hydrotherapy and encouragement, Brian and I gradually learn to walk, and are fitted with our callipers together. Little do we realise that this means we will soon be separated, never to see each other again.

The day my life changed is etched in my memory. I was up early as usual: breakfast and bath. But there was something different. There were tears in the nurses' eyes as they collected me for my bath. Afterwards, I was dressed in special new clothes: a little fawn-coloured pinafore, a pretty little blue jumper, new socks, a ribbon for my hair. My callipers were polished. I was excited by the clothes, but also suspicious. Why new clothes? Why the crying? Why was Linda fussing over me at this hour? I didn't usually see her until later in the day. She grabbed me and held me as tight as she could. Her tears wet my face. I started to become alarmed.

The head sister told me I was to meet my mummy and daddy. Mummy and daddy? What did they mean by that? Me and Brian were Mummy and Daddy, and I told her so in no uncertain terms. But she insisted that my real mummy and daddy were coming, and they would take me on a long journey. I was going home, she said.

'But I'm already home.'

'This is a hospital. You came here when you got sick. Your mummy and daddy are taking you back to your real home, the home you came from before you got sick,' she responded.

Eventually, confused and scared, I was taken into a room where there stood two people who seemed as though from another planet. They were introduced to me as my parents. I remember recoiling in horror as they handed me to the strange dark lady.

'This is your real mummy,' the nurse said in her most soothing voice.

I would have none of it. 'She's not my mummy! He's not my daddy! They're black!'

I remember tears streaming down their faces. How my words must have hurt.

I know now that it was not their fault they couldn't visit me in hospital. They were two people without money, living in a society where Aboriginal people needed permits to work and to travel. There was no independence for my parents back then. You had to have permission from the powers that be to do anything at all, really.

The circumstances of the time meant there were no gentle introductions, no reorientation programs. There was no scope for us to get to know each other. I was thrust into the arms of strangers with no warning and they, in turn, had no idea what to do with this screaming child who looked at them as though they were monsters.

I was allowed to say goodbye to Brian, who wept and screamed as much as I did when they finally managed to prise us apart. To this day, I still think about Brian and Linda the cook and the little girl with the badly burnt body and wonder what became of them.

The strange couple carried me, still screaming, into crowded Central Railway Station, trying desperately to ignore the suspicious stares of strangers. All their comforting and stroking was to no avail. I continued to weep as we boarded the train. Eventually, with a shudder, it pulled out. We passed through suburbs with poky backyards and thin children who raised their hands to wave and grey washing flapping on clotheslines that stood like drab sentinels of late 1950s Sydney.

Then we were in the countryside, and my childish interest was piqued. Cows, sheep and horses grazed in green paddocks. I had only seen these animals in books until now. I stopped crying long enough to ask if they were real. The two strangers grasped the chance to connect with me at last. Each animal was pointed out, named. I calmed and started to relax into the warmth of the dark-skinned lady, who seemed soft now that I was not struggling against her. Her eyes were big and brown and tear-filled. She stroked my hair and whispered, 'We're going home now, baby girl.'

‘Back to the ward?’ I asked.

‘No, baby girl, home to your real home. You have a brother and a sister. They’re called Buddy and Lulla. You have a grandma, a grandpa and cousins. There are horses and dogs. You’ll see. We’ll take good care of you.’

The journey seemed to last forever, but the kind, gentle lady held me throughout. I became sleepy and nestled my head into her breast. Her blouse was damp from our intermingled tears. I finally slept.

*

The next morning, the train pulled up at a small railway station in the middle of nowhere. There were a few ramshackle houses and what looked like vast expanses of red dirt. There were no trees, just scrub. Connie Francis’s ‘Lipstick on Your Collar’ was blaring from the stationmaster’s radio. We stepped off the train, the only passengers. The stationmaster greeted Mum and Dad like long-lost friends. He smiled at me and welcomed me home. We walked into the searing heat, with only the echo of the station radio breaking the eerie silence.

I began to think that these people might be aliens. They had taken me to some far-off planet. I whimpered in fear. The man who I now know is my father, seeing my distress, hoisted me onto his shoulders and we continued across the red earth, bare except for strange little trees every so often.

We seemed to walk for miles. It was so hot. An emu darted past us, and lying in the shade of the saltbush was a goanna.

Then the sound of laughter and children’s voices floated over on the wind. I could hear someone playing a guitar and singing ‘Mona Lisa’ as we walked into a clearing where there were huts made from scrap, tents and a caravan. Dogs and kids were running about, and all the children and adults were the same colour as the people who had brought me here. And, as I soon realised, the same colour as me.

People surrounded me. An old man with silver hair and twinkling blue eyes took me from my mother’s arms and held me tightly as he whispered, ‘My little Topsy is home at last.’

I was passed to a woman named as my grandmother, Edie, and then to uncles, aunts, cousins. Finally I was introduced to the little people: my brother, Buddy, and sister, Lulla.

My new home was a far cry from the quiet, sterile hospital I was used to. A caravan had been bought especially for my homecoming. The toilet was a deep pit over which a wide wooden seat had been built, and it was enclosed in a tin shed with a wooden door. Dad knew it would be impossible for me to use, so he built me my own little toilet He painted it blue and adorned it with pink cabbage roses cut from a magazine.

Somewhere between the hospital and my new home, something had shifted in me. I lapped up the love that was showered on me like rainfall.

*

Soon I forgot about the convalescence home. I came to love my family. We moved to a bigger town with a river and paved streets. Dad bought a block of land and got a job with the Department of Main Roads, New South Wales (now known as Roads and Maritime Services). I settled into my new life, but little did I realise that this was not the end of my tumult and upheaval. In a way, it had only just begun. For the next decade, I was taken twice a year, kicking and screaming, from my mother's arms for the seventeen-hour train journey to Sydney, to a place called the Drummond Far West Children's Home, for more treatment. The Far West Home in those days was a cold and forbidding place. The playground was all green concrete and high fences. No trees, no flowers, no grass, just a solitary merry-go-round, or 'hurdy gurdy' as we called it. Particularly galling was that it was directly across the road from Manly Beach. The inmates and I could smell the sea, fairy floss, toffee apples. We could watch beachgoers laughing and having fun. We soon learnt that if we pressed our noses against the wire, these people would sometimes take pity on us and slip us bags of lollies.

To break the monotony, there were occasional outings to the beach and to the marina and fun fair at Manly Wharf. Sometimes television, movie and music stars of the day would visit. We were treated to concerts by Jimmy Little and Col Joye and the Joy Boys, taken to meet people such as Donna Douglas, who played Elly May on *The Beverly Hillbillies*, or to meet visiting royalty. One friend met Princess Anne and I got to meet Princess Soraya while in Camperdown Children's Hospital, but mostly it was the same dreary routine. I think that's why I have such a hatred of routine, and why I've never really fitted into a conventional workforce, with its rules and its nine-to-five mentality. It was so different from home, with all the chaos of a big family. At home there was life, animals, a river, grass, trees – and when it rained, the unbelievably beautiful smell of water on dry earth. At home I was black and went barefoot, except to school and on outings. At Far West I was unsure just what colour I was, and I wore those hated callipers from six in the morning until seven at night.

My family didn't have the money to come and see me, and in a way I was grateful for that, because while there I could adjust to my life as it was without the distraction and longing that seeing them would have brought. Instead I developed a rich and wonderful gift: the ability to be in the moment. Where I was, was where I was.

I formed a rich inner life. I learnt to treasure solitude because when alone I could be anyone I wanted; I could be anywhere I wanted. My legs may have been encased in callipers, but in my mind's eye they were strong and muscular. On my feet I wore delicate silken butter-soft slippers and danced like the ballerinas I had seen in films and on the stage. Or I was barefoot and ran like a streak across vast expanses of beach and desert. I wasn't tethered to the earth. Oh no! I leapt onto strong stallions and rode bareback beside princes and warriors. I flew like a bird and rode on magic carpets and cast pity at the people below as they scurried across the earth, harried and worried and unable to see me smiling down on them.

I never saw myself as disabled. I was unaware of my pronounced limp. I was always so surprised when a child or a cruel adult at Far West pointed it out. I would look around to see who they were talking about. The realisation may have momentarily hurt, but never for long. There were too many adventures and romances – there was too much magic – to conjure.

Lying on the ground watching clouds, tracing the streams the jets left as they streaked across the deep blue sky, I would imagine the people in those planes, wonder at the places they'd been or where they were going. I was sure I would be in one of those planes one day. I could not countenance a life where this was not possible.

*

Others did not share my confidence in this future.

When I was twelve, my mother took me to see the local doctor for my dreadful migraines. He said to my mother that they should start looking into getting me on a disability pension before I finished school. I went into a fury: 'I don't need a pension. I have a brain!' My mother knew then that I would be alright in life.

She and Dad did everything they could to ensure I had the best possible education, because they knew that would help me achieve any dreams I had.

A scholarship to a prestigious girls' high school in Sydney gave me entrée to a society with people who understood me. I made lifelong friends there and, on leaving, found work easily.

As an adult, it came as a fabulous surprise that I too could have boyfriends and know the loving embrace of men, that I could give and receive sexual pleasure. Men loved me, and it didn't seem to matter to them that I limped. They always looked surprised when I mentioned it, and were often puzzled as to why I brought it up. They saw the inner me. I lived a gloriously happy life for many years, full of music, laughter, food and friends.

A decision to move back home would change me. At first, it was wonderful to be with my family and in my country. I met a man I thought was the answer to my dreams, and we got married. But I had married an illusion, for no sooner was the ring slipped on my finger than he turned into a drunken, violent monster.

Eventually I was able to gather enough resources and leave him, returning to Sydney, but I was flat, emotionally stripped. People said I'd lost my glow. I kept up a front for a while, and suppresed my deep hurt and anger as I dealt with the onset of post-polio syndrome, which resulted in the loss of mobility that resulted in me living in a wheelchair.*

---

* Post-polio syndrome (PPS) is a condition that affects polio survivors years after recovery from the initial acute attack of poliomyelitis. The most common symptoms are slowly progressing muscle weakness, fatigue and gradual muscle atrophy. Pain from joint degeneration and increasing skeletal deformities such as scoliosis are also common.

It's hard to pinpoint when my mojo went walkabout. But it was probably when I stopped wearing lipstick and started going out in trackie daks and t-shirts. I gave up my beloved Chanel No. 5, lost interest in flirting and couldn't pick up on the signals from men. Eventually I took to sleeping incredibly long hours, and sometimes felt so weighed down by life that the simple act of rolling over in bed became a chore. I would lay there with my ear hurting but lacking the will to simply turn onto my other side. My mind, with its seemingly infinite capacity for imagination and pleasure, was failing me, clouded in a miasmic fog that I couldn't think my way out of. For the first time I could remember, I was tethered to the earth and merely physical. It was a scary place to be. I sought help but could not relate to the white psychology. The drugs I was prescribed didn't make a difference, and drinking only exacerbated my blue feelings.

I knew I had to find my way back. The alternative was too devastating to contemplate. I needed to look deep inside and reclaim my wild and free self, with its capacity to discover joy. I needed my silken, butter-soft dancing shoes again. They were still there, I was sure. I just had to dig through the mental wreckage to recover them.

I started by sifting through all the anger and hatred I felt towards my husband. Although my thoughts were dark and murderous and filled with rage, I revelled in these extreme feelings because they made me feel alive again. I then began to let them go, one by one. Each day I became lighter as I discarded the emotional detritus. Those feelings of wrath turned to pity, and soon thoughts of him became feather-light, desiccated husks that I simply sent away upon the softest of breezes. He could no longer hurt me.

Next I had to deal with my feelings about my loss of mobility and come to terms with using a wheelchair. I could no longer sustain a full-time job. I had to find new ways of making a living and of living in general. I decided to become a writer, and told my friends about my plan so I would not be able to back out. I entered competitions, pitting myself against other would-be writers, and to my amazement I started winning. I submitted articles to various newspapers and journals, and they published them. I wrote a book, and this took me all over Australia to talk to readers.

I have since written five children's books, as well as many articles and short stories. I speak at conferences, I run writing workshops and I teach children. My life is organised to suit my needs now and not the needs of others. I have a five-second commute from bed to desk. I can wear my nightie to work if I so choose, and my natural nocturnal ways rule. My friends say I keep rock-star hours and know never to call before noon.

I have my dancing shoes back. I am no longer anchored to the earth by the past; I can go anywhere I want. I have my lipstick, Chanel No. 5 and pretty dresses back. I have my blokes back. I have my life back. I have my mojo back.

I knew the return to myself was complete when I travelled to Europe and visited all the places I'd dreamt of as a child. Flying home after a wild and wonderful trip, a mere hour away from Sydney, the plane tracked over my home town. I looked out the window through the mid-morning light and smiled. I was finally in a plane leaving jet streams in the sky. I was the one returning from faraway lands. As I looked down at the disappearing speck of my childhood home, I wondered if there was another little girl gazing up and dreaming of one day travelling on a plane that briefly left an ethereal signature in the sky. I hoped so.

Born Special

Kath Duncan

I'm glad I don't remember being born. My mum describes it as horrific. It was a breech birth – bum first. Mum says she heard a woman screaming and thought, 'Poor lady, I hope they help her,' then realised she was the one screaming.

I'm a researcher. I need to know *everything*. Naturally I applied for my birth records. They show that Mum received a local anaesthetic as they performed the episiotomy that brought me into the world at Sydney's renowned King George V Memorial Hospital at 1.20 pm on Thursday, 13 April 1961.

Condition at Birth

Class:	B*
Weight:	6.13
Length:	21 3/4
Sex:	Female
Foetal distress:	Cord around neck – loose
Deformity:	Left arm – right leg not formed Toes 4 on left foot

I was my mother's third child, so she was used to the birth routine, but she passed out at some stage and when she came to there were many heads staring at her through the delivery room window. 'That's odd,' she thought, before losing consciousness again.

---

* The other options are Class A, Class C, Class D, or Stillborn.

My mother was taken to her own room, separate from the other parents. That was strange too. She asked for her baby, but I was not brought to her. A whole day passed and Mum started protesting as loudly as she could until her gynaecologist arrived. He sat on her bed and spoke earnestly. 'Your baby has one or two abnormalities.' He listed them.

My mother replied, 'Is she behaving like any other baby?'

Her gyno declared, 'Yes, she's doing everything. All her reactions are the same as any normal baby.'

Mum quipped, 'Okay, I'll add on the rest, then. I can do that.' And I was brought to her.

Mum loves the end of this birth story. I'm not sure what she meant exactly, but Mum's own father was an arm amputee, having lost his right arm via a Gallipoli sniper in World War I. She was used to armlessness. But Mum also might have meant – typically of her time – that my physical and neurological differences at birth were important to her. This sort of differentiation affected how you were treated growing up disabled in Australia

I was born Special. I can't entirely recommend it but lots of us survive it. I was claimed by the Special sector from the start, and the experience, while privileged if compared to what happens to kids born like me in other countries, has been hairy and scary and complicated and weird. Weirder than me by a long shot.

My parents, my four siblings and I were launched into 'special' communities: doctors of 'special' patients, 'special' schools with 'special' students, and a 'special' prosthetic crew who lurked in ill-lit buildings with power saws, fibreglass, sweaty limb socks and talcum powder. War veterans, people who had been through accidents, ill older people, and other congenitally differently limbed children, all of us were on the eventful ride of 'special' treatment that ultimately affects pretty much everything: employment opportunities, access to education and medical treatment, income, social events and venues, and career paths.

After a long two weeks of testing at the hospital, my mother and father took me home to Sydney's then bushy south-western suburbs. My parents had a sprawling wooden house on brick stilts at the top of a block that rolled messily and scrubbily down to shimmery, shallow Salt Pan Creek. It was lush.

I've been told everyone was shocked by my appearance.

Growing up, I didn't realise my body was such a minefield, as to me I felt perfect. This has remained the most bizarre thing to me – the contrast between how Right I feel within myself and how apparently Wrong I am to everyone looking at me. This started very early. My mother describes family members and neighbours as having to 'adjust' to me, as though their usual new baby congratulations were awkward. And publicly I was managed differently from my mother's other children too.

By 1962 I was registered with the New South Wales Society for Crippled Children. By 1963, I was attending their 'special' preschool. That same year the *Australian Pre-School Quarterly* asked teachers: 'Can school staff really accept a disabled student as a person and be objective about the handicap while being warm and friendly?'

By the time I was five or six it had become obvious how different I was, and it wasn't a happy realisation. I was now at the special school – which felt like a cradle-to-grave establishment, a furtively ugly institution with barbed wire around it and an underground entrance, built on a former dump site in suburban Sydney.

I went to special school via a long 'special' taxi ride. My older sister and brother went to our local school on the local bus, which I travelled on outside of school time.

At special school I could be taken out of class at any moment and questioned, tested and examined. Once, two ladies in green observed and timed me with a ticking stopwatch in a closed room while I took off both prostheses and all my clothes and put them back on again. I found the tension of wondering when the ladies in green would come for me again very frightening.

It was confusing; it felt like punishment for being me. It felt also dangerous. In 1968 a few hundred 'special' educationalists met in Canberra for the consultation called The Provision of an Adequate Education for the Handicapped Child. They faffed around for a day before unanimously agreeing that the 'basic purpose of education for the handicapped child' was to accept 'that the handicapped child is not a whole person but damaged'. This declaration says a lot about what it felt like to be in special education in Australia. That was a national consultation, so it affected all kids and young adults in the Australian special school system. At the time, I was seven years old.

The school and my prosthetics clinic were more like places of torture than places to grow. We were treated like objects. If that isn't 'damaging', I'd like to know what is. It's still surprising to me that these people could not perceive how destructive their practices and attitudes were to us.

In the 1960s you stayed in Special Ed if you couldn't go to the toilet by yourself or get up stairs. I worked out how to do both those things. I started to have regular sessions with the Special School psych, and I really enjoyed them. I remember playing games with toys and telling stories. In the spring of 1969 I started mainstream schooling.

Wow! I was a Freak Superstar for a few weeks, and at the start of every new school year I copped teasing and bullying. I was perpetually a sports failure and excluded, and I learnt how to fight using my prosthetics – but it was amazing to have so much freedom! The public school wasn't boarded up, and there was no barbed wire, no fucking Special taxi trips, and the hundreds of students running around looked as beautiful as butterflies to me. The front gates were always open, and the back of the school emptied into gorgeous scrubby bush.

Home was not always fun. My three sisters were wonderful buddies, supportive and fun, but my mum had married two drunks – her first husband, whom she had my eldest sister with, then my father, an impossible person to get to know or like. I feel only reluctant gratitude for his single sperm. I was envious of my friends' fathers, who seemed happy and family-focused, while my father was always working, drunk or hungover, especially as I got older. My parents were conservative, white, middle-class, Anglo-Scottish atheists, who turned right-wing politics into their religion.

At sixteen I was secretary of my local Young Liberals branch, and by eighteen I had changed my views and was studying political economics at Sydney University and learning how to read and research. I love my mum dearly, and appreciate her guts and industry and the way she pushed us all to get an education, but we do not talk politics now. Turning away from conservative politics was a huge and positive leap in my life, opening up my world to new experiences and adventures.

I moved out of home after my eighteenth birthday. I struggled financially and with keeping up with my studies, but in Sydney's then creative, youthful and experimental inner 'burbs, Freedom was all around me.

Part of my growing up included discovering how difficult it was to be taken seriously as a creative person. I was offered all manner of hideously boring jobs – and unpaid training – by employment services, while my attempts to get funding and support for my creative goals (to perform, to make art, to be a creative rebel and producer of bizarre works, to collaborate with others to break boundaries, to write poetry, to make films – some of which I was already doing) were rejected.

What changed this was finding the community station Radio Skid Row in Sydney and volunteering with them as a trainee presenter/producer. It was the early 1980s, and you would not believe how important it was in those days to question the -isms Australians had all unconsciously grown up with: sexism, racism, ableism, classism, etc. Ableism is the systemic discrimination against bodies and minds judged to be 'different', and the valuing of those judged to be 'normal' above ours. It is still prevalent everywhere, so much so that disabled people also suffer from internalised ableism – in which you apply these discriminatory ideas to yourself and other Deaf and disabled people. At Skid Row I hung out with people from all sorts of backgrounds and cultures who treated me like they treated everybody else – as a curious equal. I found out what a collective was. I heard music that wasn't vacuous pop. I met people who were politically engaged, savvy *and* great electronic storytellers and reporters.

In those days, the federal government actually gave a shit about ordinary people, and they put funding into community organisations to employ and train people. By early 1984, Radio Skid Row had applied to the Community Employment Program to set up a five-person news team and were successful, and because the program came with quotas to employ culturally and linguistically diverse (CALD) folk and people with disabilities, *I got my first job in the media*. These were amazing days, working with fantastic people whom I would meet again over the next decades through other media organisations, in universities and at conferences, and in every place where people fight for a better planet.

Skid Row changed my life for the better. My first job propelled me into other media work, including television, and further study, and media teaching, and gave me the confidence to keep doing the wild and fascinating shit I do. But the biggest gift Skid Row gave me was my comrades, whom I still treasure nearly forty years later. Thank you, Skid Row, for proving to me that I could do more than labour in a sheltered workshop, or fade away dreaming and filing in the suburbs; that I too could find a place in our cultural sector.

By the mid-1980s I was working as a casual radio journalist for Triple J and studying Film and Video Production at the University of Technology Sydney. I wasn't rolling in dough, but I found out that I could apply for a thirty-dollar per week Special (that word again!) Study Assistance payment through the Department of Social Security. On the day of my appointment to see the DSS consultant I also happened to be working for the Js, so I had my audio gear with me. I explained myself to the lady there and requested the assistance. She said point blank, 'No one will employ you as a journalist.' I pointed to my CV and my gear – slathered with ABC stickers – and said I was already working as a journalist, but she scoffed and refused my application.

It takes a lot of guts to be born different. And self-belief. And friends and supporters.

I have not done this alone. I can thank my friends and colleagues – disabled and non-disabled – and my family, especially my sisters, Beth and Clare, for my surviving and thriving.

My escape from special school had left me with scars, including internalised ones. I actively avoided disability altogether and kind of pretended I was different – not like those other cripples – from the age of eight, until I met my first cool disabled person, Kali Wilde, when I was twenty-four.

I was working for Radio Skid Row that day, and Kali was staffing an information stall at the community services event I was sent to. I saw Kali was disabled, and interesting-looking with her short hair in a groovy cut, so I approached her and we chatted. We stayed in touch and became friends. I was scared at first. In my experience, claiming your disability could mean getting excluded and locked up, left to rot, but Kali introduced me to other very cool, very politically engaged disabled people, and my eyes opened wide. I have never looked back.

I accumulated three degrees and am working on a PhD. While I was getting my BA (Hons) at Southern Cross University in Lismore, I was introduced to the world of Disability Studies by an awesome mentor and colleague, Gerard Goggin. How can I describe what it was like to finally see my situation theorised and validated by the academy? Even just the memory of opening the book Gerard loaned me and starting to read it makes me cry after nearly twenty years.

I had a great full-time job with ABC Radio National by the early 1990s, again because of visionaries who set quotas to employ people like me – those who are talented and ready to work but have been considered too different to fit in. Thanks to Nicola Joseph and Anna Schinella, the Women's Unit at RN (now defunct, natch) had an intake quota of one disabled, CALD and/or Aboriginal trainee every new year, and a number of us outsiders received the best media training ever. This absolutely would not have happened without quotas. Quotas gave me my career. I can't speak highly enough of making all organisations that receive public money accept quotas to employ marginalised groups. This is one clear way to have a career, and money, and credibility, like pretty much everybody else.

I could wax on about my love life, which has been, and remains, colourful and unconventional, but it would take up too much space. LOL. It is fair to say that I suggest that those disabled people searching for love primarily check out progressive causes and collectives.

By the time I was in my late forties, I was living in Melbourne and finally returning to my performing roots. I co-founded a troupe called Quippings, where my sexuality and performance aspirations would mesh and grow.

Quippings drew together mainly queer, all Deaf and disabled performers and emerging performers on an accessible stage, to strut our stuff and show our pride. I was feeling strong. Bold. I was also seeking to redefine myself.

It was my Quippings performance in 2013 that allowed me to grow up and love my Freak and my Freakiness.

'Freak' is marked as different. Freak is stared at. Freak is irresistible. Freak has shock value. Freak is strong. Freak is one of many great words starting with 'f'. Freak is something you could be called as an insult. Freak as a title for oneself is an act of defiance.

I embrace Freak. Freak is powerful. Scary.

> **freak, n.** a thing, person, animal or event that is extremely unusual or unlikely and not like any other of its type.

Not only do I like being a Freak, I like to think like one. Permanently strange: irreparable, incurable. Unmistakable. Resistant to treatment or cure.

Claiming Freak is, philosopher Elizabeth Grosz says, 'a political gesture of self-determination'. What am I resisting?

I'm resisting being the preferred cripple: the normalising 'nice' model promoted via incestuous, secretive, oppressive partnerships in the governmentalities of the Moloch-like medical and disability industries.

Freak is Congenital. Or close to that moment of birth.

Freak is circus and performance; magnetic and magic resonance. Among Freak performers, our contempt is that of insiders towards the uninitiated. The sucker who comes to the show is on the outside, not the exhibit.

'Freak' is a frame of mind, a set of practices ... Loved, loathed, feared, despised, worshipped; exhibited, exploited, applauded, laughed at AND shut away.

Calling myself Freak is an obvious insubordination against the norm: oppositional, rebellious, difficult, resilient.

So I'm at a Tropical Fruits New Year's Eve party, buzzing, and a guy I know – he serves me coffee at a local caff and he's nice – comes up to me pilled OUT! and he grabs me, Kath! I have got to show you something. Please! At a nearby hay bale he takes his shoe off with ceremony and props his left foot in front of me.

'There!' he says.

I look at his foot, at him. 'What?'

He says, 'Look!'

'Uh huh,' I say, looking at his foot. Fuck, I must be *wasted*, I'm totally missing it …

So he points to his second toe, 'My secret!'

I look and, yes, it kind of turns up and to the side a little. 'Aha!' I say.

He bursts out with: 'From the first time I saw you, Kath, I knew I would one day show you my toe. I knew you would understand because I understand you. All my life I've never gone barefoot 'cos *the toe*! And I'm breaking my long silence to show you. Finally!'

He's crying by the end. He can't possibly know what I've seen, where I've been, and the insignificance of his toe difference to me is flooded by the significance he puts on it.

I hug him. I say, 'Shame is fucked. Let that toe breathe, the toe is beautiful, man. It makes you unique …'

You can't police Freak.

In ancient times, the arrival of the Freak baby's body was an interpretive occasion inciting regulation. National struggles, climactic events and religious conflicts have been read in the unexpected or unusual bodies of babies. Research suggests disabilities in Western antiquity fell into hierarchies of social acceptability. For example, deafness, blindness and intellectual disability were more acceptable in comparison to my sort of disability, the congenital absence of limbs, which was considered a source of religious terror and the reason for fatal exclusion. By the Middle Ages, exhibiting and selling freaks and/or their body parts and corpses was a top earner.

Freak is obviously troubling, and child Freaks especially so. I bet you're uncomfortable even seeing the word 'Freak'? That's how much power it has.

But really, who wants to be just A Person with a Disability?

I wear the uncanny mantle of Freak as blessing and curse.

My sister Beth and I discuss Freaks. Beth says Freaks are born. A Freak is someone who has been touched by God – something is added, not destroyed. An added bonus.

I ask Beth: 'How do you think being a Freak since birth has affected me?'

She says: 'It makes you an outsider, puts you in your own tribe. It doesn't matter whether you are physically different or have language differences, because of the structure of where we live and what we think everything is built around this philosophy of people who are constructed in a certain way. It's an analysis that developed via feminism, being outside of the norm of male privilege, but you're a more extreme example – your club is more elite, and so you also have lacked shared opportunities to develop your own languages to describe your experiences, so I can see you're dying to use the word Freak – because you need words that will articulate the experience itself.'

I'm ten at my second cousin Sue's birthday party. It's a lovely cake-stuffing event until suddenly Sue starts screaming. We all run over, me and my sisters and other kids, to find Sue on a flight of stairs, wailing and crying. 'What's wrong?' someone asks her. 'I've broken my nail!' Sue yells (yes, another digit story! I have a million) and she waves her hand in the air. No blood, no mess, just fingers, fingernails, whatever. I don't get it. I stare at the scene as all those little girls cluster around Sue, comforting her. I back off like an alien. Fuck knows how many scratches, bruises, muddy bits and whatever nail thingies I have on me at this moment, plus two bulky prostheses (one ending in a gleaming silver hook), special shoes, a loud limp ... How does Sue see me? If a nail can freak her out, what about me? I'm falling into a lonely, self-loathing abyss of weird until I feel beside me my sisters. Warm next to me. I see they're as baffled as I am. We start laughing. We run away. We laugh and laugh.

I am the biggest freak, but that day they stood with me.

Show the freaks some love. We're the ones who make history. Every day. We are speaking out, sharing secrets, gathering in freaky company, freaky community; we are resisting being nice.

No Middle Ground

Yvonne Fein

Lithium probably saved my life. I was never in danger of not taking the drug during my many depressive episodes. It was during the much rarer – and possibly rarefied – highs that I was vulnerable, because it was then that I thought I was invulnerable.

I am a manic-depressive. That's not the PC term. In polite company it's now called having bipolar disorder. But a rose by any other name …

Coping mechanisms are a vital part of living with the condition. So what really works? In a depressive state I've found the most important step is getting out of bed in the morning. In the clinics where I've stayed, that is the policy. No matter how gloomy, threatened or bleak you're feeling, they insist you get up. When I haven't been bad enough to need a clinic, my sister has stepped in to help. She would sit on my bed for however long it took for me to rise. Once up, things do feel different. I've never really understood why.

Those people who don't have any back-up – the cruellest predicament – are most at risk.

Another vital coping mechanism is taking meds. But bipolar is a condition of extremes. You're either up or your down: Arctic, Antarctic. No nice warm middle ground. Middle ground is where the rest of the world lives. So as soon as you're feeling better, the classic response is to throw the lithium away. That rarely has a positive outcome.

Therapy? It's never really worked for me. I now see a benign therapist once every four to five weeks. She prescribes and I take the medication. We chat for a while and afterwards I do feel lighter, but in the depths or at the heights there's not much she can do except adjust my cocktail of meds.

Bipolar is hereditary, but just because it runs in the family does not mean the next generation will necessarily inherit it. Environmental factors – abuse, mental stress, loss of a loved one or any number of traumatic events – may contribute to or trigger bipolar disorder.

While I was not a victim of abuse, I nevertheless ticked too many of the above boxes. My mother had it. I believe my maternal grandfather also had it, but we'll never know for sure because he died in the Holocaust and my mother was too young to recall him clearly. The rest of my ancestors are long dead at the hands of that same enemy, more bitter than illness. There's no way of discovering how their cerebral activity functioned.

I think the Holocaust was the trigger for me. I didn't live through it. I am what they call a second-generation survivor, who grew up with both parents dealing with PTSD from what they had experienced in the death camps. Of course, in those days no one called it 'PTSD'. Identifying post-traumatic stress disorder was a long way in the future.

A family friend, who also supplied zippers and yarns to my parents' clothing factory, used to besiege me at every opportunity, for reasons I still don't understand. 'If ever there was a lost generation, it's yours,' he would say ad nauseam, each time believing he was telling me something new. His accent fractured his speech. 'I know it was my, *my* generation who lost *you*. Some even say that all we managed to pass on was pain from the camps. But if we admit it, will it stop you from keeping psychiatrists and divorce lawyers in business? You're lost and sick. Blame us? Sure. But the point is you're the ones who are sticked – stuck – with it.'

As soon as I could, I would flee from him because, at some level, I knew he was right. I was sticked with it.

I was a teenager when it first began, in my tenth year of school. I didn't want to go out, let alone participate in the elaborate premating rituals of my peers. I found I could not study or even engage in class discussions anymore. I failed every mid-year examination.

When my parents berated me for my academic failures, I remember thinking: 'I came across some figures once, Mum, Dad. Did you know it was the ones with degrees, the Jewish academics, who perished first in Germany? They were so well-educated, they knew they would always be safe in *das Vaterland* ...'

But I never dared say it.

Between episodes of darkness or a light that was far too bright, I understood the ache beneath those volatile surfaces of mine. I knew that trying to measure up to people who had become rag-trader millionaires after surviving Hitler was a feat of death-defying magnitude. And more, they had done so in a strange land, learning a strange language, at the end of the world. How could anything in my life approximate the terror and the passion, the beauty and the obscenity experienced by those who had endured to give me life?

My mother came to Auschwitz at seventeen. She watched her mother and baby brother being forced by Mengele into the line that led to the gas chambers. The soldiers dragged my mother to the right, into the line for the young and strong. They pulled her hands from her mother's as they both cried, an image that plagued my dreams for many years after my mother shared that information with me (she was manic at the time).

The first tale of romance I ever heard was that of my parents meeting across the barbed wire of a labour camp. By the time it was told to me, I had developed a concept of reality that was congruent with that of my peers. I grew up in the company of second-generation survivors and most of us had evolved to find the abnormal normal. At a class reunion not so long ago, someone read out a list of those classmates who had died before their time. The number of suicides was disproportionate.

Then there were the feelings of impotence which exacerbated those interminable times when I visited the dark side. I could not have saved my parents. I could not have prevented that whirlwind of blood and slaughter in which they became caught up. There was nothing I could have done. My anger, combined with a toxic mix of self-reproach, shame and guilt, hurled me deeper into the gloom.

I felt impotent too, when confronted with the opinions of those people who deny the Holocaust, the David Irvings of the world. It does not matter to them how much evidence Spielberg, Wiesenthal, Ságvári, Paulsson and countless others accrued. In the times when equilibrium shone its brightness upon my brain, I was able to accept that it was beyond me to change anything about the phenomenon of Holocaust deniers. At some level I knew they did not believe their own words. I understood that their goal was not freedom of expression, that they were malevolent and hate-filled towards persecuted minorities in general and Jews in particular. By arguing that six million never died, that the Holocaust never happened, they conjured another reason for Jew-hatred: lying Jews, silver-tongued and deceitful Jews. If Hitler had wanted to persecute them, he would have been entitled to, but he hadn't and his reward was Jewish lies. Or so the denier narrative maintained.

But the blue numbers tattooed on my mother's forearm, which I saw every day of my childhood, were proof. As were my father's cries in the night as he fought with sleep-generated spectres of the baby brothers he had lost – the ones *he* couldn't save from those Grimm Teutonic ovens.

Once, a sympathetic psychiatrist told me that when he asked my mother if she thought it would be a good idea to have the numbers removed – surely it would help her forget? – she looked at him in some surprise. 'I don't want to forget. That would give them victory,' she said. 'I survived in spite of their *ekldik* numbers.'

I am a high-functioning manic-depressive. I did nothing to deserve bipolar, and by the same token it was good fortune rather than good deeds that made me one of the high-functioning ones. It's simply the hand I was dealt.

My father told me – his mind still hustling, agile – 'Think how many died in the camps. Just because we survived doesn't mean we were braver, stronger, smarter. Maybe we made a sharp choice or two, but in the end we were just luckier.'

I have lived with this rose by any other name for fifty years.

I take the lithium.

I read somewhere that it works on 80 per cent of sufferers in their early manic phases, but the success rate is far lower in its use as an ongoing treatment. It doesn't work for everyone.

It does for me.

Just luckier, I guess.

A Polio Story

Fran Henke

My mum was young and pretty, a promising pianist and pilot, flying flimsy aeroplanes practically held together with safety pins. Dad was sent away to war in an ill-fitting uniform but returned quickly to his career as a Gippsland stock and station agent, thanks to a minor illness.

As soon as I could walk, I chased bullocks down the nearby stock route – much to the horror of drovers heading to Leongatha's saleyards. We had an English sheepdog called Hobo and a duck called Donald. That sort of thing – a fairly normal childhood for the 1940s.

Allegedly, at my third birthday party in June 1946, I hit a kid with a croquet mallet. Retribution was swift. I began to feel ill. Too fat to walk. The last thing I remember is being lifted out of bed to see white horses that had come into the yard, a misty remembrance of them capering around Hobo's kennel. Maybe Mum told me about that later.

The next seven years are largely blank: according to Freud, it is a blessing for children to have unpleasant beginnings locked away, like a security box at the bank. A community health centre nurse described my black hole as 'childhood trauma amnesia'.

A local doctor soon diagnosed the illness as infantile paralysis, or poliomyelitis. An isolated case in Leongatha. It meant a life-threatening coma and fever, the local doctor knew that much. My left side was affected, particularly my leg, which had a flaccid, scrunched-up pedal extremity.

Poliomyelitis has existed since Ancient Egyptian times. Epidemics of it began sweeping the world in the late nineteenth century, hitting Europe, the Americas, Australia and New Zealand. It was described as a disease of social progress, the epidemics brought about by cleanliness, oddly enough as toilets came indoors. Previously, when sanitary conditions were poor, children were exposed to the virus at a very early age and developed natural immunity to it.

At first, doctors were helpless. They had no weapons against it; only general nursing care was given to patients. There was no cure and there seemed no pattern for the course of the disease. Some patients escaped lasting ill-effects; others were permanently paralysed. Thousands died. In Australia after World War II, outbreaks occurred annually – 1951 was particularly bad. The polio scare emptied cinemas, swimming pools and shopping centres.

Mad schemes involving nasal sprays and clothes pegs were recommended to halt polio's spread. Peter Colville was a young doctor working for the Victorian Department of Health at the time. I interviewed him in 1990 in an attempt to find out what happened to me and why symptoms were returning. 'It was an acute illness and acutely devastating in the early stages,' explained Dr Colville, himself a polio survivor. 'There were the waves of crazy preventatives like the pegs, a lot of misinformation. It was actually a bowel infection, rather than the upper respiratory virus first thought, and it went through the blood to knock off the anterior horn cells in the spinal cord. It is a normal bowel infection still in the community.'

Large-scale immunisation against polio began in Victoria in 1956, after the development of a vaccine by American virologist Dr Jonas Salk.

There is a cheeky view among survivors that we 'polios' (as we call ourselves) have an indomitable spirit and are stubborn, determined to achieve despite physical limitations. Survivors may be found climbing the Himalayas or riding camels across a desert. Or we might become president of the United States, like Franklin D. Roosevelt, who founded a polio rehabilitation centre in Warm Springs, Georgia.

'In Australia, doctors kept under their hats the serious potential for the disease to spread further out of control with the movement of migrants around the country,' Dr Colville recalled. 'Migrants came in with young children. They were put in camps, created a culture, then the virus affected the camp. The families were moved, say, from Bonegilla to Somers camp (north-eastern and south-eastern Victoria respectively), bringing the virus with them. We were very worried by this movement.'

That information never got out. The media was different seventy years ago. No panic, no backlash against a group of people who already had enough problems.

My memory remains empty about most aspects of the illness, but the spectre of Dr Dame Jean Macnamara is large. She had rooms in Spring Street, Melbourne, on the first floor. Mum had to carry my sister and me, one at a time, up two flights of stairs. While Dame Jean was the source of what seemed like torture then, it is her (and Mum) I can thank for my ability to indulge in ridiculous exploits like climbing to a mountain-top temple in India.

My late mum remembered Dr Mac only too well. (I interviewed Mum too.) 'Dame Jean was an extraordinary personality,' she recalled. 'She campaigned for the introduction of myxomatosis, a viral disease, to control rabbits, and also suggested to Prime Minister Robert Menzies that he encourage the Queen and Princess Margaret to wear fox furs in order to reduce the number of foxes in Australia. Dame Jean was a very single-minded, determined woman. Welfare House [in Prahran] had been founded by the Red Cross for the children of airmen to stay in while their mothers were ill or in confinement. Dame Jean used you as an example to make Welfare House available for country polios. Later, she organised it to accommodate spastics too.'

This was particularly relevant to our family because a year after I had polio, my sister Janet was born with cerebral palsy, thanks to the Rhesus (Rh) factor. I guess they didn't know then that the first child might be alright but that a second could be born seriously ill.

I spent around eight years in and out of Welfare House and Lady Dugan Home in Malvern as new splints, plasters and corrective techniques were tried. Being a test case triggered rebellion. For instance, in the ablutions block at Welfare House, there was a 'potty book' where the doings of each child were recorded. While waiting my turn for a bath one day, I filled in the book with red ticks so each child could be seen to have done their best. The system was subsequently abandoned. In retrospect, harsh punishment in relation to the potty might have caused me to do this. Polio friends have talked about being locked in bathrooms or cupboards for hours. Hello, claustrophobia.

In those days, there were no lightweight materials for splints or other body-correcting devices. One of Dame Jean's specialties was to immobilise and straighten paralysed and twisted limbs via metal splints. Mum said the first time she and the Welfare House matron, Lois Ditchburn, had to strap me into the appalling iron frame called the Double Thomas, they offered an aspirin to relax me and then closed the door, anticipating screams. None came. The following morning they crept in to see how I'd survived the night, and found me sitting on the pillow. 'Got myself out!' I said triumphantly. Houdini couldn't have done better. I still can't abide being tied down or sitting anywhere without windows.

The next instrument of torture was a heavy brown pram, long enough to push me strapped in calipers or the Double Thomas. The pram was not the vehicle you wanted to be seen in publicly – attracting well-meaning old ducks with ample bosoms, chucking you pityingly under the chin. That kind of attention breeds strong determination not to be different.

Mum and Dad fought to keep me at home, but when Janet came along – in worse trouble than me – I stayed longer at Welfare House, with its peppercorn trees and the gravel drive that grazed knees during forbidden caliper races. Those trees hold pleasant if unreliable memories, representing shade, climbing, rare childhood adventure.

Dame Jean came up with really strange theories for treating my sister. One was a papoose board. The notion was that when spasms occurred, the head or limbs would hit the sides of the board and train the patient not to spasm. Another suggestion was to throw the patient from a height face-down onto a hard surface, forcing them to put their hands out to save themselves. But there was no control over spasming limbs, so Janny could never save herself – couldn't they see this? Mum could not bear to do it, even on a bed, so she trailed around 'quacks', looking for other solutions.

The TV adaptation of Alan Marshall's *I Can Jump Puddles* contains an agonising scene in which Alan's parents had to force his polio-twisted legs flat every night, despite his screams. But they did it, as did most of our parents, because Doctor said so. Doctors were treated like gods. Parents didn't argue. As Mum said, we had to try everything.

And she did. I had not grown enough, so I went to the growth unit at the Royal Children's Hospital, where we short kids were lined up naked, measured, prodded and discussed. At art school sixty years later, we were tasked with painting a painful memory from childhood. Mine was a kid naked but for a bow in their hair. A legacy of that incident is painful modesty – donning bathers at the pool is agony.

After the growth unit came a doctor targeting 'aspirational parents' with remedies for height problems. I was given steroids to make me grow. Years later I discovered that the *British Medical Journal* warned at the time not to give steroids to children. Side effects: migraines, obesity, infertility – check, check, check. Tall kids were given diethylstilboestrol, resulting in rare cancers that were transmitted to their daughters, plus surgeries to correct limbs that grew unevenly. My anger remains raw over that unconscionable experimentation on children.

I was more fortunate than other children though. Some parents couldn't bear the fight, abandoning stricken children to institutions. One friend's parents were embarrassed by his illness, didn't know what to do – so they kept him in a shed. Polio was seen as dirty. People crossed the road to avoid houses where polio lurked; families were snubbed. Our home was quarantined.

School was torture for those of us in boots, splints and special chairs. Being different was the pits, being short was the pits. Tied into a chair at boarding school to stop me running around, I became a target for bullies. I did badly in everything except English. I could write, and was encouraged by Mum to read, to adopt new words. I realise now that I had concentration problems related to a polio-affected brain.

Then my sweet, highly intelligent, Liberace-loving sister died, aged eleven. Mum and Dad had decided to send her to a school for 'crippled children' to broaden her horizons. On the very first day, staff placed her face-down on pillows to drain her nasal passages and left the room. She suffocated.

Mum never got over my sister's death, blaming herself. I became the focus of her concern. I left home as soon as I could to become a journalist – Albury, the Gold Coast, Canberra, London, Sydney. I loved my mum, but three days were long enough in each other's hypercritical company. There were many questions I could have asked to better understand what she and Dad had gone through, but in her later years Mum became too distressed to talk about the past. How did two young people manage with two 'crippled' children, and the related costs, post-war? Cousins have revealed recently, thinking I already knew, that my parents were so desperate at one point they put us both in the car and planned to drive over a cliff.

When the late effects of polio hit me in the 1980s and doctors claimed it was 'all in my head', my childhood distrust of the medical profession resurfaced. I had been fortunate to avoid doctors and hospitals until then, preferring so-called alternative age-old treatments such as homeopathy, iridology and chiropractic. Then I found an article in a South Australian newspaper about American polio survivors being diagnosed with post-polio syndrome.

Aha! I decided my communication skills should be used to spread the word in Australia. It was not all in our heads. I wrote letters and articles, went on radio and lobbied. I was invited to a Polio Network Victoria meeting. Being among people in wheelchairs, or wearing calipers or on sticks, again was confronting. I cried all the way home. That wasn't me. I thought I'd concealed the limp, any obvious disability, like so many who were told never to mention polio again.

Then the Australian government donated one million dollars to Indonesia for polio vaccination, and I thought, 'What about us?' I was back on track.

'Us' meant the comfortable fraternity of polio survivors, among whom I was not the odd one out. 'Us' meant understanding that physical exhaustion was caused by having to work damaged nerves and muscles twice as hard, that there may be swallowing and speech problems, heat and cold intolerance, and an inability to manage noise and crowds, and that it's okay to ask for a lower chair with arms (took years, that one).

Now seventy-six, I have never regretted polio, or asked 'Why me, why us?' I've had a marvellous life, travelled widely, married – no children, which allowed us both to take risks to benefit society.

In recent years, I've come to understand that some some survivors of polio carry baggage in the form of post-traumatic stress disorder. The most distressing part of my own baggage is the debilitating fatigue and loss of memory.

But for me, there have been some silver linings. Being four foot eight-and-three-quarter inches led me to a family of tall men who all married short women like their mother – and gave me the guts to knock items down from top shelves with my elbow crutch at the supermarket, loving the freedom afforded by my mobility scooter Being 'disabled', however disguised, forced me out. Mum always said, 'Make yourself known.' So I did, meeting and writing about extraordinary people, chalking up, so far, twenty-three books and thousands of articles. My lack of tertiary qualifications seriously bugged me, despite these achievements. So, aged sixty-five, I went to TAFE (shingles, term one, from fear of failure) for a diploma in Visual Arts, majoring in sculpture and printmaking: I got seven high distinctions.

My shoulders may now be wrecked from carving stone with a scutch hammer and hauling my overweight self out of chairs, but hey, I've got the certificate.

A friend says I am the least disabled person she knows. I'll buy that.

Lady Lazarus

Carly-Jay Metcalfe

I have done it again.
One year in every ten
I manage it.
*A sort of walking miracle** of bacteria, antibiotic and flesh,
this biomedical poultice in a Petri dish,
spinning brindle like the wolf at my feet
as we walk by the river's brim.
It would get down to this, plain and simple:
a regiment of women in white
priming lines, tapping burettes and wiping licks of blood
off broken skin
as I'd yell, thick-throated and venal,
that they cannot do what they are about to do.
But they do and I would smell it
like a cow smells the blade of a knife in a kill yard.

Dying
Is an art, like everything else.
I do it exceptionally poorly.
1. Yeast in my blood (11)
2. Dead lungs (21)
3. A bloodied mass in my lap (31)
4. A head full of small brutalities (41)
The bones worry when you dig your own grave with one
finger, they do.
It's true. They do.

They worry when you dredge up a salute to your old life
under the guise of ending another.
Fracturing a fall forward,
your hunger becomes an exercise in mercurial discord.
But when you've mended your chest with a bagging needle,
learnt to pray over a burning arc,
made your yearly pilgrimage to the dying room,
the silence is tempered and you must sit in your mercy seat
and sing, sing, sing euphorically.

* *from Sylvia Plath's 'Lady Lazarus'*

Surprising Myself

Isis Holt

This piece is the result of an interview between Isis Holt and Carly Findlay.

Winning a medal at the Paralympics is one of the best feelings in the world. Nothing says 'I can do this' quite like crossing a line in first place. The crowd is so loud you almost can't feel the ground beneath you vibrate. That atmosphere is the most addictive thing about my sport. Circling the stadium with our flag and my teammates gave me a sense of satisfaction and pride I can't really find anywhere else. It reminded me that I am capable, something I think everyone deserves to be reminded of, particularly those of us who sometimes feel we are told we're not.

I am eighteen years old and I have diplegia cerebral palsy (CP). I am a professional athlete – I competed at the 2016 Paralympics – and a student. Personally, I feel very lucky and experience few barriers due to my disability. Often it has just been a matter of having to do little things differently to make life easier. Sport has been a huge enabler for me. It has helped me to rarely perceive things as impossible and instead try to find another w ay around situations or a happy compromise.

My disability usually presents pretty early in life, but I was diagnosed fairly late, at the age of eight or nine. Because of this, I spent most of my childhood oblivious to disability or any association it might have with me. Any of the differences I had to other kids I put down to a quirk, and never thought too much about it. My inability to hop or balance like other kids certainly didn't stop me from trying. When my CP was explained to me, since I hadn't encountered disability much at that point, I was confused because I didn't look like what I thought disability looked like: i.e. wheelchairs and severe impairment. I struggled to understand exactly what it meant for me, and came up with my own definition: 'One of my legs is shorter than the other one and it makes some things difficult.'

I don't think I was ever explicitly bullied for my CP, but I do remember becoming very self-conscious about it when I wore a leg brace. It attracted looks and stares from lots of people, both kids and adults, and I remember finding that disconcerting. It sometimes left me wondering if my leg brace (with its awesome patterns and butterflies) was weird rather than cool. People would often ask me if my leg was broken or if the leg brace 'stretched out my leg' to make it the same length as the other one. In retrospect that's pretty funny, but when I was younger I was a bit confused about what to say in response, and I think it perpetuated those feelings of self-consciousness, particularly in late primary school and early high school.

My parents were perceptive and provided the freedom for me to choose the things I wanted and helped me understand what I needed. I was never treated any differently and that really helped when I was first diagnosed. Another thing they provided, which I think is really underrated, was humour. We would often joke – and still do – about my CP and the things people would say, particularly if what they said upset me. I think it is so easy to treat disability as something serious and taboo but when it comes to family and people who truly understand the nature of your condition and the way you feel about it, humour makes conversation easier. It also made me feel like I had something to be proud of, rather than something to be ashamed of.

When I was around fourteen I started calling my CP 'Paul'. My friend made this name up out of 'Cerebral Pa[u]lsy'. So whenever I did something that was characteristic of my CP, such as drop something, trip over or walk funny, we would say, 'Oh hey, look, it's Paul!' This developed into an affectionate little character, which my parents and close schoolfriends now refer to as well. Nothing made me accept my disability more than giving it its own personality. It became a kind of confused sidekick rather than something that was out to get me or make my life harder.

I was always a pretty active kid and I really enjoyed horse riding and equestrian events from a very young age. I first learnt to ride when I was around seven and fell in love with it. I continued to take lessons and ride regularly until I was about twelve. At this point I had started at a new school and joined their athletics program as a way of keeping fit and having fun. I still had my leg brace and was proud to participate with everyone else despite it. Outside of sport I'm quite creative and love any excuse to write, read or paint. I think that's why I was so drawn to sprinting and athletics: it required my full attention and concentration in a similar way.

The best thing about my athletics career was that it seemed to happen almost accidentally. I started off just participating in my school squad until the coach, Nick Wall, asked if I wanted to try running competitively with other kids who had disabilities. Initially I was hesitant as I had hated competitive sport in primary school. I was never as coordinated or fast as the other kids. However, he managed to convince me, and I ran at a competition the following weekend. In that race I qualified for nationals in Sydney that year, which was so far from what I thought I could do that I was shocked into going. That was where it really started. A year or so later I qualified for my first world championships and everything happened from there. What kept me going was the empowerment of it. I had found a way to show what was possible outside and alongside my disability. The thing that I loved so much about what I was doing was that I could present ability alongside disability – and that is a whole other kind of cool.

I trained as part of an able-bodied squad, so my disability was never a focus, except for my coach when he wrote my training programs. As far as I was concerned I was just like everyone else. I often felt frustrated, as the fatigue and muscle spasticity that comes with CP can be limiting, as well as the energy it takes to concentrate on drills and exercises that require a little more coordination. Outside of that, though, it was fantastic. When I was running I always felt physically strong regardless of what happened once I had crossed the finish line. I loved the challenge and I loved proving people wrong. I think at the heart of it sport really gives you that opportunity. I'd be lying if I said I loved the 300-metre time trials and speed endurance sessions, but I did love what they amounted to in the end.

I had been running for about three years when I attended my first Paralympics, in Rio. The whole experience was incredible. It was the first time I had been on a team with other sportspeople, beyond athletics. One of my favourite aspects of Rio was the Paralympic Village. Athletes from all the countries' teams lived here for the few weeks of comp, and walking (or wheeling) between the buildings and to the dining hall was brilliant. It was like a small town filled only with other people with disabilities and the effect was pretty surreal. To this day I think it is the one place where I lost that sense of self-consciousness, because in this setting I was just like everyone else and we were all there together to show that to the rest of the world. This contributed to a pretty cool vibe once competition actually started. Competing itself was obviously fantastic in its significance, but I'd had some injuries and other issues in the lead-up to comp, which really put the pressure on. So being part of that community really reminded me why I was there and why I do what I do.

Being a Paralympic athlete is more expensive than being an able-bodied athlete. There are more physio appointments and doctor check-ups, as well as additional maintenance that needs to be done for me to keep up with the physical demands of training.

The Paralympics offers such a vast range of opportunities so I'd encourage people to get involved in any way you can. There are heaps of talent search days and occasions for people with disabilities to participate in sport. These events welcome anyone and everyone with any level of experience. You have absolutely nothing to lose and everything to gain.

My goals as a sportswoman seem to change each year! Right now I want to challenge myself and see what I am capable of. I would love to promote the Paralympic movement as one that is exceptional and vital. I do what I do because I love it and so other people can do it and love it too.

As cheesy as it sounds, my friends, teammates and training partners inspire me. Of course, so do the superstar athletes like Usain Bolt who are an example of human performance at its finest, but it is the people who I share the experience with that I find most inspiring. The way we all have to deal with different things in order to be the best we can be and watching how they overcome their own barriers and setbacks is not only inspiring but motivating. If I didn't have equally committed teammates and training partners, I know that most of the love and competitiveness of the chase (pun intended) would be lost.

Some of the most important friendships I've ever had were formed through sport. When I first made a team, at the age of fourteen, I was instantly adopted by the other athletes as one of their own. I was never treated like a child but always provided with the guidance I needed. Some of those athletes are still both friends and mentors to me now, and I have grown up with many of them. I always expected a team environment to feel like a school camp, but it feels much more like a family (cheesy, again, but true!). These are people I may only see four or five times a year, but in those few weeks away we are in our own little bubble and I miss that feeling as soon as I leave. After a time of high stress, like competition, you always return to a group of people who remind you that sport is so much more than medals and world records.

I am currently taking a break from training and competition until I finish Year 12 at the end of this year, but when I was training was when I learnt the most about myself. I'm currently studying for my Victorian Certificate of Education (VCE).

When I was still in full training last year, I adjusted my school timetable to allow for extra training sessions and more study time to get homework done. At the core of it, though, was communication between everyone I was working with, and my coach and my parents played an integral role in getting that balance right. My training was always very flexible in terms of sessions, as we often had to adapt what I did to how my body responded, which could be unpredictable in times of high training blocks and rest. Flexibility and intuition in each aspect of life were so important. Ironically, now that I'm not in full training, I often use exercise of any kind as a stress reliever. Once I graduate, I want to go back to training and keep on my sport journey. In terms of education, I would like to do a Bachelor of Arts, majoring in Psychology and English.

The advice I'd give to other young people with disabilities is to not let the fear of the unknown stop you. I think disability is such an interesting and ever-changing topic, and it's important to think about what you really want to do and then set about doing it. Of course there are barriers and things that may come up along the way, but if you have a cheer squad or support crew of even just one other person then take advantage of it and give yourself the opportunity to surprise yourself.

This Is My Song

Lucy Carpenter

Have you ever been in that awkward situation when you're thinking of a song but can't remember the name of it, no matter how hard you try? Think about the frustration of being able to hum the tune perfectly, with a few mismatched lyrics thrown into the mix, but not being able to think of what the song's called. I like to use this analogy to explain what my vision impairment is like. I'm able to see the colour of an object perfectly, like the tune, and I can sort of make out the size and shape of the object, like the lyrics, but I'm not able to identify what the object is, its name. Now, I know not everybody gets this metaphor, but in my opinion it's easier to grasp than some of my previous explanations, including the 'I don't know how to describe it, I just can't see' approach.

Throughout my eighteen years of life, I've regularly had to explain different aspects of my albinism. Whether the question is about my skin, hair, eye colour or vision, I can safely say that I've heard almost everything. 'How many fingers am I holding up?' has always been a favourite of mine, because when the embarrassment of genuinely not being able to answer the question hits, I embrace it and say something silly. My go-to answer is 'seven and a half', and although I may not be able to see the person, I'd like to count their presumably confused facial expression as a win. My ability to laugh at these sorts of comments has increased over time. Something that never fails to make me laugh is when I get asked ridiculous questions out of real curiosity. Being asked – sincerely – what planet I was born on remains one of the most hilarious ones so far. It's always a challenge to keep a straight face while I explain that, no, I do not bathe in bleach to make my skin and hair this white, or that no, I will not melt if I go in the sun.

I've always found it difficult to explain my condition. I will never be able to tell you what I can't see, because, well, I can't see it. I can't describe my vision loss because I never had vision in the first place. To me, my vision is perfect, I can see everything that I've been able to see since birth, I've never seen any better, and therefore I don't understand how people can see more than I can. I always try to make people realise that no matter how many times I explain what my vision is like, they will never actually know what I see. The only person who truly knows is me.

That said, quite often I've also been on the receiving end of explanations that don't make sense. For me to understand something that I can't see, the person needs to use specific descriptions that I can easily interpret. I can see colours perfectly and shapes fairly well, but I have no depth perception, am very light-sensitive and can't see fine details. So you can imagine that it isn't the best help when somebody says to look 'over there' or to go 'that way'.

People also don't seem to grasp that descriptions of faces mean nothing to me. If I'm close enough I can tell who people are, but if somebody described the way my mum looks and asked me to guess who they were describing, I would get it wrong. Friends and family members often try to describe people's looks, but no matter how well they do I will always think that every tall girl with long brown hair looks exactly the same.

This doesn't just apply to people. My method of recognising things by colours has failed me on a few occasions. For instance, I was leaving my weekly djembe drum lesson a few years ago. I carried my drum out to the car park and got in the car. After getting comfortable I looked over to the driver's side, only to find that it wasn't my mum who was sitting there. I'd simply seen a white car around the same size as Mum's and hopped in. The embarrassment started to kick in. I remember awkwardly saying hi before grabbing my drum and getting the hell out of there. Thinking back to this moment, I've realised that I don't have the best relationship with cars.

One beautiful summer night, my older brother and I were riding our bikes around our neighbourhood. During our intense game of real-life *Mario Kart*, which in hindsight probably wasn't the best idea, I was lucky enough to get a boost. I didn't think about how dangerous it was to speed ahead of my brother, who had been leading me the whole time, until I was lying on the ground, limbs tangled up in my purple Bratz bike. I'd hit a parked car. I don't know how, but I didn't see the large silver clump of metal until my face was literally pressed against it. Everything was kind of a blur as my brother rode back to our house to get Mum and Dad, who thought I'd been hit by a car. Then they were suddenly beside me, thoroughly inspecting my face to see how many teeth I had left. After discovering that the alarming amounts of blood pooled around my face and left knee were just the results of small cuts and not, thankfully, any missing teeth, I was driven home with a feel-better slushie from the servo in my grazed hands. Now, every time I go past that spot I look at the faint bloodstain that remains after seven years and am reminded why I'm walking past it instead of riding this time.

Although most things in life have been explained to me, it is quite easy to miss a few. I was fifteen when I found out that M&Ms have a little white 'm' on one side. I was even older when I found out that people could see through other people's car windows. This specific realisation put an abrupt stop to backseat jam sessions with my earphones on.

My top two blind moments have occurred very recently. At sixteen I once brushed my teeth with foot cream, thinking it was toothpaste, and about two weeks after my seventeenth birthday I discovered that brown dry shampoo exists. This particular discovery came about because I mistook the product for hairspray and ended up with a fairly large brown patch in my snow-white hair.

These stories are just a small part of a plethora of unique things that come with growing up with albinism. I'm going to be honest: they are not all good.

Other people perceive me as different, and my parents made sure I was aware of this from a young age. I'm extremely thankful for this because, truthfully, the world is a cruel place. Because I've been aware of the way others perceive my condition for almost my whole life, I've been able to build resilience and a thick skin when it comes to comments about my albinism. Some things still bother me, though. I don't particularly like the fact that if you looked at a picture of my class – or of me and my friends – you could most likely spot my white head of hair in an instant.

I don't really have a problem with looking different. But when you grow up in a coastal town in Australia, summer isn't the best time of the year for self-confidence. The beach is busy with locals, and the crowds are amplified by people escaping the city. One of my best friends is one-quarter Malaysian, and the juxtaposition of her bikini-clad, naturally tanned skin and my covered-from-head-to-toe milky white skin is almost comical. I love my albinism, but sometimes I find myself wishing for smooth caramel skin instead of my white-chocolate tone.

My favourite thing about my albinism is my hair. Compliments come daily. 'People pay hundreds of dollars to get their hair to be your colour, and it doesn't even work half of the time,' they say. I like to express my personality by dyeing it all different colours. Hues of pink, red, purple and blue have all covered my head at some point. Red probably wasn't the smartest idea – it stained my hair for a good six months before disappearing. I loved it, but I don't think my school did.

Growing up with albinism has taught me many things. I don't need others to accept my disability for me to accept myself. I've worked out how to deal with all the hardships that have come along with it. This has shaped my personality and attitude towards life. I have learnt to accept myself for who I am, and would not change anything.

I don't need to search for the name of the song anymore, because I'm writing my own song. One that is unique, possibly embarrassing, but nonetheless mine.

Catching Meaning

Natalia Wikana

You have an IQ of below 70.

If you don't know or you have questions, just ask!

Do the quiz again. Don't be lazy with your answers.

Each comment pounded into my six-year-old head, making me more conscious of how wrong my brain was. I sulked in embarrassment. I tried my best to hammer at the mental block lodged in my mind.

I used to think that struggling through school and interpreting things in a certain way was normal. Kids think differently. But as the years went by, the other kids grew smarter, capturing the meaning the teacher was searching for in a sentence; they absorbed things quickly. I would get there the next day or a month later. And I cursed my brain for humiliating me, not helping me with schoolwork and class or saving me from judgemental faces.

No matter how hard I stared at text on a paper in front of me, there was always a block. It was heavy and pulsed like a headache, stopping me from understanding. I would tsk at myself, willing the words to get in my head and make sense; I would've ripped them off the page if it would've helped.

Teachers would explain things, but I'd forget within a few minutes. Sometimes I did stay focused on what they were saying, but sometimes my mind wandered off unintentionally.

When my attention returned, I would whisper to my friends, 'What are we doing now?'

'Weren't you listening?' they'd grunt back.

They'd then reluctantly help me get back on track. Guilt biting at me, I'd promise not to ask for anything again. But that never stuck. Surprisingly, my friends did stick around.

What's wrong with me? Why am I like this? Why can't I listen and absorb words from my teachers? Whatever was wrong with me, I grew to hate it.

What did keep my attention were movies and other forms of pop culture. They were the only things I could absorb and 'get'.

I also marvelled at how objects were made and functioned. Intensely. I would stare at their edges and colours until they broke into pixels. I would study the lead of a pencil and its sparkling trails on paper – even the scratchy sound it made when dragged across paper was fascinating.

This obsession grew to include bringing out all my toys from their containers, especially my classic Polly Pockets and Starcastles, with their detailed features, to examine and fiddle with. A recurring story would stir in my head while I played with them. I would act out the story with the miniature houses, cafe, aquatic centre and castles. I imagined them having a vibrant life, but then desolation coming, so I would take the toys apart. Remove a hedgerow from a house, remove a flower and balcony from a castle. I then got a kick out of restoring them again.

When I was done with playing, I would return my toys to the containers in order of preference. From least favourite to most favourite. The orange Polly Pocket witch house with the pink roof first. The blue stone Starcastle with a huge flower on top that blew bubbles last.

Other people, including my family, thought it was weird that seven-year-old me could get so absorbed in an object, twirling it around. 'What are you doing?' they'd ask. This question persisted for years, until I grew to hide my tics by age fourteen.

I would blush in embarrassment. I didn't notice how weird the things I did were. I was just having fun with my toys. I soon found out that no one did what I did.

I'm weird, I should stop being weird and be like everyone else. The thought boomed in my mind every now and then. But I still couldn't help but do my own thing.

I tried to be better at school. I struggled and worked through trenches that closed in on me, pushing hard on my head and chest. Only to reach just below average grades, enough to get to the next year level. I didn't feel good.

Little did I know that a new demon would manifest when I was about eight. Anxiety.

Can you please enunciate? I can't hear you.

Speak up.

I had been talkative, with a quick tongue. Whatever had a hold on my brain waited for years to attack my vocals and gnaw on the cord linking brain to tongue and voice. As if it had conspired with anxiety. *How do we make our host suffer more?* they asked as they rubbed their little hands, grinning.

I needed help, but I didn't want everyone to know I was a 'dumb' Asian. Asians were either geniuses or 'stupid'; being the latter was inconceivable. What would my family think? What would white people think?

I ended up going to Special Ed, starting from around Year 5. Somehow word spread that I was 'new to Australia'. I didn't say anything. Being 'dumb' and 'weird' was enough humiliation. Everyone already had a false idea of me.

My friends corrected me whenever I mispronounced words, not gently but in a condescending way. They would do the same thing when I misunderstood words.

'Bicentennial?' I asked when my friend told me she was planning her tenth birthday party in Bicentennial Park. Then I blurted out, 'Oh, the place is made of metal?'

'No, bicentennial means you live forever,' another friend replied, almost shouting.

I felt myself shrinking. I had been making a reference to *Bicentennial Man*, a movie about a robot. I thought bicentennial had something to do with metal – it sounded like a type of metal – but I was wrong. My friend was wrong too, but she wasn't corrected. None of us knew the actual meaning at the time.

I let my friends correct me even if they were wrong. I just wanted to fit in.

As time went on, despite Special Ed, my journey to reach the meaning of words and their context was torturous. I still couldn't form my own interpretation to let my teachers know I understood, that I was a good, smart student.

'Are you writing that paragraph with your own words? You're not just copying?' My Year 6 teacher spoke to me as if I'd committed a crime, startling me from creating a duplicate of the textbook in my hands.

We were meant to paraphrase some pages from it.

'Yes,' I lied in a slightly hoarse voice, disused most of the time. My brain refused to translate the words in the book. I tried to unravel them, but time was running out and I wanted to get the task done by the end of the day, so I copied the pages. I was hoping my teacher wouldn't notice and I would try to work it out at home.

The teacher gave me a sceptical look, eyeing my notebook placed in the textbook, open for her to see. Her lips were thin and tight.

My cheeks reddened.

'Alright,' my teacher said in a strained voice. She didn't believe me.

She would later yell at me because I wouldn't talk during peer support sessions. Anxiety and whatever else infected my brain didn't care about my education or social skills.

I was forced into piano lessons so I wouldn't be 'lazy' anymore. All I wanted to do on the weekend was play with my toys like any normal kid. I wasn't interested in piano.

Those lessons were torture because:

1. my teacher was Asian.
2. most of the other students were Asian (that was a lot of pressure)
3. the lessons were performances. I had to play.

I got the hang of the notes and which key was which, but when it came time to play, reading the sheets and touching the keys at the same time was hard. My fingers froze up and my brain lost its grip on how piano worked. The notes shifted into a foreign language.

My teacher got frustrated one day. 'Did you even practise at home? Watch me. Pay attention. Are you paying attention? You're not focusing.'

Did you even practise? Pay attention. Are you paying attention?

My face and chest burnt with hurt and anger, and I couldn't hold it in any longer. I burst into tears and shouted, 'I did practise at home, I did pay attention!'

I focused on the teacher with all my energy and willpower, capturing the music and the way her fingers moved. But my stupid brain blocked me.

But I didn't tell her about that last part. Wasn't bursting into tears in front of another person humiliating enough?

'Sorry for being hard on you,' my teacher said afterwards. She changed tack and used the nurturing method. Gave me a tissue as a peace offering.

Eventually I felt better and poured all my concentration and effort into the piano. My teacher kept up her new method for future lessons and slowed down to my pace. I blinked away grateful tears, clenching my jaw to avoid a broken dam and more embarrassment.

There was an end-of-year performance where everyone showed off how smart and gifted they were. I didn't want to do it, but I had to. I demonstrated my skills by playing an extremely basic beginner piece. It was one of the only few pieces I could learn and remember. The performance took about a minute. At the end, I quickly got up, bowed and left, my eyes avoiding the audience.

I didn't reach the next level. But even though I didn't like piano, I felt a twinge of joy that I had made some progress with it.

Around ten or eleven years old, I was sent to a speech pathologist. They went through sentences, grammar and the basics of writing at a kindergarten level with me. Yes, I was ashamed and cried on the inside. I was so glum that my pathologist noticed. They told me I never smiled and I looked angry.

You should smile more.

I didn't.

Eventually, though, I improved, and I did smile because my brain finally worked! My pathologist was happy. Our business was done and we shook hands in farewell. I was ready for the big school, despite my still almost below-average grades.

Little did I know high school would be a nightmare. My weird and stupid brain never went away. Under its influence and also anxiety's, my tongue slowly turned inflexible and my voice diminished. Teachers spoke a different language; subjects like Maths and Science were especially hard to decode. Why did we need to learn about Pythagoras' theorem?

The school arranged special sessions for me, held in between my classes and after school. My tutor was my speech pathologist.

That was when I found out what had infected my brain. Intellectual disability. It was written on my file, but no types or categories were mentioned.

I didn't know what to do with this information besides thinking 'Intellectual disability sounds like a polite, smart word for dumb.' I felt resigned, embarrassed. There wasn't much hope to fix it since my progress remained slow.

I still found myself in the trenches, trying to hammer through that mental block.

Blank pages for exam essays had me reeling. At least I managed to translate my thoughts and ideas onto paper. But my answers were so short compared to the other students' – I noticed the never-ending scratches of pencils and pens around me in the classroom when I was done. I peeked at one of my neighbours and they were writing two full pages in answer to a question! How? I'd only written half a page and my writing wasn't small.

In the end, I faced comments such as *Please explain* or *Elaborate* and the words from hell: *Please see me after class.*

My anxiety grew. Words and thoughts became harder to spit out. I became quieter. My friends drifted away from me. I found it difficult to make new ones. I struggled to stay focused on schoolwork. Stressed out, my mind wandered to imaginary worlds and my dreams of being the same as everyone else. Anger at both myself and everyone else intensified.

No matter how much the teachers tried to help me and get me to open up – one even tempted me with lollies as a reward – I was failing. My anxiety overpowered my senses and thoughts. My tongue froze. My voice shrank from a whisper to a croak. My social skills became stunted. And my articulating thought process rewired into a lesser version of what it used to be.

I got to the point that I couldn't take it anymore, so I dropped out of school at sixteen. Not without criticism from my teachers. 'You're not going to get anywhere if you leave,' one said.

If I didn't leave, then I would suffer and fail even more.

I continued to struggle through the HSC at TAFE, but something changed in me in that environment. My brain opened up and absorbed a lot of information. I wrote more words. I understood and absorbed, understood and absorbed.

I even wrote a novel for the first time, at nineteen, after reading a young adult book. It inspired so many possibilities for my imaginative and wandering mind. This book also sparked a love of reading, and not just for studying. I started devouring every book that caught my attention.

My brain still glitched when I read and wrote stories, but it didn't stop me from finishing.

Though my sister found my novel to be too similar to the book that started all this, I worked on it to make it my own. I did some research on things I wasn't sure of, like object names, and on words that I thought I knew the meaning of but was still uncertain about. I looked to other authors and their works, and tried to mimic their style.

I sent samples of the book to agents and publishers. I got back rejection letters and emails. I was hurt, and immediately blamed my stupid brain. I fought against it by revising the work, listening to expert industry advice, and reading all the do's and don'ts about writing novels and query letters.

I failed. Again and again and again. Each failure grew more hate towards my disability and, to be honest, people. I started to become jaded and disillusioned. I wanted to give up. There was no place for writers like me.

Yet I kept going. I couldn't stop writing.

Ten years later, I would have the strength and confidence to write more novels of over 50,000 words – with one exceeding 90,000 words. Younger me would've been shocked.

Uni came and gave me the best years of my education life. I'd never thought I would make it. Let alone complete an English degree. To my surprise, again, I understood and absorbed. I grew out of my shell. I participated in class. There was zero sense of being in a prison, trapped in one particular way of thinking and doing things.

I still struggled with essays in exams, but my grades were higher than the ones I had in high school. I achieved Distinctions on my 2000- to 3000-word essays. I noticed that the ones relating to my favourite subjects had the highest scores.

Maybe the 'cure' for my weird brain was being in a certain environment and studying subjects I had passion for.

Maybe there was no 'cure' for my intellectual disability. Only things that would work for me.

At twenty-eight, I still jumble things up when I read or write, so I have to read and revise carefully. Reread until I'm 100 per cent certain I understand it. I also have friends who help me shape my stories, much to my surprise. I haven't driven them away with my weirdness.

I still stutter when I speak. My voice drifts and cracks, and words sometimes scrape my throat. My verbal communication skills are a roller-coaster ride. Most of the time, my thought process doesn't work like that of 'normal' people, especially when it comes to hard conversations or interviews. It has been a battle and complicated my path to success. I have to write what I need to say. But I can't bring notes to an interview or into a social space. I guess I have to practise more.

Sometimes I still think:

Oh my god, why am I like this?

Why can't I do things like a normal person?

Think and talk and solve problems faster and clearer like a normal person.

But I remind myself that if other disabled people can achieve milestones without changing themselves, then so can I.

Social media has helped me accept myself, and learn from other disabled people about ableism and all the things I wish I'd known about as a kid.

I'm still learning how to block ableist thoughts and words, and navigate a world full of them. A world that values able-bodied and 'smart' people.

I remind myself of my achievements to keep going.

You have an IQ of below 70. I don't know what my IQ is now because it's a lie, rooted in racism.

If you don't know or if you have questions, just ask! I ask questions by writing, mostly. I'm still battling anxiety, but I do ask, either verbally or by writing, when I don't know something.

Do the quiz again. Don't be lazy with your answers. I had years of exams, assignments and tests on job applications. I got them done.

Are you writing that paragraph with your own words? You're not just copying? I've written four novels. Two of them are in revision. I've written about five short stories for contests and programs. I have a blog and update it regularly. I write content for a pop culture publication. The only copying I've been doing lately is translating my words into Mandarin. I'm learning bit by bit.

Did you even practise at home? Are you paying attention? I wouldn't have got one partial and two full manuscript requests from literary agents if I hadn't practised or paid attention.

I'm still learning to love myself and the way my brain works, but I love myself more than I did when I was a kid.

The Bedridden Astronaut

Melanie Rees

It was an innocent question, but when the nurse asked what I wanted to be when I grew up the conversation left an aftertaste worse than my medication.

'She's training as an elite gymnast, but after that she wanted to be an astronaut and go to the Moon.' Mum's voice was like soda; it sounded bubbly until those bubbles reached the surface and popped.

Wanted?

'I guess she could still work in the scientific field,' Mum continued. 'Something at a desk.'

Desk?

'Sounds exciting.' The nurse rolled up the sleeves of my oversized hospital gown and connected a bag of saline to the needle in my elbow crease. 'We will just give her some fluid to help her kidneys.' She talked to Mum about disability financial support, as if I were the Invisible Man's child.

Disability? I naively associated that with amputees or paraplegics. Sure, they had just discovered the kidney disease I was born with, and I was tired and vomiting regularly, but I'd just been selected for a junior training squad at the Australian Institute of Sport. I was physically fit and capable.

That night, as I attempted and failed to sleep, I stared at the IV line – like a safety tether connecting my spacesuit to the shuttle during my spacewalk – and gazed at the cardboard cut-out stars dangling from the ceiling along with Disney characters. The stars could have been real. The IV pole and infusion pump could have been part of a spaceship; the glowing green numbers on the pole could have been data on the ship's dashboard.

The cystic fibrosis patient in the adjacent bed, coughing up blood into the nurse's bedpan, wasn't another person waiting for their organs to fail. She was my fellow astronaut.

Your suit's running low on oxygen.

The display panel showed three hours and forty-five minutes until re-entry.

Go! I'll fix the heat shield. I'll save you. Go back to the ship!

Eventually she did go.

I wondered whether the nurse asked her what she wanted to be when she grew up, and whether the nurse knew that she wouldn't get that chance.

After numerous hospital stays, endless appointments, and surgery, I began to realise why Mum had said the stars were out of reach. Maybe the only way to travel to the stars was via heaven, like other patients I'd met.

I knew astronauts were checked for even the slightest hint of an infection before taking flight. I guessed that my potential for organ failure and need for in-flight dialysis meant I wouldn't be considered. Even after a transplant, the medical complications, risk of infection and rejection would be an issue. I was like the Invalid from *Gattaca*, who was never given a chance.

What I didn't yet realise was that an elite gymnastics career was now also a ridiculous dream. Cramps, fatigue and nausea became the new norm. During high school, the doctors convinced my parents that my body couldn't cope anymore. Although I didn't speak to them for a week, I was almost relieved they made me quit the arduous thirty-hours-a-week training schedule. It gave me the chance to sleep.

Sleep. That was all I seemed to do during my school and university years, leading up to complete organ failure and kidney dialysis.

On peritoneal dialysis, restful sleep became a forgotten pleasure. Like a scene from *Aliens*, a catheter emerged from my stomach, connecting me to my dialysis machine, filling and draining my stomach with fluid to remove toxins. Every. Single. Night. It was hard to imagine the tube from my stomach was an astronaut's safety tether now. Cramps pierced my calves and shins, and as I attempted to walk the pain off, I tried to believe I was flying back to my ship.

But my tubing only let me walk a couple of metres, and that floor space was cluttered with the bucket containing my last night's dinner and the plastic bag with the yellow waste in it.

I was trapped by my tubing, unable to sleep or escape. The display panel on the dialysis machine mocked me with its bright green words suggesting I have a 'good night'. Toxins accumulating in my blood made sleep even more elusive: my skin itched so much I made it bleed, and restless leg syndrome caused spasms throughout my body.

Each morning, the yellow complexion of Frankenstein's monster glistened in the mirror and bloodshot anaemic eyes greeted me, as I spat out mouthwash to remove the taste of bile and urea.

During daylight hours, when I wasn't in the emergency department for high potassium levels or the fluid building up on my chest, I wrote in my diary, which had been my confidant since high school.

Dear Diary,

Nightly dialysis sucked. Again. I didn't travel to the Moon or go for a spacewalk; instead I spent the whole night reading between the spasms and cramps.

Morning also sucked. Took tablets. Injected EPO. Tried going for a walk until my swollen ankles hurt too much to stand. Looked through the classifieds for a job suited to my degree and flexible enough for my dialysis schedule.

Afternoon was okay. I'd passed out from fatigue at the kitchen table until the alarm awoke me for my midday dialysis exchange.

Drained. Depressed. Desperate for sleep.

Signing off until tomorrow, when we will do it all again. Or leave to heaven and the stars. Dear Diary, tell me which is really the worst option?

Months and years blurred by. During another sleepless night dialysing, I was reading *The Hitchhiker's Guide to the Galaxy* for the umpteenth time, trying to find out that elusive meaning behind forty-two. I must have fallen asleep, because I awoke with a stomach cramp like nothing I'd ever felt before. I placed the waste bag over my book to check the fluid for infection and, through the usually clear yellow liquid, I couldn't see a single word. The cloudy solution concealed everything. I should've been scared of the potentially life-threatening infection, and yet a tranquillity settled over me. Like galactic hitchhiker Arthur Dent, I suddenly understood everything as my Babel fish translated the invisible prose: *Why waste time on pointless ramblings in your diary and pining for something you know to be impossible? Why write about disadvantages and what makes you unhappy? Write about what you want, what you imagine, what you dream behind that cloudiness.*

When I was too swollen to walk, I could still write. When I was tethered to drips or emergency haemodialysis machines, I could still write. And even on the darkest, most painful days, when my bones ached too much to type, I could still create new worlds.

Maybe in an alternate reality, like *Stargate* or *Sliders*, I would be looking out a portal at the approaching Moon.

But why should I mourn the loss of a single trip so close to home, when I could visit a thousand worlds and moons?

That's why I'm happy and thriving in my reality, resting on a lumpy hospital bed tethered to tubing, after a failed transplant and more years on dialysis. I'm not staring at the flickering fluorescent light above or dwelling on biopsy pain and boredom. I'm holding a pen in my spare hand and gazing at distant stars, wondering which will be next.

Falling

K.Z. Barton

As I walked up the stairs from the school canteen, the heaviness of my legs was all-consuming. It felt like I was trying to lift my knees through liquid cement. All around me, students and teachers bounded up the insurmountable climb, while I kept stopping to cling to the handrail. I was about two-thirds of the way up when I heard laughter. Friends – not my closest friends, but close enough – were discussing my progress from down below. My cheeks burnt and I willed the molecules of my body to separate. Separate so that I could simply dissipate into the air around me. At least then I could experience lightness. Just when I thought my mortification was complete, an unfamiliar teacher came up behind me, clapping her hands and saying 'chop chop'.

When I try to explain what it was like to grow up with invisible, undiagnosed chronic illness, this is the moment that always comes to mind. My condition was both seen and unseen. I existed in a peculiar space between well and unwell. It meant looking normal enough for a teacher to attempt to hurry me along, while always falling in some manner or another. Falling on the last step, with laughter ringing in my ears. Falling out of sync with the lives and expectations of my friends. Falling behind in school until I was forced to drop out. Falling into the dark crevices of my mind that told me I was just crap at being alive, that I was somehow deficient and so incompetent at being a human that I had conjured up all these pains and problems. Falling into doctor's chair after doctor's chair with another strange injury or malady. Falling into packets of antidepressants because the same doctors told me those drugs would solve most of my problems. The weight of my invisible, undiagnosed conditions meant I could never stop, or even understand, the falling.

Even now, as I approach my thirtieth birthday, and I write in my office to the background noise of my husband trimming his beard in the bathroom and the hum of the baby monitor next to me, I don't know that the falling has stopped. But it has slowed down, and I can now name it. It has a first, last and middle name – Ehlers-Danlos syndrome, endometriosis and adenomyosis – and it is very pleased to make your acquaintance. The falling is no longer an uncontrollable plummet after being unceremoniously dropped from a great height with an anvil attached to my leg; rather, it is more of a different way to travel. Inconvenient at times, limiting more often than I'd like to admit, and something that I'm always aware of, but I own many brightly coloured parachutes. And I'm getting better at steering. It is less falling away from the life I want to have, and more manoeuvring towards the life I can achieve.

Each of my brightly coloured parachutes serves its own purpose in slowing my descent. My purple parachute unfurled the night I went to the Van Gogh exhibition, when I couldn't handle the severity of my abdominal cramping and didn't think I could walk for any length of time, let alone make it through the whole exhibition. This parachute took the form of a hired wheelchair for the evening.

My blue parachute is well worn and I always carry it with me. This parachute is for the moments when I decide not to do a seemingly normal task, like cutting a sweet potato or pushing a pram up a steep hill, because I know it will cause my joints too much pain and possibly end in an injury. This parachute also opens when I tell friends that I have to stop chatting with them on Messenger because typing on my mobile for any length of time hurts my fingers too much.

My pink parachute is my awareness of my energy stores. It's knowing when to say that a trip is too far because my fatigue might make it impossible to get there and back.

My green parachute is acceptance that I'll never be able to do as much as the other mums I meet at playgroup.

Using my parachutes means allowing my conditions to be seen; they also mean thriving, and at times floating, instead of falling.

I no longer consider my conditions a burden. They are an aspect of my identity, an integral part of how I engage with the world around me. I still sometimes hate them and wish things could be different, but this is not the norm. It took a long time for that girl on the stairs, the one who thought herself not good enough, to find her way here. She had to battle her self-doubt and she had to self-advocate. It took me years to realise that I was worth more: more than letting the pain and fatigue in my body isolate me; more than believing my pain was just a reflection of a broken mind; more than trying, and failing, to live in the same way as my friends.

I wish I could pinpoint what caused this shift in self-belief. It was so gradual that I don't really know when it started. I just know that after being bedridden for months, some part of me realised that I had to fight or this was how I would stay, stuck in a bed and entirely dependent on my mother.

In the process of getting diagnosed and learning how to manage my chronic illness, I lost faith in many members of the medical profession. My lived experience, my pain and my knowledge of my body were dismissed at every turn. Specialists blurred together and became an amorphous darkness almost as scary and uncertain as the chronic illness itself. For a decade I searched, asked for new referrals and yelled over the constant background hum that says women's pain is insignificant, a product of hysteria. Eventually I didn't have to yell anymore. The blurry blackness lightened to the crisply ironed shirts of doctors, both male and female, who listened to me speak and told me that my symptoms could be explained and treated. They had magic pieces of paper in the form of referrals for the right tests. They let me be valid. I began to sew my first parachute.

The girl on the stairs still exists in my moments of self-doubt, the moments when I feel like a fraud even though I know my symptoms are real. But I think I've done her justice. Because I fought so hard to be seen, to receive the treatment and support I needed, I have a son. He is the love of my life, but he might not be here if I'd allowed myself to be dismissed. If I'd listened to those doctors who told me that my pain was in my head and that I really should leave the emergency room, I never would have had the surgery I needed at eighteen weeks pregnant.

I was already pregnant – I just didn't know it yet – when I was diagnosed with Ehlers-Danlos syndrome. The diagnosis meant that my obstetrician knew what complications to look for. He was able to save the pregnancy when my cervix was failing to hold everything where it was meant to be. He told me afterwards that if they hadn't been specifically anticipating that problem, they never would have known there was an issue …

I don't like to finish that thought, because I can hold in my arms the most definitive evidence that the struggle, all of the learning how to slow my descent, was worth it.

I am an adult, and a mother, and I am able to thrive while living with chronic illness, but I still don't feel grown up. I'm not sure I ever will. I have a family, I have my parachutes, yet I still constantly have to learn and adapt. My condition is degenerative, so there will be times when I forget how to thrive, or I'll throw out one of my precious parachutes because it's no longer working. I'm sure I'll have to start sewing new ones again. While there are many challenges I'm yet to face, I like to think that I'm no longer fighting but living the epilogue of the fight I waged for so many years. Existing in the epilogue is a beautiful thing, but it is not without fear, and the knowledge that I can never allow myself to become complacent. The constant parachuting takes a lot of work, energy and focus.

Perhaps I'll take up hang-gliding instead.

Umbrellas in the Rain

Emma Di Bernardo

I'd never read a whole anthology of stories about other people's disability and illness without drinking a strong cup of tea first.

Maybe for you it's a large glass of wine, or a stiff beer.

It's not because these collections are too sad, and it's certainly not because they're too boring. It's because some tiny part of my chest tightens, my breathing pauses, and mentally I need to hold up a small umbrella. A nice little umbrella of emotional resistance that lets me sit through the rain of relatable stories about perennial grief, about finding beauty in ugliness, about never taking the little things for granted. So that not a drop of emotion touches me.

My advice to young people who are growing up disabled is to get ready for resilience.

I grew up, for the most part, as an able-bodied person. Somewhere around the age of fifteen, I started experiencing severe period pain. More than a decade later, I'm a woman in her late twenties with a condition and a list of unexplained symptoms longer than the scrolling text at the start of a Star Wars movie. Officially, it's chronic nerve pain in the pelvis, vulvodynia, vaginismus and mast cell activation disorder. Truthfully, it's been years of wasted youth stuck in doctors' offices, being told that something's wrong with my nerves but nothing concrete, even after enduring every available procedure with the suffix -oscopy. Treatment and management are a stab in the dark, with more plot holes than the aforementioned Star Wars movie.

As a maladjusted youth I had to forgo the rites of passage – parties, partners and periods – that take up your teens and early twenties, so I am used to the word 'resilience'. Acquaintances marvel at my resilience. Resilience is equated with bravery, as in 'you are *saaaahhhhhh brave*' for struggling against the odds. People think you are born emotionally tough, with some inherent or genetic ability to go the distance. I want young people like me to know that resilience is different for the able-bodied, and the reality – the truth of staying strong when faced with barriers – is that it doesn't occur as naturally as one might think.

Inevitably, you will need to hold two kinds of umbrellas: one against a torrent of people, and the other against the pelting rain of yourself. It's not the storm that will overwhelm you in the end: it's the rain – gradual, drop by drop – that can threaten to take you under.

The people umbrella is neon-pink with fantastic sparkles. It's so bright and cheery it's almost ironic. You need it to face all the well-meaning people who say you can cure endometriosis with yoga, or the nosy colleague who serves you a backhanded compliment about how well you seem. It shields you from the people wanting to tell you about their own experiences (or those of someone they know tangentially, or have just heard of) because they don't know how to react in a positive, understanding way to the news that you have a disability. This is not their fault. It's how humans connect. But it's a kick in the teeth to the girl who's just found out she needs to freeze her eggs at age twenty-two. Hearing how someone else struggled or triumphed is rarely constructive. So as you open your glittery umbrella of resilience in these moments, here are some tools to help you endure: quickly direct the conversation elsewhere; an easy smile can end the interaction.

During the first year of my chronic-pain journey, I was so desperate for answers that others' tips and stories filled me with hope. But over time, as the deluge continued and none of these ideas worked for me, I had to get out my umbrella. I'm not suggesting rudeness when you face unsolicited medical advice or well-meaning compliments. Instead, be aware that this is a storm that never ends and equip yourself with the proper glittery protection.

The second umbrella is needed when saving yourself from … well, yourself. This might be pessimistic, but I think it's realistic to be prepared for the possibility that your health will go south, or you'll have a flare. Depression and anxiety go hand in hand with the grief of living with ongoing health crises. I have been emotionally crushed during medical appointments, in a state of shock for two days, or crying immediately at the familiar injustice reigning within my body. And because of those moments, I have learnt that we all need to hold a little black umbrella. Maybe this one is tough, like leather, or comforting, like soft velvet. Whatever style your umbrella takes – hold it strong against yourself.

When I was nineteen, my body was betraying me in the worst way: I had pain in my vulva and vagina, even though I hadn't ever had penetrative sex. That betrayal was nothing compared to the utter devastation and shame I felt as a doctor made an offhand comment that I shouldn't have had this transvaginal ultrasound if I was a virgin. Looking back, perhaps he simply meant *he would have been gentler in administering it if he'd known this in advance.* I had fully consented, and yet my world tipped upside down with this one stray remark. Was I a bad girl? Had I destroyed something pure inside me? The answer was no, but I didn't believe that, not for a long time.

Awful experiences, in which you and all you stand for are laid bare, prepare you for this resilience against yourself. I know now that I may emotionally break down during appointments, so I have better strategies in place, such as calling a support person and going to counselling. I am not to blame for those bad experiences. But I raise my little black umbrella to make sure that metaphorical hail doesn't hit me smack-bang in the face.

Your little black umbrella might indeed be a stiff drink some days. It might be a call to a crisis hotline. It might even be talking to a friend or getting a hug from someone you love. Your little black umbrella is there when your health turns ill, or your mind, or both.

Resilience is not a virtue you're born with. Unlike disability, it's not congenital. Unlike mental illness, it's not genetic. It's not diagnosable and it's not prescribed. It's sure as hell not on the PBS. It's something you learn in the face of adversity. Growing up disabled means you experience adversity – whether physical, mental or social.

But you and I can make a pretty cute pair, standing strong with our umbrellas in the rain.

Dressing to Survive

Jessica Newman-Marshall

I am woman. I know how to dress for each of life's occasions, fluent in acquiescing to her demands of poise and propriety. Each sliver of my life hangs from a black velvet clothes-hanger in a sedate oaken wardrobe – spaced precisely one inch apart, my life *before* illness split sharply from my life *after*.

*

From the darkness of my mother's womb, I am born raging in my nakedness, *vernix caseosa* scrubbed from my wriggly newborn flesh and cast across the fiery lands of Kariyarra country.

Family albums record the arrival of Little Venus, bare-bummed in the ports of the Pilbara. I'm unaware of the rules of fabric and flesh, as rich, pindan earth squishes between my piggy toes. My summers are spent nude and careless – the very best way to spend them. Until a puffy display of budding nipples brings an end to my summers of naked sprinkler-hopping and in their place a suitcase of rules: Blue and green must never be seen (unless there's a colour in between). A woman's belt and shoes must always match. If legs are daring, breasts must be concealed. Women must never show both at once, nor neither at all; the line between fusty and fucking-asking-for-it is a capricious one.

Despite all this, I am going to be somebody – I am *going places*.

But life has other plans.

Thirteen

What makes a high-school uniform Catholic? Dad argues it's the cost. I think it might have something to do with the great big yellow crucifix embroidered on the left breast of my woollen school jumper.

On the first day of high school, Mum excitedly lines my brothers and I up along the eucalyptus-framed verandah to document the occasion, camera in hand. Dad wryly remarks that it's like herding cats.

My comically long Mary Janes jut from beneath a woolen skirt suspended two inches above my ankles. 'You'll grow into it,' Mum says to nobody in particular. I stand with my brothers, a spidery slip of a girl abuzz with awkward adolescent energy, smiling for the camera – what may have been, frozen in time.

I don't remember the last day that I ran, or jumped. The last tree I climbed, or the last time I felt hot bitumen beneath my feet as I played street cricket with my family.

I do remember my screams the morning I could not walk, and how they hollowed me out inside.

How did I not see this coming? It all makes sense now. The whispers my parents overheard at my tap-dancing recitals: 'Don't her parents *feed her*?' My joints continually collapsing onto themselves as I played with my friends in the front yard. My parents laughing when the ER triage asked if we wanted to use our Flybuy points. My limbs: too long. My palate: too high. My joints: seemingly made of rubber. My spindly fingers could stretch across one and a half octaves by my thirteenth birthday. And yet, I was like my Dad. I was like my siblings. We teased Mum for being the odd one out. 'You're so short,' we giggled.

Would I have done anything differently if I'd known this was coming? Was ignorance bliss? I can't say for sure, but I torture myself with these questions. Nonetheless, I am grateful that I had one last perfectly normal supper before my universe was turned upside down. I went to sleep a child, ignorant of the pain ahead – what a gift that was.

My runners – the ones Dad worked overtime for, justifying the cost because they would 'last really well' – are the first to go. Shoes are no good when your legs don't work.

I take to wearing fluffy bed-socks to insulate the cyanotic blue of my newly resigned feet, much to the delight of our family's golden retriever, who is allegedly responsible for ninety-one odd pairs of socks. My school dress waits patiently in my bedroom, next to copies of *Girlfriend* and posters of Delta Goodrem.

Girlfriend becomes *Dolly*, and Delta turns into Adam Brody. Two full moons cycle past without me leaving a footprint.

'Dad, I'm in pain,' I whimper.

He takes a sharp breath. 'Darling girl,' he pauses, before continuing carefully, 'you're always in pain.'

The world has a short memory. It takes only eight weeks to shift from *Jess can be anyone she wants to be* to *Jess who?*

I have no idea how to dress for the part of 'fifteen-year-old kid in a wheelchair'. I have no idea how to dress anymore at all. Each morning is the same: my spindly fingers, which once danced across piano keys, curl raw-boned in a fist, too weak to zip closed the wool skirt that hangs from my hollowed-out pelvic girdle. My hips grip in protest at the pressure from the band of my underwear, and I allow a single, harrowed cry to escape.

Dad paces up and down the hallway, banging his coffee cup on the kitchen bench.

'Jess, you have to go to school. Even if you just go for one hour: once you get there, you'll be fine.'

'You. Don't. Under–stand,' I heave between screams, as ligaments in my hips twist in protest, unforgiving. Ever the peacemaker, Mum hands me a glass of water so that I can gulp down my morning round, powdered life-rings. 'Once you get there, maybe you'll feel a little better,' Mum offers gently.

'I don't know what we're going to do, darl!' Dad shouts.

Dad always has the answers. I don't know what it means when he doesn't. I feel the earth fall from beneath my rotting limbs. If Dad is falling, I'm falling: we're tied together in a parachute without a ripcord: where will we land?

'She can't keep not going to school!' he yells again.

Mum wipes the tears and spittle from my face. But no scrubbing can erase the tattoo I now wear – The Girl Who Didn't.

I think of the summer classes just months earlier, when I would lounge on the hot grass with my friends as we baked our lithe legs in the afternoon sun, lazily eating sandwiches. The daily ritual of having 'anorexic slut' yelled at me across the yard. My friends and I, smelling of Sportsgirl fake tan, watching wasps lured into soda-bottle traps. I think of those wasps now, sticky and seeing their world from within a plastic bubble. I silently promise myself that I'll never trap a wasp again.

I wish I knew how to tell Dad that I want to be at school more than he doesn't want a mortgage, but I know he won't believe me. I wouldn't believe that from a fifteen-year-old girl either.

Fifteen

I have pubic hair.

I catch sight of myself as Mum transfers me from wheelchair to toilet. After she closes the door to give me the illusion of privacy, I take a closer look. In spite of myself, I reach down to feel the soft, downy wisps of hair. The brown hairs that I rub between my fingertips are in stark contrast to the natural blonde atop my head. Another deception from my flesh – I am an imposter. Should I dye it? Or shave it? I don't even know *how* to shave it.

My fingers snap back with an instant shame when I'm interrupted by a loud knock at the bathroom door, and I hurriedly promise: 'I'm almost done!'

Each day, the routine is the same. Mum removes my clothes with the tenderness of a mother with her newborn, careful to avoid provoking my screams as she persuades my limbs, emaciated shadows of their former lives, to conform. When I haemorrhage puddles of crimson, she wordlessly mops the floor and tucks me between clean sheets. My straggly blonde hair is always washed, brushed or plaited. As a hairdresser, Mum knows that clean hair makes everything better.

Weekly, I am cushioned by an assortment of pillows and rugs in the car, a hopeless attempt at comfort. We drive two hours to the Royal Children's Hospital, one way. My doctors are kind, and they are male. They hand me a standard-issue white backless gown.

'Wear the gown with the back open at the front, and leave it untied,' the doctor reminds me, turning to his computer while Mum changes me. 'You can keep your underpants on,' he reassures me.

It takes precisely five minutes to transform me from a regular fifteen-year-old girl who just grew pubic hair and loves the Essendon Football Club to '15 y.o female p.t presenting with Marfan syndrome–type morphology and ectomorphic composition, current BMI of 12.9 at 5 feet 10 inches tall. Generalised ligament laxity correlates with reports of severe, chronic musculoskeletal pain. Arachnodactyly, high arch palate and scoliosis are present. Positive for Walker and Steinberg signs. Significant joint hypermobility. Mitral valve prolapse and regurgitation present. Aorta currently stable.'

I am moved onto the examination bed. My doctor keeps his eyes downcast and hands me a towel in a pretence at modesty. He asks me to lie on my side, facing away from him, chest exposed. He lubricates the echocardiography ultrasound transducer. 'Sorry, it's going to be a little bit cold,' he says.

In the darkened room, lit only by the computer screen, the cold new sensation of the transducer approaches my nipples. My small buds stiffen. I am pert, and I am a paediatric patient. I don't know how to make sense of this contradiction. I listen to the shame ringing in my ears, perfectly in time with the *whoosh whoosh whoosh* of the transducer – a Marfan metronome. I wonder if he will laugh with his colleagues about the girl with no breasts.

When he is finished, he hands me a white towel. 'You can use this to clean yourself up.' He pauses. 'You did really well,' he reassures me.

And he exits the screen-lit room, leaving me to wipe the sticky muck from my xylophonic chest.

As I wheel to leave, I feel the eyes of every person waiting in reception seeing through my blouse to the viscous shame across my chest.

I feel like I've done something wrong. I just don't know what it is or why.

Once I'm cleared to return to school, my House Leader pushes me to my first class in an 'act' of solidarity. Wheeling past the portable classrooms, I am acutely aware that my head is rapidly floating past the windows at a comedic height. The sound of 200 chairs scraping, so those seated in them can stand and stare at me in silence, rings in my ears. My cheeks blanch, incandescent with shame.

Later in the day, as I wheel past the toilets, a popular girl from my year level calls out to me across the yard. We've never spoken before. She looks around, ensuring her audience is engaged.

'Hey, Jess! Can you walk *at all*?!'

My tongue stumbles. I don't yet have the language of disability: part-time wheelchair users; ambulatory wheelchair users; relapsing-remitting impairments; wheelchair users who don't have spinal cord injuries. I don't yet know how to say, 'Fuck off.' Instead, I fumble, looking down at my feet resting on the pedestals of my wheelchair.

'Um. Not really. Um.' The heat rises in my cheeks. This feels like a public undressing.

'So how do you go to the toilet then?!' she shrieks. The flock of raucous laughter ripples through my bones.

I wonder if she can somehow see the new tuft of hair that rests beneath my clothing. How easily she strips me naked.

We may wear the same uniform, but she will never wear my genome. Somehow, hidden as it may be, deep within each and every cell of my body, she can see the truth – I do not belong.

Seventeen

After three years of Dad working overtime to put my brothers and I through private high schools, my Catholic-school blazer is exchanged for a public-school knit jumper.

I tell people that I changed schools because my old school was unsupportive. In reality, it began with a toilet, and ended up with a bag of golf clubs.

'No, we don't have any wheelchair toilets,' the vice-principal tells my parents, smiling sympathetically, his eyes averted from the wheels beneath me which seem to have their own gravitational pull – sucking into them all common adult sense and decency. 'But if Jess needs to use the toilet, one of you can leave work, pick her up and take her to a wheelchair toilet at McDonald's, and bring her back.' They smile broadly. There's that term again. *Wheelchair toilet.* Is that a wheelchair-meets-commode? Is it a toilet you can race, bobsled style? Whatever it is, I'm not sure I want it.

Later, I wait in the school office for Mum to collect me from school, so that I can use the magical wheelchair toilet at McDonald's, between Maths and before English. Sitting idly, I spy a door plastered with a giant 'Accessible Bathroom' sign. Tentatively, I push the door open. Sporting equipment spews out noisily: a cacophony of ableist discomfort. Cricket bats, tennis racquets, basketballs, nets and countless sets of golf clubs.

I stare in disbelief. There is no space for me to use the *accessible* toilet. There is no space for me at all – this is space for golf clubs.

Prior to beginning at my new school, I spend months in Melbourne's Royal Children's Hospital. I learn to walk again, dress myself, feed myself. I do everything asked of me, and more. To fail to do so would mean I am non-compliant. I don't yet know the words 'medical model of disability'. But I know how suffocating the corset of its control can feel.

Deviance is advancing or rejecting that which violates social norms as dictated by medical social control. I am the Good Girl. A Goody Two Shoes. I do not break the rules. I do not deviate.

With morning light across my spine, I dress myself in a woollen skirt, one inch above the same knees that make me cry in the night-time. My arachnodactyly fingers button up my white cotton shirt, heat-pack burns hidden for the day. My black knit school jumper warms my body as I prepare to attend another lunch for one. I smooth Maybelline Dream Mousse bronzer across my cheekbones, as Adriana Lima nods approvingly from the cover of *Dolly*. She knows how to wear bronzer – and she never eats her lunch alone.

Sometimes my friends permit me to eat with them. They are kind like that, you see – so long as I follow the rules. I must not tell stories that are too funny, too long, too serious or too short. I cannot speak about my brothers and I *definitely* cannot speak about *their* brothers. Most importantly, I am not allowed to talk about my 'conditions'. Besides, *they know* I am making it all up for attention. That's what deviants do. They've told me so.

Instead, my role is to listen. I listen to stories about the parties they have thrown, and the fun that is had in the throwing and the throwing up; the filthy, sexy fun in the next-morning landings with pounding heads and vodka on their breath. I reassure myself that my invitation must have been lost in the mail and pretend that it wasn't posted on Facebook.

I remember the day I am finally invited. It will be my first party.

Mum takes me shopping at Sportsgirl. That's where the beautiful girls buy their clothes. The ones who have summer boyfriends instead of summer admissions. I buy a grey knit pullover, and I slip sheer black stockings over my Bambi legs, which are still finding their footing on land. I will be a six-foot, size-six doe with a melon Cruiser in my hand. I complete a smattering of cosmetics with a glossy soft-pink lip, and imagine how it might feel for a boy to kiss me.

Mum's car is hardly in the next street after dropping me off when I am met with shrieks of laughter.

'Is that outfit from the Salvation Army?'

Their pointed fingers move from my body to my face in rapid succession.

'Didn't anyone ever tell you that lipstick is only for grannies?'

'Wait, you actually paid for that outfit?'

'No guy would ever look at you.'

They beckon me towards their tipsy perch atop a backyard trampoline, wry smiles upon the faces of the cruellest among them.

'What are you sitting down for, Jess?' they tease.

'Stop being so boring, you're always so boring. Go on: jump,' one demands.

The others soon join in, feverishly. 'Jump. Just jump, Jess, it's not hard.'

With each creak of the trampoline springs, I realise I am not a Sportsgirl. I am just bones in Grandma's clothes, and I'm not going to be kissed tonight – or any night.

'Jump, Jess. Jump. Jump. Jump.' Their supple bodies bounce in freefall together, the sounds of the trampoline springs mocking my creaking bones as their laughter echoes into the night

I am the deviant, the noncompliant. Even when I follow the rules, it's never enough.

Later that year, they almost get their wish. I almost jump.

Eighteen

Sick kid communities are a bustling necropolis – but the cost of connecting with your physical likeness is walking in the shadows of those who came before you and creating a path for those who will come after you. There is always another anecdote, another tragedy. You never know who will be next. It could be you. Every story begins with the fact that once they were okay, like you, and finishes with: 'And then they died.'

We don't think about that on sick teen camp – there's a lot we don't think about. The one thing that everybody does think about, though, is their camp costume. The competitive extremes that forty sick and dying teenagers reach in the name of a themed slumber party are unparalleled. It's not a testament to our 'inspiring' determination: we just really need to get a fucking hobby.

While our able-bodied peers are eating Tide pods for clout on TikTok, my friends and I jostle for space in front of the single, overcrowded mirror in our camp cabin. In a frenzy, I slick glitter mascara over my lashes and dust lavender eyeshadow across my fluttering eyelids, before smacking bubble-gum pink lips together in a pastel kiss. Dressed in a pink tulle tutu with matching antennae, an elastic snap of my wings announces my metamorphosis is complete.

Deep within the gums of Wathaurong Country, the camp recreation hall has been haphazardly dressed for the occasion. Rainbow paper chains lazily drape from the ceiling, brushing atop the duck of my head through each doorway. Darwin's theory of evolution is flouted in a sequined, shimmying *fuck you* to a world that necessitates sick kid camps. Beneath the watchful eyes of doctors, nurses, officers in blue and CPR-certified volunteers, my friends and I rewrite the laws of the jungle, survival of the fittest be damned.

Wheels waltz with feet and monkeys tango with tigers. As Katy Perry booms from the speakers, another electrical storm alights the brain of my loving, loyal lion. His giant paw had been the first to reach out to mine four years, one wheelchair and his ability to speak ago. "I'll look after you," he had promised, never letting go. Tonight, lying on the carpet he returns from the place only lions go. We sip soda, and then he takes my hand. May he have this dance? My last dance will always be saved for him.

My eyes follow oxygen tubing across the forest floor, which gives breath to dance monkeys. Nearby, leopards pose for selfies with a physician giraffe, and kings of the jungle ask baby zebras for the next twerk.

My chest is overcome by a spasm, and I walk into the cool night air to catch my racing breath. Outside, beneath a stretched fabric of black velvet and golden beading, I listen as forty of my friends dance, cough and laugh to Lady Gaga, the blended melody melting into the night sky.

I don't allow myself to wonder how many of us will be alive in fifteen years' time, or even five. Instead, I straighten my wings and re-join my pack.

Nineteen

I am wearing a shrink-wrapped black pencil skirt, which stretches gamely across my pert bottom, its shadow creating a starless eclipse of two perfect half-moons. The white Milky Way of my flesh wobbles beneath the knit fabric with each sway of my clicky hips, which have suffered one dislocation too many. Matching vintage Jane Debster pumps signal my arrival at the Royal Women's Hospital gynaecology clinic. This is what I am wearing on the day that I am told I almost certainly cannot conceive or carry children.

I look down at my spidery hands, and marvel at their emptiness. I am alone.

My gynaecologist hands me a tissue. She is soft and kind. She is the type of person you want in your corner in a moment like this.

I stare at the floor for a long time. She is wearing leather flats with detailing in the shape of a doe. Little leather Bambi taunts me as she speaks. The fawn with no mother, bleating at the mother with no fawn.

'Surrogacy is now legal in Victoria for women who cannot carry due to medical reasons,' she ventures kindly.

It had never occurred to me that being too sick to have a baby could be illegal.

'I know you're very young. But it's never too early to begin this conversation.'

Last year, I shared my virginity with someone. My adolescence was spent learning how not to get pregnant, banana and condom awkwardly in hand. Now I will spend my adulthood learning how to navigate the red tapes of a pregnancy nobody wants me to have.

Who will ever want me?

Sitting on the V/Line train home, I consider for a moment stowing my aching heart in the large luggage compartment and leaving it there. It can ooze across the carpet, strangers tracking my pericardial fluid from Ballan to Brunswick, only stopping that to wipe the goop from the soles of their shoes onto the nature strip.

As the moon rises, taunting me with her round belly, I seek safety in pastel-pink pyjamas that stretch nearly as far as my joints. I slip my pencil skirt down past a belly that will never blossom and lift my blouse over breasts that will never swell. I curl into the foetal position; cotton softening the irony.

My bedroom door creaks open, and I pretend to be asleep. Mum curls in beside me, her face wet with an apology that isn't hers to make.

'I'm so sorry, my baby girl. I'm just so, so sorry.'

We stay there until morning.

Twenty-One

Mum weaves black satin through the eyelets of my cherry-blossom corset, pulling until my breasts swell and my scoliosis softens, cushioned between bone and boning.

Thigh-high fish-net stockings settle above my knees – even Extra Tall are no match for Marfan syndrome. My blonde hair bounces with the knowledge that my statuesque figure commands attention. I've never felt so fucking sexy in my life.

Fifty of my closest friends have made the trek to my family's hobby farm to celebrate my twenty-first birthday. They have travelled by V/Line, Jetstar and Nissan Pulsar. They have risen early in the morning, or absconded from hospital under the cover of darkness and black hoodies disguising in-situ PICC lines. They arrive as strangers to one another – chronically ill, disabled, able-bodied, straight, queer, black, brown and white – their friendship with me their only connection:

Changing into their costumes, they strip their preconceived notions and leave them lying in a heaped pile on my bedroom floor. They greet each other in burlesque and gangster costumes.

Mum mixes vodka jelly shots and Dad pretends to play security, helping himself to the odd jelly shot for 'quality-control purposes'.

My friends and I dance together beneath a sky of fairy lights, my parents' furniture shifted against the plaster, serving as both leather wallflowers and 'I need to sit, I can't breathe'. There are no rules in this gangster's paradise. We move our strange bodies freely against a swell of suits and stockings, absolved of all consciousness. Long legs, short torsos. Short lives, long G-tubes. Tiny G-strings, giant realities. Atrophied arms punch the air, and bellies shimmy with ostomies between. Girls kiss girls, boys flirt with boys, there's inter-abled fucking and disabled lovemaking down by the stable.

Mum hears a telltale cystic fibrosis cough from outside on the trampoline, where a group congregates, kept warm by blankets and morphine. 'What if they get sick?!' she panics.

Dad looks at Mum, her famed potato bake in his left hand. 'Darl, they *are* sick. Let them have this. They're just kids.'

Overnight my friends and I sleep sprawled on mattresses across my parents' living-room floor. An occasional snore escapes our ageing golden retriever, who competes with a drunken friend for possession of one of the mattresses. I can hear the titters of a shared sleeping bag somewhere over to my left. To my right, two of my best friends are drunkenly regaling each other with tales of a Ballarat farm–sized moth. A little further south, other friends whisper deep and meaningful nothings, while an oxygen concentrator hums in the background.

When dawn approaches, I am tempted by the haze of sleep, still wrapped and bound in corset, satin ribbon tying me together. My false eyelashes cling on for another day.

In spite of everything, I am grown. As I soften into sleep, for the first time I find myself thinking: *This might be the type of life I know how to wear.*

Today

I am woman.

I'm now twenty-eight years old. I have occasion to wear many of life's splendours, and I savour these moments. Sometimes I dress in more than my pyjamas. I wasn't prepared – for any of this. I am the firstborn in my family, I am chapter one of an inherited, incurable connective-tissue disorder. The epilogue was written with invisible ink.

For thirteen years, I prepared to dress for a life that was never going to be mine.

My oak wardrobe pays homage to my various lives – the one that was; the one that could have been; the one that will be. I will not bid goodbye to my Year 12 blouse with its final-day scribbles from my peers. Ballgowns mingle with embellished dresses worn for friends' forever-farewells, and itsy-bitsy bikinis that remind me to jump into summers with my family, despite the pain. Always despite the pain.

And there are some new additions to my closet these days. On Tuesdays my golden retriever, Willow, and I dress in matching red pet-therapy uniforms. We volunteer at the local primary school. Recently a student asked me, 'Do you have human children too? Or just Willow?' 'Just Willow,' I replied, smiling. 'That's fair. She's pretty cute. Can we go back to reading now?' she responded. What I really wanted to reply was: *I have all of you, too.*

Hospital gowns continue to drape across my shoulders with mundane regularity. I'm just another six-digit number typing essays in the waiting room, hoping that the hospital gets my menu order right.

My future will remain a fusion of flannelette pyjamas, pet-therapy uniforms and hospital cotton gowns. There will be pencil skirts for my first job interview, cotton jumpsuits for summers spent at the beach with Willow, date-night red nylon negligees, and my scarred and striated birthday suit for making love – or entering the operating theatre.

I do not know the exact order I'll wear them in, nor the timing. I do not know how my life will unfold, where or why.

But I do know how to dress to survive.

It Is 1975, I Am Newborn

Ricky Buchanan

It is 1986. I am eleven.

There is a school excursion to a roller-skating rink.

I fall.

I tell the teachers I hurt my arm. I tell them I don't want to skate anymore. I sit down.

My teacher thinks I am embarrassed or afraid. He does not believe my arm is seriously hurt. He insists on 'helping' me overcome my 'shyness'. He tows me around the roller rink by my hands. He is trying to be helpful.

Later, my parents take me to the hospital. My wrist is broken.

I feel vindicated.

It is 1987. I am twelve.

I have never had as much stamina or physical ability as other kids. Our class at school has to jog to a nearby sports oval for PE. I can manage it at a walk, but I cannot run. I am the slowest student by a large margin. The teachers encourage me to try harder, assuming I need more motivation.

The sportiest kid in our class laughs at me.

It is not my fault.

I feel like it is my fault.

It is 1989. I am fourteen.

My wrist has been dislocating all year, over and over again. It hurts a lot even between dislocations. Nobody knows why either of those things is happening.

I go on a study camp. We are supposed to do trust falls. I volunteer to go first. My fellow students drop me.

I tell them I cannot help catch, because my arm hurts. The camp staff assume I am embarrassed and encourage me to participate. When I refuse, they pressure me until I agree to help catch. They tell me it will be fine.

It is not fine. Pain explodes through my wrist at the first catch. I refuse to participate any more.

My wrist hurts badly for most of the study camp. I keep it in a sling. When the pain is less, I take off the sling so I can write.

The camp staff assume I am either lazy or faking my injury for attention. They 'know' this is true, because sometimes I write.

Someone examines my wrist. It is excruciating. I cry out in pain. The camp staff 'know' this proves I am a faker, because it could not possibly hurt that much.

I do not know words like 'allodynia' or 'hyperalgesia', so I cannot explain to them what is happening.

I feel I cannot win.

It is 1993. I am eighteen.

Six operations later, my wrist is still unstable, agonising and mostly unusable. The surgeon does not know why it won't heal up properly. The surgeon keeps encouraging me, saying it is temporary and will improve. I believe him.

I am at university now. The disability liaison officer helps arrange support because I cannot take notes in class. One of my lecturers refuses to give me a copy of his notes, even though he has them prepared. I ask and ask. Eventually I get the disability liaison officer to speak to him directly. The DLO tells him he is legally required to help me.

Finally, a long time after the start of semester, the lecturer agrees to give me the notes. He tells me when to come and pick them up. I arrive at the agreed time. He takes me down to the photocopy room. He makes me wait for forty-five minutes while he copies the notes, so he can lecture me about how I am lazy and will almost certainly fail his course.

I come top of the class. I wish I could have seen his face as he marked my exam.

I feel vindicated.

It is 1993. I am eighteen.

I am finally referred to a pain specialist. It takes him less than five minutes to diagnose me with reflex sympathetic dystrophy. He tells me the pain is real. He tells me the pain is not my fault. He tells me he believes me.

I cry with relief.

It is 1993. I am eighteen.

The university DLO, himself disabled, invites me to go with him and other disabled friends to the Pathways conference in Brisbane. It is about disability in higher education.

I am nominally there 'to help push his wheelchair'. I have just had yet another operation on my wrist and my arm is in plaster.

Everybody there, including me, assumes that I am not really 'properly' disabled and just a helper.

It is 1995. I am twenty.

I have glandular fever.

I decide to take a year off university to recover and then perhaps travel before study resumes.

I do not get better, though. I get worse.

For three years, the doctor tells me I will definitely be better in a few months. Eventually I yell at him to stop saying that, since I have been getting worse the whole time and it is clearly not true.

The doctor explains he was trying to be encouraging.

I do not feel encouraged.

It is 2005. I am thirty.

I am still chronically ill. I have chronic fatigue syndrome. I identify as disabled now.

I poll people in a chronic illness community on LiveJournal, asking why they don't identify as disabled. They tell me that the word 'disability' means giving up on ever improving, that it means failure and that their lives will never get any better.

It does not mean that to me.

I feel alone.

It is 2010. I am thirty-five.

I have finally been diagnosed with Ehlers-Danlos Syndrome, dysautonomia and mast cell activation disorder. I stop telling people I have chronic fatigue syndrome, because I desperately hope it is true and because it is such a stigmatised condition that I get significantly better medical treatment when I don't say those words.

The medication for my newly diagnosed conditions improves my disability level more than anything else ever has, but it does not stop the progressive deterioration.

My ability level starts to decrease again.

I go back to saying 'chronic fatigue syndrome'. I say it last, after my new labels, even though it is by far the most disabling thing I have.

People treat me better when I say it last.

I know this is wrong.

It is 2018. I am forty-three.

For the twenty-plus years I have been mostly or completely homebound/bedridden, I have wished that somebody would do real advocacy in this area. Even most disability advocates don't realise that homebound/bedridden people are a population that exists. I am especially worried that homebound/bedridden people like me often don't have any access, or don't have enough access, to the medical system. There are no patient groups, disabled people's organisations or peak bodies that represent homebound/bedridden people. I realise that nobody else is ever going to do this. My frustration boils over.

I somehow manage to write the 35-page *Just Invisible* report in three months. It permanently worsens my disability to do so. It is worth every bit of pain and fatigue that it causes.

People use the report to advocate for themselves. People use it to educate politicians and bureaucrats. People use it to remind themselves that it is not their fault that they cannot find accessible heathcare, that the system is stacked against them.

I am proud.

My Early Years (Conductive Ed Preschool)

Oliver Mills

Good morning, good morning
And how do you do?
Good morning, good morning
A happy day to you.

This is how to stand.
This is how to reach out your hand –
Feet flat, head up,
Knees apart, straight back.
Sticks, rings, wooden plinths,
Ladder backs, arm wraps.

Hang upside down
Swing like a chimpanzee
Dangle from parallel bars
Slide face-down on a slippery dip.
Swim like a fish
Out of water.

Listen to a percussion band –
Bells, tambourines, triangles, drums.
Bristly brushes scratch skin.
Bright lights flicker in a cave.
Stiff plastic boots to walk in.
A legion of helpers
Move my head, my arms, my legs
Like a crash-test dummy.

Good morning, good morning
And how do you do?
Good morning, good morning
A happy day to you.

Awakenings

Tully Zygier

Every year, Mum, Dad and I pack our bags, close up the house and swap the Melbourne winter for the oppressive heat of Tel Aviv, to visit the other half of our family. It just so happens that the trip coincides with the annual familial dysautonomia (FD) get-together. Israel is the epicentre of FD.

Familial dysautonomia is a rare, genetic condition only carried in the recessive gene of Ashkenazi Jews (who come from northern Europe) – probably from millennia of inbreeding. It affects the automatic nervous system. The symptoms I experience include low blood pressure, which causes me to be always on the verge of passing out; dry-retching in the morning due to morning sickness and anxiety; no tears due to a lack of fluid in my tear ducts, causing my eyes to be dewy and sensitive to touch; constant fatigue because walking isn't automatic for me, and I have to tell myself to lift up my legs in order to move; unwanted dribbling because swallowing isn't automatic either, and I have to remind myself to swallow; and, last but not least, excessive sweating with accompanying unsociable body odour.

At first, even though I have the same condition as the other attendees of this one-day-of-the-year support gathering, it was confronting to see the variations of FD. Some people are hooked up to oxygen tanks 24/7. Many have feeding tubes due to difficulties with swallowing. Others can only get around using walking frames. And most of them have never worked or driven a car, and have never left the country – because they might pass out at high altitudes, not to mention all the life-support equipment they would need to take with them.

Although I was one of them, I was healthy by comparison, and a proud owner of a mostly able body, naively ignoring the signs of things to come.

Then 2008 came around. That was the year Mum made me see what everybody else already could. It began with her usual questions about the FD gathering.

'So, how was it, Tul?'

Oh God, I really don't want to talk about the scary things I've seen.

'It was alright, I guess.'

'Just alright?'

'Not really.'

'Tell me.'

Change the subject! Change the subject!

'Let's go to Shlomski's for pizza, I'm starving.'

Not really.

'Okay, let's go.'

It wasn't like Mum to stop interrogating me. What was she up to?

All through dinner, Mum did not do her usual act: telling everybody exactly what she thought in nuanced detail. Instead, she remained silent – and that silence was heavy with angst. I avoided it by making small talk with Dad.

Mum's silence hung over me for the remaining two weeks of our Israel holiday. But my denial had put me inside a bubble full of delusions: 'I only stumble once in a while, it can happen to anyone low on energy', 'It was the jet-lag kicking in', 'Over-exhaustion can make anyone stumble, and trying to fit too much into the day doesn't help', 'Cobbled stone paths can make anybody trip', 'It's easy to lose your balance walking on beach sand', 'Anyone can miss a step when rushing', 'Everyone trips over a loose rug or bumps into a pole on the footpath at some point', 'Window-shopping can distract you from watching where you're going', 'Finding your footing is not easy when you're getting out of bed half awake'.

I failed to see it coming. I was too proud to walk unaided. My delusions helped me believe that nobody noticed my feet were turned out, or that my left leg was dragging along behind me whenever I got tired. My delusions blocked out the stares that followed me. The way I got around was awkward, to say the least.

But the pretence was hard work and getting harder by the year. Only when I was on my own did I use furniture and walls to help me walk. This wasn't always easy, and because I was holding on to one side, my balance was uneven and I'd often fall over.

But at Tel Aviv airport, my mother completely bowled me over.

We were walking to the departure lounge. My eyes strayed to a handsome couple with a baby and I lost my balance and tripped over my own two feet. There I was, floundering on the floor, and I looked up to see my mother's fearful face as she grabbed my arm and lifted me back up. Seconds later, she exploded with the sound and fury of a parent worried, disappointed, frustrated and angry. Her home truths burst my bubble of delusion wide open.

'It's about time you took responsibility for your health. I won't put up with your denial anymore. I've remained quiet but I've been watching you ... And the way you've handled yourself around Israel ... I could see how difficult it was for you to get around. And the social worker from the support group could see it. Everybody could see it. But not you! No, not you! You're still too bloody stubborn to see it for yourself ... I can't keep looking after you. I'm not getting any younger, and I can't grow old being your carer. I don't have the energy anymore ... It's time to look after yourself once and for all ... It's time for you to GROW UP!'

It was hard to hear, but I knew that everything she said was true. So when we got back to Melbourne, I made an appointment with an occupational therapist to be assessed for a walking frame. Mum and I went together.

I named my walking frame after the heroine of *Gone with the Wind*, Scarlett – a stubborn woman like me. That put a smile back on Mum's face. When we got home, I pushed my reluctance aside and dared to take a walk around the block (something I had avoided for many years) with my new walking companion. I listened to Crowded House's 'Weather with You' on repeat as I set out on my first adventure with Scarlett.

As I walked along, the autumn leaves crunched underneath Scarlett's shiny new tyres, the sound suggestive of breaking new ground together. The previously twenty-minute walk to the corner of the block now took ten minutes. That corner had always been my limit. This time I walked not one, not two, not three, but all four sides of my neighbourhood block – thanks to Scarlett. She opened up a world that I had only seen fleetingly whenever I travelled in my parents' car. Now I was the driver, able to stop and see whatever I wanted to. I walked into the library and perused the true crime section. I stopped at Sissi & Co. for a coffee and a lamington. I dropped into the local nursery and bought a pot of rosemary. I took a little detour to a nearby friend's house for a catch-up.

Along the way, the gentle breeze in my hair rekindled the flame I had felt as a child, running around without a care. I began to realise that I was independent. As long as Scarlett was with me, I could achieve my greatest ambition: to free my parents from full-time worry and responsibility. And I could sit down whenever I wanted! But when I leaned back on my seat and breathed in the fresh air and the joy of freedom, sadness welled up within me. Next thing, I was crying for all the world to hear my anger and devastation. The thrill of four-wheeled freedom and the grief of being officially disabled were at loggerheads in my mind. Scarlett made it possible for me to move more easily through the world, but she also showed the world my disability. This stark realisation accompanied me all the way back home. When my mother opened the front door to congratulate me on my big step forward, I broke down and cried in her arms. She cried with me. Together we shared the joy and the sadness: for me, of being a woman with a disability; for her, of being the mother of such a woman.

I wasn't ready for the transition from living with a chronic illness to living with a disability. There was still a little of my old delusional self, hard at work convincing me that I could hide my dependence on Scarlett from the wider world. And so I would only use her in the house and when I went out with my family. The rest of the time, I continued to struggle from A to B and would stop myself from falling by clinging onto friends, lampposts, rubbish bins, fences, shopfronts and window frames. Wherever there was a bench, I would drop down onto it, gasping for air. There, I would wait for the next burst of energy to get me up and going.

The greatest feat of all was my three-month placement as a social work student at the Royal Women's Hospital, while completing my Bachelor of Social Work at the University of Melbourne.

If getting on and off public transport wasn't herculean in itself, it was miraculous that I was able to spend three months rushing from ward to ward, attending to pregnant women, and anticipating the demands of obstetricians and nurses – pretending all the while that my disability wasn't slowing me down. Looking back, I don't know how I did it without causing a disaster to myself or others. Self-deception was the driving force that got me through it all. It blinded me to the truth but, paradoxically, empowered me to stand on my own two wobbly, fragile duck feet. But how long could I sustain my everyday life within this bubble of delusion?

I discovered the answer during my second placement, at Yooralla, one of Melbourne's biggest disability service providers. For the first four weeks I navigated the open-plan office spaces as if nobody would see me grasping onto partitions, desks and windows. My job was helping people with disabilities access government funding, housing, therapy and counselling. Around the fourth week, I was assigned to run a peer support group. I still didn't consider myself a fellow person living with a disability. I didn't join the dots between my walking frame at home and the wheelchairs around me every day at work. Until then, I had always been surrounded by able-bodied people. I grew up in the mainstream. Living with a disability was as foreign to me as it was to non-crips in an able-bodied world. That and my wishful thinking were a double whammy of denial.

The physiotherapists and occupational therapists I worked with couldn't help but notice me stumbling from office cubicle to office. They were too busy, too polite or too afraid to bring up the subject of my disability denial.

Except Trudi.

Trudi was an old-school occupational therapist and hobby dressmaker. She was the type that would pull up her handmade culottes, lift someone out of their wheelchair, strap them into a sled and push them down the mountain. But by 2010 OH&S was her mantra and everyone had to follow workplace policies and procedures. Because I was completely terrified of her, I was determined to please her in any way I could. I got my paperwork done on time; I was extremely respectful with the clients and put them at ease; I always greeted her with a hearty hello and how are you; and I even lent her my DVD of *The Big Chill*, which she never gave back and I never dared to ask her to return it.

She was a very hands-on manager and regularly touched base to see how I was going. Even though I was green in the disability sector, she saw my passion and drive as raw materials for tailoring me in her image. Meanwhile, I got on with my daily responsibilities, oblivious to the many eyes witnessing my exertions and accompanying pretences of being able-bodied.

On the Monday morning of my fourth week at Yooralla, I was sifting through my email while sipping on my second coffee of the day and eating my usual strawberry-frosted cupcake. Trudi came over to my cubicle and asked me into her office for a chat. Her tone of voice suggested that this was definitely not the time to ask for my DVD back. I reluctantly left my coffee and half-eaten cake behind and made my awkward way to her office. Thankfully it was next door so I didn't require much grasping to get there.

She was sitting behind her desk with a heavy look of concern on her face. Clearly this was not going to be a friendly chat. She rose from her chair and gestured for me to sit beside her. Before I'd stumbled in, Trudi had positioned the visitor chair beside hers. To get to it, I had to clutch her table and clumsily make my way next to her. Trudi's silence was deafening, like my mother's had been in Israel. As I struggled, my mind was flipping through all my clients for somebody who might have put in a complaint. My underarms were sweaty and my hands were clammy, leaving skid marks on her desk as I gripped it to leverage myself to the chair. I couldn't think of any possible complainants. Had one of the physios or OTs criticised the way I interacted with clients? Surely not. They were all so open and honest with me, and supportive too. Meanwhile, my nerves activated both my sweat glands into uncontrollable overdrive. First was my eccrine gland, secreting its odourless, clear fluid to cool down my rapidly rising body temperature. Next came my apocrine gland, discharging a thick fluid that, when it makes contact with my skin, produces that potent body odour I dread. My t-shirt clung to my armpits and my face flushed red, dripping with perspiration. By the time I reached the seat, I was drained of all energy. And to top it off, my mind was as blank as an empty page.

So here we were, the two of us, sitting side by side behind her beige desk, which was ordered with military precision. Her Montblanc pens (a red one, a blue one and a black one) were lined up like legionnaires ready for duty. Her matching royal-blue stapler and tape dispenser were placed next to her National Gallery of Victoria diary, which displayed elegantly scripted entries of her week's appointments.

Trudi gave me a few seconds to regroup and launched into it.

'Tully, I've noticed the way you walk around the office. And it has been brought to my attention that people are worried about the way you're getting around. We're all worried that you might fall over.'

Her words hit me like a bullet in the heart. *How had I missed this? How had I not seen what everybody else was seeing?*

'It's not safe to be holding onto furniture and clinging onto walls while you're trying to make your way around the building.'

Oh my God, I didn't realise how obvious it was, I thought I could …

'Our clients also have issues with their walking, and it's our job to look out for them and their safety. And if you saw someone walking around like you do, you would be worried about them too and would want to help them.'

Of course I would! But …

'It's our job to give them the resources to live their lives safely and independently. What would you do if you worked with a client in a similar situation to you?'

Similar situation to me?! By now, I wanted to cry and could no longer look her in the eye. My head dropped down to my chest. *Please, earth, open up and swallow me whole right now.*

I felt Trudi's arm rest on my shoulder as she gave me a moment to answer.

I pulled myself together and took a deep breath, hoping that an answer would come to me.

It had been there all along: 'I … would … tell … them … to … use it.'

Trudi smiled.

'Good,' she said, and gave me a nice little half hug. 'So I can rely on you bringing your walking frame to work from now on.'

How does she know I have a walking frame?

'My walking frame? Oh yes, my walking frame. Of course.'

She accompanied me to the door.

'We all have to get advice sometimes, Tully. I know it's hard for you to accept your disability, but I also know how remarkable you are in going about your work. The two are not mutually exclusive. So as of tomorrow, I expect you to use your walking frame.'

I nodded and walked back to my coffee and cupcake, feeling an acceptance of who I am in this world. From somebody I couldn't ignore. Trudi was a mentor in the truest sense of the word – empathetic, trustworthy and straight down the line.

As I sat at my desk, the memory of my mother dishing out home truths at Tel Aviv airport came back. That had been the beginning of my awakening. Then there had been my walk around the block, and mother and child embracing within a new paradigm. And now Trudi. All three moments were part of the same epiphany. I had gradually come to acceptance, and Trudi gave me the courage to be my true self – a beautiful young woman living with a disability.

To this day, I continue to grapple with this, but the little awakenings along the way remind me that it's okay to not be okay.

Blurred Lines

Iman Shaanu

'You're too beautiful to hold that ugly thing in your hand.'

I paused, standing at the front door. I'll admit I wasn't exactly shocked by this comment. I was used to my family being fairly materialistic and focused on appearances, whether that be social norms or what someone on the street was wearing. But I was somewhat taken aback by this comment, made by a family member whom I am close to and respect.

It was the holidays, and I was over at a family member's house. We were off to lunch. I had everything ready: jacket, bag and cane. Yes, I'm vision-impaired, and no, I don't have a dog, I use a cane. For the record, I hate dogs and would prefer a guide cat if that was a thing. You know, because cats are far superior beings, in every sense.

Being vision-impaired and from an ethnically diverse background is challenging, to say the least. But not in the ways you may expect. It wasn't a case of me struggling to accept my vision impairment. I grew up always knowing and accepting it. Instead, I had to learn to navigate my parents' attitudes and perceptions, as well as those of other family members. This is where the above encounter about my cane comes in – although my family loved and valued me, they often worried about the societal implications of my disability. There was also the whole language barrier, which proved to be more of an issue in the earlier years. It's very difficult to advocate for your child, and to teach your child to advocate for themselves, when you don't have the language to do so. This contributed to many of my family's uncertainties. Adjusting to a new country and its language is difficult on its own, but adding the complexities of having a disabled child makes it even more so. Yes, interpreters help, but support services and government schemes can be hard to navigate, even if English is your first language. The NDIS is a clear example of this, as it is so convoluted and ever-changing.

When we had just moved to Australia, we lived in a quiet area filled with many other people from our home country. When I was with cousins, my mum felt comfortable letting me run around like other children my age. She knew I was safe, and she could easily communicate any concerns she had. But when I was about four, we moved to a predominantly white neighbourhood, where immigrants were few and far between. This was pretty scary for my family as they lost their safety net of family and close friends, and felt alone. This led to them being quite overprotective and unsure how to deal with my vision impairment.

When I began my first years of school, I noticed that my mum was careful and hesitant with me. My aunts and friends' parents weren't like this with their children, so why was she? I wanted to run around and play like the rest of the kids.

It must have been around this point when I stopped using my cane. Honestly, I don't remember using my cane in public, except for going to school. This was partly because of my family. I guess they thought that I could walk along with them, holding onto some relative's hand, no big deal. Which is fine … when you're, like, seven. When you're nine or ten, it becomes a little awkward and embarrassing. I now understand that this notion of me walking along, being guided by them, came from a place of love. My family wanted me to be safe, and to take care of me, and they thought that this was the best way to ensure that. Also, back then the idea of a mobility aid was new to them. Besides, we were a brown family in a predominantly white area, so people were already staring at us and thinking we were different. And I didn't want to look different in two ways.

I didn't even use my cane when I started at a mainstream school. Looking back now, I don't know how I didn't walk into anything or injure myself. But I just wanted to fit in. Again, I always had this sense that I was different to kids my age, and pre-teen girls are great at exclusionary tactics. I felt an overwhelming sense of loneliness during this time in my life. Add on the pressure of dealing with ongoing family problems – well, I guess I was that kid who sat alone at lunchtime, looking lost. At recess, I would sit in the canteen, trying to make my packet of chips last as long as I could, so I didn't look like I was sitting with nothing to do. I felt isolated at school. Kids would come up to me and ask me how many fingers they were holding up, and walk backwards while doing so. My friend W* commented on this recently, telling me that his way of sticking up for me was to say, 'You know she's not totally blind, right? She can see you walking away.'

It's not like I didn't have any friends. It's just that they went to different schools to me, with the exception of W. But I still felt awkward telling them what was going on. Remember, at eleven, even *you're* not sure of what exactly is going on, and finding the words to explain something you don't quite grasp yet is virtually impossible. I had another vision-impaired friend, who could relate in a way, but her parents spoke perfect English and were her biggest advocates. She knew what AFL was, she ate the same food as everyone else at lunchtime (my parents' idea of a sausage roll was to wrap up a sausage, with sauce, in flatbread) and she never had to explain why she was fasting or quickly think of an excuse when the teachers handed out chocolate. So how could she possibly understand?

Skipping forward a few years, high school was pretty much the same, in terms of feeling lonely and dealing with the inexplicable problems of having an intersectional identity. My sister was lucky because she had a best friend of the same nationality. She had someone to relate to in that respect. And my cousins went to schools that had ethnically diverse student populations. But there were mostly white Australians at my school. I didn't really connect with anyone during the first half of high school, but I did develop a crush on a boy in my year level, and this somewhat added to my worries. I wasn't one of those secretly-go-behind-your-parents'-back-to-see-a-guy-and-go-to-parties kind of Muslim girl. But my parents and I were definitely not the types to talk about boys and crushes. I'd gauged that in their opinion, boys were off limits. I could never understand how my aunties and friends' mums were so open on the topic; I relied on them for this. And I was a little envious of my friends and cousins as well, because their mothers were so open and acted like it was a normal thing to go through, which it is.

Growing up in a Muslim family and being vision impaired certainly has its challenges. In terms of wanting to learn more about my religion, I mainly rely on the internet; however, the lack of resources and information for blind and vision-impaired people is frustrating. For me, it's not as simple as being able to pick up a hard copy of the Qur'an and starting to read. And learning the braille Arabic alphabet seems complicated. The rise in popularity of e-books and audio books have helped, to an extent. And I will always be grateful to the family member who took the time to physically show me the correct way to pray and described how to perform the obligatory ablutions before prayer. Regarding disability, Islam encourages the inclusion of disabled people in society; in fact, the second caliph of the Prophet, peace be upon him (PBUH), built a house for a blind man so he would be closer to the mosque. And the prophet (PBUH) himself would visit and spend time with those who were sick and disabled.

My overseas family treated me differently to how my Australian family treated me when I was young. They treated me like anyone else, and accepted my disability and my cane as a part of me. This was partly because attitudes regarding disability have changed, but also my overseas family didn't face the struggles my Australian family had faced when I was younger. One of the factors behind my family's treatment when I was young was that their ableism stemmed from Australia's racist society, not Islam, as some might believe. The acceptance and support I received from my overseas family, and that I now receive from my Australian family, reflect Islam's attitudes towards disability.

As I don't wear the hijab and could pass for a number of different ethnicities, I hear a lot of negative comments in passing about my faith. I've never experienced any direct racism because of my appearance, but I've also never felt completely comfortable either, as I didn't have culturally diverse friends to relate to until the end of high school. The only time I felt represented was in books like Melina Marchetta's *Looking for Alibrandi*, and Randa Abdel-Fattah's *Does My Head Look Big in This?*. With *Looking for Alibrandi*, I could relate to the over-involved, gossipy family, and the main character's struggle with her ethnic identity. With *Does My Head Look Big In This?*, it was the character's attempt to balance her faith and culture, while being a young person. The fact these books were written and set in Australia had even more significance for me personally and made me feel like I wasn't quite so alone. Also, one of my favourite movies growing up was, and still is, *Mean Girls*. I don't remember exactly how old I was when I first watched the movie, but there was one particular scene that stuck out in my young mind: the iconic rap scene with Kevin G, the rapping mathlete. His demeanour reminded me of my male cousins, and sons of family friends – and later on, I saw him personified in some of the boys I met when I was older. But more significantly, here we had a brown man, who – surprise, surprise – wasn't a terrorist or evil. In fact, Kevin G was the best thing in *Mean Girls* and had some of the most memorable lines.

As I grew older, and progressed with high school, I became more socially aware, and gained more self-confidence and began to develop stronger friendships, which I have kept until today. This increase in my social awareness meant that I became more of a realist in terms of society's perceptions about immigrants and Muslims. I can recall scoffing at a comment made by a marker of a creative writing assignment, which stated, 'I don't know what is so bad about your culture.' I wasn't comfortable mentioning my country of origin when I wrote of my struggles with my ethnic and religious identity, although I did mention I was Muslim, and most people are aware of how we are perceived. I can also recall feeling incredibly uncomfortable when telling my friends my nationality, despite the fact that they were all of different nationalities themselves. You'll notice I haven't mentioned my country of origin in this piece either. I was once asked if I was hesitant to disclose my nationality because I was ashamed of it, but that's not it. It's more that I've always been seen as the 'other' by society already, because of my disability. I can remember being out with my mother and sister when I was younger, feeling the looks of strangers and hearing comments about 'that lady walking with the two blind children'. This made me feel small, awkward and uncomfortable. My attempts at repressing my ethnic and religious identity were my way of trying to fit in. I didn't think these attempts were even noticeable when meeting new people, but my friend H* commented that it does seem as though the topic makes me self-conscious.

I can recall feeling angry when a white co-worker stated that I couldn't go around assuming everyone was racist or Islamophobic, despite our right-wing government and the media's portrayal of Muslims. Her justification? She wasn't racist or Islamophobic because her 'best friend was Asian'. My best friend was white and would never think of saying anything so insulting. On the day of the Sydney Lindt Cafe siege I cried because society hated Muslims and blamed us for everything that was going on. I also scoffed at the news reporter who claimed there was an ISIS flag with 'Islamic writing' being displayed by the terrorist. Since when had Islam become a language? I was also saddened when I heard the reports of the refugee crisis of 2015, because if circumstances had been different, that could have so easily been my family. I should feel grateful to live in this country as a disabled person. It is incredibly upsetting to see the rise in cases similar to that of Kinley's, where simply because a family member has a disability the family is at risk of deportation, as the government feels they are a burden on society. Again, that could so easily have been me, who has known no other home but Australia. Living in this country is all I remember. I was angered and upset when people like Pauline Hanson and Donald Trump gained popularity due to their hate for all Muslims, immigrants and POC, as well as their mockery of disabled people, and when the Australian government vilified asylum seekers and tried to convince us they were illegal, like with the case of the Biloela Tamil family. It terrifies me that people like this are being voted into power, and are given a platform to spew their hate.

I can remember feeling shocked when, on the way to uni, I heard of the attack at Ariana Grande's concert. I have also been upset and shocked when other acts of terror have occurred and the perpetrator has only been labelled a terrorist because he's a POC or Muslim – and when all Muslims are blamed for his actions. I am angered by the double standards in the media when a similar act of terror is committed by a white man and it is blamed on his traumatic past or mental illness.

But at the same time, I was also touched by the Twitter hashtag #IllRideWithYou trending when a Hijabi was scared to ride the train by herself. I was also grateful to the teacher who, during a conversation, made a passing comment about how Muslims weren't terrorists. I was thankful when my best friend A* wrote a heartfelt post on Facebook about checking in with all your Muslim friends after the New Zealand mosque attacks, and who then checked up on me personally to make sure I was okay. I was moved when a boy in my class made a speech on Islamophobia in the media, because for so long my people have been, and are still being, attacked, blamed and criticised by the media, public figures and politicians, and I had never known a non-Muslim person who was willing to stand up for us. I felt surprised and happy when 'Egg Boy' Will Connolly threw an egg at a racist politician who had blamed Muslims for the Christchurch attacks, because someone was angry on our behalf. And I felt accepted by my friends who were angered about the way Muslims and other minorities were being mistreated. It showed me that I wasn't quite so alone with my cultural struggles, and that there are great allies out there.

In the blind and vision impaired community, I've found that there is a lack of diversity, and the struggle of being both vision impaired and ethnic is somewhat isolating. A lot of members of the disability community are clueless on a number of issues, especially regarding race and religion. Apart from my sister, I knew no other blind or vision-impaired person when I was growing up who could understand my mixed-up feelings from balancing my multifaceted identity. My disability and my religious identity are the two most significant aspects of my identity; I cannot talk about one without the other. Although I struggled to make friends when I was younger, in the last year of high school and in university I found people who I could relate to in terms of culture. More recently, I became friends with someone who is both vision impaired and ethnic, and having someone to connect with over the challenges I had experienced growing up, with cultural rules and wanting to be independent as a vision impaired person, is a huge relief.

My experiences of being a vision-impaired Muslim have certainly been unique and filled with ups and downs. Navigating the confusing mess of being a teenager was made more difficult because of my struggle with my ethnic and religious identity, rather than my blindness. My hardships have made me better appreciate kindness and acceptance from people. I'm grateful for my white best friend, A, who never ridiculed me because I wasn't allowed to do certain things as a kid or enjoy the same degree of independence she had. For my other friends, who have accepted my family and are open to our culture, and who never see my vision impairment as something that gets in the way. For my manager at work, who treated me like anyone else, and who was the first person to invite me out socially. This was surprising, because as much as I don't like to admit it, in the past I have occasionally been excluded from gatherings and catch-ups. For the girl, who on my first day of high school, offered to help me if I needed. For the friend who, to my great surprise, invited me to their birthday party, the first high school party I attended. For my friend S*, who approached me in a class we were both taking and struck up a conversation with no awkwardness about my vision impairment, just because we were the only ethnic-looking people in the room. For my friend's boyfriend, who knew the correct way to guide a vision impaired person, although I had never met him before. For other friends, who are more than willing to provide image descriptions, and play taxi driver when I need them. For my friends at university, who included me in their banter and as one of their own, and who weren't awkward about my vision impairment, and were more than happy to assist me if I needed. For the professors and teachers who went above and beyond, ensuring I wasn't left at a disadvantage in class. And for my family, who now crack the occasional blind joke with me.

Although I'm a little more open now about my ethnicity, it's a topic that still causes me to feel awkward and uncomfortable. I've never had a choice about disclosing my vision impairment though, and I think I'm at peace with that. I'm happy to say the relative who made the comment about my cane is more accepting now, as they have a better understanding of why I need it. If someone were to make a similar comment to me now, I would explain to them what was wrong with that comment, and why exactly I need the cane. Even if it might provoke ethnic aunties.

Learning My Place

Chantel Bongiovanni

'This place isn't meant for you,' said Mr Robins.

He said it so offhandedly that I was briefly stunned. This always got me: how casually lines could be drawn in the sand. I could be anything, provided it fit in with everyone around me first.

This place isn't meant for you. I repeated the words in my head.

We were at a careers expo, I was fifteen years old, and Mr Robins was my Special Education teacher. We were there as a cohort of able-bodied and disabled students to look at our futures. Although all the kids with disabilities were usually integrated into classes with able-bodied students, for this excursion Mr Robins had put all the students with disabilities in one group and separated us from our peers, because, well ... I still don't know why. I think the school wasn't sure what to do with us most of the time, and relied on the Special Ed teachers, who knew how to *deal with* the disabled students, to make the right call. Mr Robins had had a long career working in disability and thought he knew a lot more than he did. Sometimes he even used to send us home with letters to our parents, relaying how much he understood the ongoing 'burden' of disability. Us kids with disabilities laughed at that when he wasn't around. But today I wasn't laughing.

I'd left his group to check out a university stall, hoping he wouldn't notice. We'd been at the expo for hours and we hadn't looked at a single university yet. I was only here for the universities, because that was where I intended to go after high school. It was frustrating me that we were basically wasting our time. I hadn't yet got a single piece of information that would help me plan my future. So when he was distracted, I wandered off.

He found me less than a minute later and said those words that now reverberated through my brain: 'Chantel, come with me. This place isn't meant for you.'

What does that even mean? He ushered me away from the stall and back to the main group. I understood the implications without him saying them: university wasn't meant for someone like me, a girl with a disability, a girl who used a wheelchair.

If I'm being real, I wasn't a standout student. I never got academic excellence awards or anything like that, but I wasn't a low-achieving student either. I never failed a subject and I constantly worked hard. My parents had always intended for me to study beyond high school, and I planned to do just that if I could get the grades. Based on the entry scores I'd seen for some university courses, this didn't seem out of my reach, even if I couldn't stand up to do it.

Mr Robins continued guiding us disabled students through the career stalls, our self-appointed leader. He seemed so blasé, like he'd already forgotten what had just happened. 'Who wants to be a pizza delivery person?' he joked, as we went through the aisles.

What? What did delivering pizza have to do with anything? Half the students in this Special Education unit had physical disabilities; it was unlikely that they would be driving cars. *Why are we talking about that? What are we even doing here?*

He was wasting our time, but I felt like the only student in the group who noticed. Some of my friends found me uptight for being frustrated with him that day, but I don't think they could see the bigger ramifications of him deliberately restricting our access to information about future careers.

At home that night, my mum raged. 'I'm calling the education department in the morning! How dare he do that! He has no right to tell you whether you can look at university degrees or not!'

'No, no, Mum, don't,' I pleaded. I had been arguing with her for a while, begging her to calm down. 'I'll work it out. Don't worry.'

I wasn't doing it to spare him his job. I understood why she was angry, but I hate a big deal being made of my disability. I hate being obvious. I could basically excuse any type of bad behaviour directed at my disability. When you have something physical everyone can see, you always feel noticed and watched, you can never go under the radar, and that was something I desperately wanted. I just wanted to cruise through and blend in. If a teacher got in trouble because he wouldn't let me read a brochure about study options, how obvious would that make me? The other thing was that my parents were tireless. They fought for everything for me to the detriment of their own health. They shielded me from every negative attitude or expectation I ever came up against, and trust me, there was a lot of that. It wasn't fair to them.

'What do you want to do, then?' Mum asked.

I thought for a while, uncertain, turning what had happened over in my brain. 'Just don't ring anyone yet,' I said finally.

The next day at school, I debated how to respond when some of the support staff asked me how the careers expo had gone. I find it hard to lie to people when they ask me direct questions, so after a brief hesitation I explained what had happened. I told several of the staff working under Mr Robins what he had said. I didn't embellish anything.

At the end of the day, as I was getting ready to go home, Mr Robins approached me.

'Can I talk to you for a moment?' he asked.

I followed him away from my locker, outside to a bench, where he sat down and I positioned my wheelchair to face him.

'I've heard from some of the staff that I said something to you at the careers expo that was perhaps inappropriate,' he began. 'I don't actually remember what I said to you when I took you away from that stall; I didn't think anything of it to remember it, so I'm sorry for that.'

I stared at him, expecting the apology to continue.

'I want to be honest, though,' he said. 'I've seen your grades on your report cards, and I can tell when I talk to you that you're quite smart, I'm not denying that …'

'Okay,' I said, waiting for more. I couldn't really believe he was apologising, that obviously he knew what he did was wrong.

'But,,' he continued, 'I believe that if you were to go to university you would fail, and it's not because of your intelligence, it's because you have a disability. You'd struggle at university. That's what I believe, and I'm standing by it.'

I faltered after that. Honestly, I was enraged by his opinion. I realised then that for his entire career he had set such low benchmarks for children and teenagers with disabilities that he almost ensured failure by holding them back. Those letters he wrote to my parents made sense now, the ones in which he framed me as a burden; he genuinely thought I was one. Deep down, he did not want me to achieve and he did not want anything to prove him wrong. My full potential was better off not being pursued.

There's something monstrous and insurmountable about such attitudes. His opinion wasn't insignificant. He taught students with a disability every day. He was meant to encourage, direct and steer them towards success. Yet here he was actively shutting down my possibilities before I'd even tried. He represented something much larger, something I'd seen all my life in different ways, but I couldn't pinpoint until years later. It was reflected in the shock strangers expressed when they realised I did things that 'normal' teenagers do. The space around me is always so reduced, so confined; I'm always at the mercy of what others think. I often feel like I'm a different-shaped puzzle piece to everyone else, and that can be a really hard thing to confront every day. Everyone else is a circle, while I'm a square. I can force myself into the puzzle, but it never quite looks right; the piece never quite fits.

But in that moment, when Mr Robins delivered the final blow of his judgement, I realised something important: I didn't have to fit in with the circles. I'd never had to; people had forced me to. The puzzle where the squares like me fit was right next door; it's just that we pretend all the pieces are circles and they have to fit in the one set.

When Mr Robins looked at me again, his face contorted into an expression that was sad yet sure of himself. I understood that what I was confronting was bigger than him and his beliefs about my life. The choice I neeeded to make was huge and difficult, but also, in some ways, simple.

I went back to class the next day, and I studied.

Motherhand

Jasmine Shirrefs

Puppa Tom snapped an inopportune picture of Mumma Katrina in a great deal of pain with many body fluids. Then a baby was born with a mushy head of hair that looked like a teen punk had tried to get fluorescent red hair but skipped the peroxide.

Young Family Fresh Baby piled into the old red Commodore and travelled across the Little Desert National Park and into the West Wimmera. A home blazing fire and a detour to the neighbours. Gates open for the sheep.

Young couple in cinema with baby. And the little toddler in the next row screamed as on-screen Mr Holland played his Opus while his deaf son sat on the speaker, trying to feel. And young couple hands were a collage of butter, salt and popcorn and they whispered to one another, 'Why is our baby sleeping through this racket?'

Little hearing aids for baby and a battery choking hazard. Speech pathology and a big push into the world of the hearing. Little Jasmine and Mumma Katrina down to Melbourne to Taralye Oral Language Centre for Deaf Children. Mumma Katrina loved early intervention. Baby Jasmine loved hermit crabs in the hallway.

Strapped on jelly sandals and headed into Edenhope for kindergarten. Dog pound across the road. Chook feed on the back porch at home, and a baby sister, and another, and then a brother. And around the dinner table a cornucopia of talent quests and daily charades. At night Enya almost played me to sleep and then I had to wake up and take the hearing aids out.

Bilateral sensorineural hearing loss, rural Victoria and sheep poop and school buses. Primary school principal told me deaf people had bad balance. A lady named Pauline came to school, took me out of class for a specialised sidelined hour. An FM system in a bag, pocket, swinging around a teacher's neck. School swimming day and the teacher's aide accidentally pushed me directly into the pool because I couldn't hear the buzzer and a belly whacker and red raw.

Three-hour drive to Ballarat Australian Hearing Services. Buzzers on the beep and ear filled with a gluey gunk and a mould made of my ear. Maccas drive-thru on the way home.

And a bookworm when the words don't disappear. Little eyes that read on the school bus and late at night and the school librarian stared me down and falsely accused me of stealing a library book. ABC News and Ian Henderson and fluoro yellow subtitles live with typos a sentence behind.

Nanna and Puppa's Golden Wedding Anniversary at Nhill Race Club and my hearing-aid batteries are flat, and the pharmacy is closed for the weekend and Mum shovels and digs through the car for a spare. A poem packed and delivered, bad rhymes like stars and Mars into the microphone. I couldn't hear myself. Afterwards middle-aged lady approached me and called me Little Miss Poetry. I wore junners.

Elderly rello unable to talk in the Ballarat Base Hospital and so I lip-read and he said something about a fire truck and Dad joked I could have a career in spying on celebrities and lip-reading gossip but that's what hacking is for. Family reunion with Mum's big Catholic family in Shepparton and one of Mum's fifty cousins introduced me to an old man and told us we'll get along great because we're both hearing impaired. Awkward silence and a speedy departure for a jelly slice and a lamington.

Gymnastics and on the uneven bar and I thought I would be less unpopular if I pulled off a black strapless shirt, but I pulled it off in another way. Hands on the bar just suspended in awkward. And cast to back hip circle and the hearing aids projectile. Sounds like a job for Gaffer Tape™.

Rural high school and proper chook handling for assessment. A bigger budget for the kitchen classroom than the Science lab. Mould on the ceilings and a kid tells the teacher and she says maybe he could become a plumber. German teacher hid in the textiles supply room to survive someone's stapler-gun fun while kids are climbing out the windows.

Boots shoved into my chest and Dad won't be wearing these any longer. A death at forty-three and a packet of Tim Tams I simply could not eat. Disappeared into the floorboards and it was Dad who stood there in the rain at netball when I had my hands over my ears and the curly girl with the hairdryer on the hearing aids at half-time.

I have always remembered 2010 like a split crack lightning bolt of triple death. And I vomited up a mixture of funeral foods and salty tears at midnight and I used to sit next to that boy in class and he would give me Zappos if I did his German workbook exercises. And local dads kept dying and crowds in black at Edenhope Cemetery.

Musical chairs around the dinner table. Swapping roles and walls with holes.

And at Wimmera Hearing Camp I dreamt of freefall after plunging on a 19-metre swing.

Boarding school funded by philanthropic rellos and a single-parent mum with two jobs. Choir and my fellow alto sang directly into my ear so I could try to pitch. Online friends and *Rookie* magazine and a bubbling grief I had forgotten to process. Tavi Gevinson at RetroStar in 2013 and I told her about the time I singed my nose on a marshmallow. Eyes on the page in literature and the sunset on the life on *Antony and Cleopatra* as they age and age well, enticing Egypt and rigid Rome. Lanyon was in his op-shop ties with patterns that looked like a cell under the microscope. Maths Methods on a Thursday morning and eyes glanced outside, and it was snowing in Ballarat.

Ten people in a little shack near Monash Uni and we weaved through suburbia on our way to Wholefoods. Lecturers that did cool topics for PhDs but have an inability to press the CC button on YouTube. Tired flirts with self-help books. And 9 a.m. therapy when I felt too sleepy to open old wounds and feet pressed into the floor and breathe in through your nose and out of your mouth. And I have always felt anxious like sunset on Sunday, when the doom of the working week kicks in, like the intensity and permanence of being three-quarters through one's first viewing of *Die Hard*.

Marns makes going to Coles an adventure. A slow evening spent talking about Polish cinema and thinking so much about

Murakami, she put my hand behind her head to feel her shunt. Quiet solidarity, mutual understanding.

So good at sitting on fences I have a permanent wedgie. And I am non-binary and queer. Late-night tweet about AI but my hearing is a computer with a start-up jingle. Becs and I put on dystopian swimwear and body paint and make a film about posthumanism. Bright blue insulin pumps and fluorescent pink Siemens hearing computers. Percentage machine.

Bed on Sunday morning with Phoebe and there's a small dog named Granny trying to claim a kiss as well. Phoebe pointed at her eye and then her heart and then at me.

Tuesday evenings with three friends taking an AUSLAN course and the teacher talks, and she doesn't write and I can't hear. Dropped out after two sessions and floated away. And I already speak with hands and I already hear with eyes. Halfway home. A deaf child thrusted into hearing. And I cannot catch your name and I cannot catch. I cannot hear and I cannot sign and so I read.

Growing up and growing home. And I cannot blame my mother that I am torn from the *mothertongue. And the mothertongue and the motherhand and the mothereye.* Tracing emotions with the arms and the hands and the fingers.

And I have lived an entire life in translation.

Amateur Linguistics

Lauren Poole

Words were my first love. Well, words, cutting and pasting, and a stuffed dog called Muffy. But it was words that hung around.

There is something magical about writing. It can be simultaneously meaningful and meaningless, priceless and useless, encompassing everything and literally nothing. For me, there is no greater magic than scribbled shapes on paper becoming new worlds, new people, new everything.

I process the world, myself, and my disability through words: linguistically, metaphorically, systematically and anecdotally. It is through language that I have understood the world and through language that the world understands me. Integrating new terms and phrases into my life feels like incorporating them into an ever-evolving personal dictionary. Albeit one heavy on medical jargon and historically inappropriate swearwords.

When I started to grapple with my emerging life with disability in very early adulthood, words were a comfort but also a nuisance. I had been thrust headlong into a new world that no one had given me a glossary for. There were so many new terms to decipher. But even though it felt like my brain had ceased to function, I could still recognise familiar symbols and syllables.

So I decided to take back the words for myself. Some were nonsensical, some jokes with friends, some lifted from the pages of medical journals. At one level, this was an attempt to regain control; if I could command language about myself, maybe I could command this uncontrollable life I'd been dealt. At another, it was the same process I'd always used: observe the world and myself and try to find words to make sense of it all.

*

***Ambisinistrous* (adj.) To be clumsy or unskilful with both hands. First documented use: 1863. Most recent documented use: yesterday, when I dropped my phone three times in a row.**

I confess, most people think I've made this word up. It sounds – quite frankly – like something designed to impress the reader, rather than a real term.

To be *ambidextrous* (perhaps a more familiar word) is to be good or skilful with both hands. It comes from Latin: *ambi* meaning 'both', and *dexter* meaning, variously, 'right', 'right-handed', 'skill-ful' or 'favourable'. You might have heard that musicians who can play with both hands are called 'ambidextrous' – they have two 'right' hands.

To be *ambisinistrous* is to have two 'bad' hands. In Latin *sinister* originally meant 'left' but evolved to also mean 'incorrect', 'unfavourable' or 'perverse'. To the Romans and Ancient Greeks, 'left' was unlucky; a bad omen. Right and left still have connotations of 'good' and 'bad' for us. When something is 'left behind' it is forgotten, neglected. When something goes 'the right way', it has gone well, or correctly.

I was never ambidextrous. I am naturally right-handed; the melody on a piano was always easier, the calluses from exams always on the right. But I am now ambisinistrous. Not in the overly technical meaning of the word, but in the sense that I possess two non-dominant hands.

Perhaps ambisinistrous is appropriate, because it suggests that my right hand became 'sinister'. That it followed the tradition of witches and demons and bad luck, and everything else that we have come to associate with the term 'sinister'. That it became, in essence, a second left hand. My right hand contained a self-destruct button, an abomination, a dizzying, ever-expanding mass of cells that threatened to take me down with it. It contained my cancer.

I had an incredibly rare, terribly aggressive and almost entirely resistant-to-treatment type of soft tissue cancer. Of all the places one might assume to find malignancy, the right thumb usually doesn't get a look in. But that was where it was for me. Given the options (rather, the complete lack of options), I agreed to amputate my right thumb to give myself the best chance of survival. I consented to removing the malignancy, to take away part of my body to keep the rest. And in removing this sinister lump, I also turned my right hand 'sinister'. I removed its dominance; removed the very thing that differentiates our species from animals: the opposable thumb. This part of me that was so historically and dexterously important became sinistrous.

Rationally, I know that my right hand is not bad luck. It is not an omen, or a foreshadowing. Yet I cannot look at it the same way anymore. I have a deep, abiding affection for my stump, for its scars and stitch marks, and at the same time it fills me with fear and trauma. It was a second puberty for my hand. I had grown used to it one way, and then it was changed, taken out of my control and returned to me permanently different. The juxtaposition of sinister and dexterous, the combination of known and unknown, the hand to which I had been accustomed replaced by an alien and immediate one.

I often joke that I'm ambisinistrous, usually when I've dropped something, or can't seem to grip an object quite right. It sounds like a throwaway punchline, but it isn't. I needed a new word to describe my new hand. One that fully encapsulated the joy and trauma wrapped up in scars and bandages. When I say I'm ambisinistrous, I'm upfront about what happened to me and how it shapes me now. Instead of a depressing case study, my hand is a curiosity. Rather than tragic, it is another tale for me to tell.

*

***Acquire* (v) To get or gain by effort, c1600**

***Acquired* (adj) Occurring after birth, thus not dependent on heredity, c1842**

I study museums. It's my degree, my vocation, my delight. The process of gaining – or, perhaps, possessing, stealing, taking – something of value and merit for a museum is called acquisition. In being acquired, an object is protected 'in perpetuity' (essentially, forever). When you acquire something, you are saying that it is special; that it is individually exemplary; that it specifically or generally has to be saved; that it tells a story that not only must be told but also recorded for all time. When museums acquire something, the act of acquisition itself can make the object more valuable.

For students of museums and heritage, there is an emphasis on realising how privileged we are to save things. I get to look at the history of everything and decide what is most important, what is most beautiful. When you're presented with literally everything, it's genuinely overwhelming. The scale of human history is so great as to be unfathomable. To acquire is always a privilege. You are now privy to an object's story, its many lives. To acquire something is seen as an honour.

But only in a museum.

I have one rather major acquisition of my own. My acquired brain injury. I was nineteen when it occurred, but as is often the case when one is young, no one spelled it out explicitly. I was 'ill', 'recovering', 'taking a break from university'. But 'ill' didn't cover it. It didn't cover the sudden removal of great swathes of my memory, it didn't cover the loss of walking, and it certainly didn't cover how I seemed to have totally missed six months of life and ended up in a brain and body that no longer obeyed me, and which I struggled to recognise.

I understood the enforced optimism in not 'naming the beast', as it were, but I didn't like it. Rather than transitioning through young adulthood at university, I spent my days in hospital, with medications rather than classmates as companions. No words were offered to describe just how soul-wrenching the change was. I desperately wanted a term that captured the severity of what I was experiencing.

It wasn't until one of my specialists had to fill in a particularly invasive form that I finally found a phrase that encapsulated it:

Acquired brain injury. ABI.

Finally, a way to explain what I knew the whole time: that I was manifestly totally changed. I clutched onto that phrase like a prize; it was the only key I had to understanding my new life and I wanted to ask everyone I met to acknowledge it. I needed something, anything, to explain this alien body. I wanted to build a new identity from it. I couldn't stand one more person telling me I wasn't different, that I was still the same as before. Because I wasn't.

The phrase 'aquired brain injury' was crucial for grasping that my life had irrevocably altered. That it wasn't going to go back to the old 'normal', and that I had to accept this. Rather than a label, it was a talisman, a way of marking this stark transition. Having been stripped of every other marker – student, writer, employee, friend, foe, person – here was finally a term for this new world.

Speaking about my brain injury – naming it – not only meant I could redescribe myself, it was also a signal to others. It demonstrated how massive and total this was, though understanding this took much longer for those around me. After the liminal limbo of 'ill' and 'recovering', 'brain injury' felt concrete. It acknowledged that there was no way back, no rescue available, and I could clutch this talisman on the way forward – wherever forward was.

*

Got the morbs **Temporary melancholy, c1880**

'The morbs' – as they are affectionately called in my house – come around quite a bit. Depression and anxiety are old friends of illness, so I have stopped being surprised by their frequent visits. Explaining my anxiety about my health is a little like walking through a minefield. I have quite a bit of it because, frankly, my health is difficult and confronting. Being fearful is entirely normal. To quote one of my favourite physicians: 'Your anxiety is exactly proportional to your illness. If you weren't anxious about all of this, then I'd be worried.'

I'm making light of 'the morbs' because most of us don't do it enough. Dark humour is ever-present in health communities, though; it's a coping strategy. If anyone tells you that you shouldn't joke about your conditions, they're wrong. I constantly joke about mine because otherwise I'd sink into a pit of pain and stress and never come out. And while the pit might be cool and damp now, within a few days I'll be trying to figure out how to make a ladder out of old tree roots. It's not a fun place.

The stigma of mental health and disability is so all-encompassing that attempting to find humour in it as a means of coping feels impossible. For a long time, I felt that the only way to talk about these massive issues in my life was to be totally serious, deadpan to camera. But a life without laughter is dull and boring. That's when the morbs sneak in.

If the Victorians had slang for episodic depression, then so can I. If calling it 'the morbs' makes it easier to get up in the mornings, that's fine. 'The morbs' sounds friendlier than depression or anxiety. Almost like a lady's companion rather than a clinician. Mental ill-health doesn't live in a hospital or a doctor's office; for many, it is present always.

It took me a long time to learn to treat my depression as a companion – rather than a visitor to be immediately escorted away. The constant suggestion that one should 'get better' – 'get better' control of anxiety, 'get better' and stronger physically, 'get better' from incurable conditions – infuriates me. This is my life, for better or worse, or even just for really boring days. Having 'the morbs' or 'that stroke-like migraine' or 'those joint dislocations' isn't my totality, but it is part of my reality.

*

Whoever said you had to 'name the beast to defeat it' was partly right. You need to name it to get a diagnosis and to have something to shout at during particularly tense moments. Give it a nickname, a title, maybe a nice accompanying mythology.

But defeating it was never the point. The aim was to live alongside it, and writing and talking about my disabilities has helped me do that. To figure out who I was – as a human being, as a disabled person, as a chronicler – I needed to give words to my experience. Did it change the visceral reality? Not particularly. The body I thought I had keeps changing underneath me, shifting what it can and cannot do; it seems reasonable that words can be just as malleable.

How else can I understand the world – and the world understand me – except through language?

E Is for Earwax

Khanh Nguyen

B is for baby (magical)

I'm back home in Brisbane, in a Vietnamese women's clothing shop, watching my mum and the shop owner – a woman I call 'Aunty Thanh' – ask a magical baby for a diagnosis. I had no idea there would be a magical baby here (had I known, I wouldn't be here). When I woke up this morning, Mum just asked, 'How about we have lunch in Darra, and then go to the shops afterwards?' It seemed harmless enough, but I always forget that Mum has a soft spot for the ol' bait and switch when she thinks she's doing things for my own good.

The magical baby is lying in one of those thingies that babies lie in: it looks like a cross between a picnic hamper and a baby's car seat. There's a soccer ball gaffer-taped to the handle of the crib (seriously!), so that the ball dangles just above the baby. Maybe to give the baby something to play with? I don't ask.

Aunty Thanh asks the baby, 'Will Khanh get better soon?' Before the baby has a chance to answer, Mum asks, 'It's not permanent, is it? Should Khanh stay here in Brisbane?'

A high school–aged girl and her mum, who aren't Vietnamese (they might be Greek?), have picked out a dress from Aunty Thanh's shop for the girl's Year 12 formal. It's shinier than I would've thought a formal dress would be. They're asking Aunty Thanh how much it costs, but Aunty Thanh ignores them completely. She's got more important things to do: she lifts magical baby Emily towards me, telling me to hold Emily's hands and saying something else in Vietnamese to do with healing that I don't quite understand.

Aunty Thanh and my mum, two grown women, are completely earnest in their belief that this adorable little baby can fix me.

About five minutes ago, when Aunty Thanh was answering the phone, I pulled Mum out of earshot and whispered, 'Uh, Mum, are we paying Aunty Thanh a lot of money for this?' and Mum was like, 'Darling, no! She's my friend! She's so concerned. She just wants to help you! You don't know how much all my friends pray for you! Hundreds of people would love to see Emily, but Co Thanh won't let just anyone bring all of their sickness near little Emily – what mother would?'

I was unconvinced.

'Darling, I promise you, we don't have to pay Co Thanh anything. If someone offered me a million dollars to bring unlucky energy near my baby, it wouldn't be enough. This is because Co Thanh cares for you! *Troi*, look at what Co gave me: it's precious!' Sure enough, Mum held up a beautiful little statue of the Buddha that Aunty Thanh has given us.

It's so important and real to them that I just go along with it all, even though I'm swimming inside, thinking, *What the fuck is going on here?*

I don't know why I'm here. I mean, I'm even sceptical of things like acupuncture. But when you get desperate enough, and I mean *really* desperate, you'll try anything.

Later, I'm recounting some of this to Janet, on the phone, and she's like, 'What? A *magical baby*? Are you serious?', and I say, 'Yeah, man, like how could I make this up?', to which she replies, 'Aw, I want a magical baby!' This strikes me as somewhat hilarious because before Mum took me to see Emily the magical baby, I would have sworn that Janet was the closest thing I'd ever met to a magical baby.

'So did the baby say you'll get better soon?' Janet asks.

'Dude, she was a baby,' I reply. 'She didn't say anything. I mean, she lay there and smiled and I sang "Twinkle Twinkle Little Star" to her, and then she got tired and her mum said she had to have a nap.'

'Aw, I *totally* want a magical baby!' Janet says.

Not being able to type C is for not being able to cry

From the beginning, it had always been a terrible thing, but I suppose no matter how badly I might've thought it affected my life, in actual fact, it had been manageable, at least to some degree. Then one morning, about five months ago, just as I was getting up, my dad calls through to my room to let me know that he's at the gate and could I please buzz him in. Dad and I were involved in an operation to move me out of here, and this was like day three of the campaign.

'Oh, hi, Dad, how are you? ... Yep, I'll be straight down.'

I look around for some shoes. I must've been so tired the night before that I just kicked them off somewhere ... There they are. I grab them, and go to untie the laces and – *oh fuck, I've been stabbed.*

It's blinding pain. Needles lodged deep in my fingers. The grogginess is falling away and I'm remembering dinner last night. Using chopsticks really hurt, and then even the fork I asked for was making the needles in my fingers grate against bone and tendon. I've had bad bullshit happen before – eye-watering, stabbing pain – but all I'd need to do was stop work, go home early, get a good night's sleep and by the next morning I'd feel okay. The sleep trick always worked. But this morning it hasn't worked. My hands might actually be worse than last night.

Okay, let's try the shoes in a gentle way, none of this brute-force business. Remember your condition and get around it.

No, my hands just won't work – there's no other way to explain it. They're malfunctioning. They're not my hands, they're only attached to my arms. I can't move them, and some batshit acupuncturist or Houdini motherfucker has pushed these needles so deep into them.

I look at my shoes and think, *I cannot foresee a time when I'll be able to undo those laces.* (Six months later, I'm writing this using voice recognition software, and I still cannot tie my own shoelaces, let alone *untie* them.)

It was never meant to come to this. The first time the pen fell from my hand while I was writing, what went through my mind was: *I am scared; I will never let it get to the point where I can do permanent damage to myself.* People would always say to me, 'Oh, yeah, a guy at my work can't type at all, he says his hands are just like jelly', and I would know that this was something to be taken seriously and that I would never let it get that bad. I run downstairs to let Dad in, for the first time seriously considering the possibility that this might be permanent, that this might be my new life.

We're back up in my room. I didn't say much at the gate or on our way up, other than that I had to tell him something. I don't know why, but it's really hard to explain – I can't just say 'My hands are gone' or 'It's all over now, Dad'. I sit there on the side of my bed, silent, every now and then opening and closing my mouth – a fish trying to breathe. Dad just waits for me to make my announcement. I end up rambling something about the last eighteen months, about progressively deteriorating plateaux, about how I know the feeling of transitioning to a new plateau, and I don't know if Dad's understanding, but he responds exactly the way I need: he steps forward and puts his arms around me. I'm still on the bed and my face is buried in his stomach – I'm too old to be doing this – and I'm shuddering and my whole body shakes and I realise I'm crying, or rather that I should be, but no tears are coming out and there's no relief. I push a little harder, but it's no use. Years ago, I must have unwittingly made the sort of trade that you normally require a devil to counter-sign: I got over Marissa, but in return I gave up the ability to cry.

*

Two weeks later, back at my parents' home in Brisbane, I get a handwritten letter from my little cousin, the one I call 'Little Bun'. I've told Little Bun never to write me handwritten letters, that if it can't be said via email or phone, perhaps it's not really something substantive enough to warrant communicating. Yeah, this anti-handwriting stance hasn't exactly made me popular with women or my writer friends, but sometimes we need to take a stand. My little cousin apologises for the handwritten letter, pointing out that I wouldn't be able to check my email. She's got a point. The letter is lovely, just the sort of thing I need to cheer me up. Enclosed is a photocopy of a high-school handout that says, 'Test Your Asia Knowledge!', which includes a map of what could well be Asia, but without any of the countries labelled (it has a handwritten Post-it note from Little Bun saying, 'Asia Knowledge!'), as well as a clipping from a Sydney newspaper of a musician I'm totally in love with, a lovely young woman named Bree, looking scared by the prospect of being photographed but still lovely nonetheless. And in the letter, my cousin mentions a piece of advice: she says I should cry. Apparently, when Little Bun was a kid, she was travelling on a plane and she felt really sick and vomited, and her mum (my Aunty Thu) told her she should try to cry. She did and it made her feel better, and she was saying that I should try that too.

On the phone, after getting the letter, I made fun of Little Bun – it's my way – saying things like, 'Oh yeah, that's some great advice, junior. Like, I'm crippled, and your advice is to cry more? Great stuff.'

But she was right, and we both knew it. I just couldn't. I made some excuse like, 'Dude, it's not that easy in Boyland; we can't just cry when we want to.' And she said, 'Boyland's so crap. Seriously, Khanh, Boyland sucks.'

D is for depression

I wrote the D entry, but I'm leaving it out. It's too much.

E is for earwax

'Mum, would you mind helping me clean my ears, please?'

Mum gets up, reluctantly. She's walking over to the drawer where we keep the cotton buds.

'Just let me ask you this, ear man: in a day, how many times do you clean your ears?'

I'm scampering along behind her, pointing my insanely itchy ear towards her and stooping a little so that my ear is at her eye level, looking more like Igor than I deserve.

Just as Mum is poised to insert the cotton bud and provide me with sweet relief, she says, 'No wonder you have to clean your ears so often – your ear canal is frightfully huge! That's why your hearing is so sharp! Who ever heard of such a huge ear canal?!'

Mum has been cleaning my ears every other day for the last five months. I alternate between asking Mum and Dad. (Will's ear-cleaning manner, while effective, is far too aggressive for me. I'm serious, if you ever watch him clean his own ears, all you see is clenched teeth and wincing. I once saw him pull a bloody cotton bud out of his ear. Even he was freaked out.) But whenever my mum does it, the width of my apparently freakish ear canals is a revelation to her. Even now, she frequently calls Dad or Will over, just to witness, to confirm she's not dreaming.

'It's because we cleaned your ears so often when you were little, that's why they're so big. We really shouldn't have cleaned them so often.'

Mum says this nearly every time. I used to laugh or protest, but Mum is adamant (like *really* adamant) that I have no idea how supple and suggestible our bodies are when we are young. To be fair, it's true. I used to have really avant garde–looking teeth when my adult teeth first came through, and I don't think we had money for braces. Mum just kept telling me how to press on my teeth with my fingers and told me to do it whenever I was watching TV, and, as crazy as it sounds, it actually worked.

When I was a kid, I wouldn't go to bed until Dad had cleaned my ears, put eye drops in my eyes and nose drops in my nose. I don't know what the fuck was wrong with me – I think I must have needed eye drops once, and then maybe the next night, when I wasn't given eye drops at bedtime, I thought I was getting ripped off. Apparently if Dad forgot even one of those three things, I'd come down a half-hour after I'd been put to bed, saying, 'I can't sleep, my ears are itchy'. We like to laugh about how one time I had a babysitter, and he must not have known about the nose drops, so after he'd put me to bed, down the stairs comes this little toddler dude telling him, 'I can't breathe! I can't breathe!' The babysitter freaked the fuck out, thinking this kid was going to die on his watch. I guess in hindsight it's not really that funny from his perspective.

Mum's finished cleaning both my ears now, and she's just about to throw the cotton bud into the —

'Wait! Mum! Was there much?'

Mum gives me the sort of look that says, 'Who are you kidding?' She rotates the bud between her thumb and forefinger, showing me its virginal whiteness. She stares at me, waiting for my reaction.

'There's quite a bit …' I say.

'Darling, there's nothing!'

'Mum, are you serious? It's so yellow! Look at it! I could use it as a highlighter!'

Mum ignores me, and just throws it in the bin.

'You know, Mum, of the various varieties of earwax, it's actually the *clear* earwax that is the most toxic.'

Mum is patient with me. She shakes her head and mutters, 'I can't believe the heavens gave birth to such an ear man.'

F is for fourth of July

I'm at the airport baggage carousel. I don't know any of these people, and I'm becoming a little distressed. I'm thinking about walking up to a stranger and asking them to buy me a bottle of water and to please hold it to my lips, but I'm inhibited and helpless. About thirty minutes into the flight, I was already parched but couldn't do anything about it, and now it's becoming unbearable.

Ah, here comes my suitcase, but there's no way I can pick it up, so I just watch it slowly disappear again. Mum and Will were supposed to be here. Dad took me to the airport at the departure end, bought me a coffee and helped me drink it; he made sure I didn't need to urinate, waited with me, telling me everything was going to be fine and that he and my aunts (my awesome aunts who came from another city just to help me pack; Mum would have come and helped too but she had to teach) would finish packing up my belongings and that, given this unforeseen turn of events (twelve hours ago I woke up to find that I could not untie my shoelaces), it was best for me to go back home to Brisbane, where Mum could look after me, while they got on with the job. Then, when the time came, he explained to the flight attendant about my hands, and said that Mum and Will would be at the other end, waiting for me. I kept thanking him and asking him to let my aunts know how much I appreciated this, and that I love them.

I can't remember the exact order in which I lost the ability to work out at the gym, play tennis, play guitar, type for more than half an hour at a stretch (and then even less), carry groceries or chop vegetables, but here's something I do know: in my two years of dealing with this, I've never yet regained any ability that I've lost. Now I can't even use a fork to feed myself. I'm so goddamn scared, and I keep telling myself that one day I'll look back and this will all just be a motivational anecdote that I tell my kids about never losing hope. If this is the rest of my life—

It's down to just the stragglers here in the baggage-claim area. I'm watching my suitcase do laps of the carousel, looking around for Mum and Will, and it's making me nervous. They're going to impound my luggage if I don't collect it soon, and I need that stuff. I'm going to have to ask that friendly-looking ocker guy over there to help me with my suitcase before everyone is gone, but in this post–September 11 world, it looks a bit suss if a complete stranger at the airport asks you to pick up their suitcase. Anyway, I'd probably rather ask him to help me get some water.

*

It's half an hour later. We're going home from the airport. Will is driving, I'm in the passenger seat (it's easier for Will to do up my seatbelt that way) and Mum is in the back. It's about nine o'clock at night, Brisbane time, and Mum is asking me if I've eaten yet.

'No, I'm starving, I was hoping we could stop at Subway if that's okay,' I say.

'Or I could make you *chao*. I know how much you love *chao*,' she says.

'No, Mum, I wouldn't be able to eat that. I can't use a spoon, Mum. I need really big food, stuff that's super easy to manipulate.'

This is the first day. I still think I can feed myself.

'Well, I could still make you a lovely bowl of *chao* with *gia* and tofu just like you like it. You could drink it through a straw! You love—'

'Mum! I don't want any *chao*!'

'Just letting you know that would be so easy to make *chao* for you.'

I explode. My face is so hot, I am enraged, and I'm yelling.

'Mum! I don't give a fuck about your fucking *chao*! I'm fucking crippled! This could be the rest of my life! Can you understand that? I've got so many goddamn things to deal with. Things are hard enough for me already. If you can't make things easier for me, at the very least could you stop making things harder for me? Do you know how much effort it's taking just to explain so I can get some food? I—'

'Darling, I was just saying—'

'Okay, you want to make fucking *chao*, then fucking make it and eat it yourself. If I have to go hungry, that's fine. As long as you get to cook the foods that make you happy, the ones that make you think you're feeding me, who gives a shit about listening to your son who is so fucking hungry and has run the fuck out of ways to try to explain it to you.'

Now I just roar pure vowel with everything I've got. I'm tearing my throat to shreds. I feel the damage to my vocal cords and the pain that I'm inflicting back on the world that won't stop hurting me. I am that beast in the cage that those motherfuckers keep prodding with sticks until, one day, the beast has had enough and it smashes itself against the bars again and again, spraying everyone with its blood, not caring if it has to die, just as long as the prodding stops. The whole car shudders. I run out of air, take another deep breath, but I'm spent.

Really, it's not an unreasonable thing that I'm asking for: a sandwich. With all that has gone on today, I haven't had a chance to really eat. Just this morning I found out that I might be crippled for life, and it's a lot to deal with. I'm basically in shock. I don't have the mental energy to quibble with my Mum, in the hope that I can explain to her that I'm starving. Considering what I've been through, a sandwich really isn't that much to ask.

The car is dead silent. Apart from some really annoying bullshit on Triple Z. No one says anything. Whenever I come back from Canberra, Will and I have so much to tell each other that Mum and Dad are always scared that we'll crash the car on the way back from the airport. But since I yelled at Mum, no one has said a word. It is so quiet for so long. I feel bad that Will had to witness that.

'You must be like, *What the fuck happened to my brother, man?*' I say to him. '*Where did this angry dude come from?* Sorry, dude, I totally forgot to tell you. You know that scene in *Born on the Fourth of July*? Where Tom Cruise flips out at his family and pulls those tubes out of his pants? Yeah, I'm auditioning for that role at this local theatre production back in Canberra. I just thought I should practice.'

This is Will's cue to laugh, to say something funny, to implicitly say 'Yeah, Mum's not great in emergency situations, but she loves you, remember that', but he doesn't say anything to me at all, he just looks straight ahead and keeps driving in silence for another ten minutes, then we pull in at a Subway.

Drawing My Way

Sarah Firth

CLICK
CLICK
BAM
BAM
And BEING CONFINED TO the GRID of LITTLE TABLES and CHAIRS just INCREASED my RESTLESSNESS.
tap
tap
tap
STOP IT.
SARAH! WHAT did I JUST SAY?
I CAN'T REMEMBER.

PRIOR TO SCHOOL my BEHAVIOUR was FRAMED as...

SHE'S JUST a BIT OVERSTIMULATED.
MAKE IT STOP.
IT IS SCARING ME.
SHE'S JUST a BIT SENSITIVE.
HONK HONK.
BEEP
BEEP
IT IS TOO LOUD!
MAKE IT STOP!
SHE'S JUST a BIT IMPULSIVE.
SHE'S JUST a BIT EXCITABLE.
SARAH GET DOWN from THERE

IT WAS CHALLENGING. OUT of NECESSITY MUM TRIED *different* APPROACHES to CALM ME...

SEE! YOU CAN DANCE the PEN.

I FELL in LOVE with DRAWING and DOODLING.

MUM LOVINGLY QUILTED JACKETS to HOLD STATIONERY, A TOOLKIT TO TAKE EVERYWHERE.

This book belongs to ZARAH

GLUE

STAY STILL KITTY. I am DRAWING YOU!

WITHOUT my Book I STILL DREW SO I COULD SIT STILL.

BUT MY TEACHER DIDN'T UNDERSTAND.

WITHOUT a way TO ANCHOR my ENERGY, it SPILLED out in DISRUPTIVE WAYS.

I WAS REGULARLY REPRIMANDED *for* MY DISRUPTIVE BEHAVIOUR. I *felt* CONFUSED. WHY WAS I NOT LIKE THE OTHER KIDS?

THIS FEELING of BEING "DIFFERENT" GREW AS I STRUGGLED with WRITING and ARITHMETIC
Sally and her dog go for a walk
JUNIOR READER
MONDAY
UH SO THE GIRL WENT TO UH GET A STICK FOR THE DOG?
JUNIOR READER
SARAH, YOU NEED TO READ the WORDS. DON'T JUST DESCRIBE THE PICTURE.
TUESDAY
BREAD PLEASE!
PLAY SHOPPE
$1
HERE YOU GO.
50¢
NO. THAT'S NOT ENOUGH MONEY.
BUT 50 is BIGGER than 1!
HA HA. NO IT'S NOT
YOU'RE SO STUPID.

WEDNESDAY
GOOD JANE. 12:30 IS RIGHT
NOW, SARAH WHAT TIME IS THIS?
IT'S UMM
UM I NEED TO GO TO THE TOILET.
TELL THE TIME FIRST. THEN YOU CAN GO.
I CAN'T! IT'S A TOILET EMERGENCY!
THURSDAY
6x1 = 6
6x2 = 12
6x3 = 18
6x4 = 24
6x5 = 30
6x6 = 36
6x7 = 42
6x8 = 48
6x9 = 54
6x10 = 60
7x1 = 7
7x2 = 14
GOOD. YES
NOW WHAT IS 7x3?
= 7
= 14
SARAH. 7x3 IS?
I'M SO DIZZY! I THINK I'M GOING TO VOMIT! MY TUMMY HURTS.
I NEED TO GO TO THE NURSE!

FRIDAY
NO SOONER ARE YOU DOWN THE ROAD THAN GOLDILOCKS THAT LITTLE TOAD...
MUM...
ROALD DAHL
REVOLTING RHYMES
??
?
AM I STUPID?
ROALD DAHL
REVOLTING RHYMES
WHAT MAKES you ASK?
UH
OH UH NOTHING...
IS THIS BECAUSE YOU'VE BEEN GETTING in TROUBLE IN CLASS?
I don't MEAN To! MRS. HAY TOOK AWAY my BOOK! AND IF I DOODLE she gets ANGRY!

!!!
OH! I SEE.
ehh heee
ehhh
SARAH, YOU'RE NOT STUPID. YOU'RE JUST DIFFERENT.
DON'T WORRY. I HAVE an IDEA.
MONDAY
???
THIS IS FOR YOU.
Dear Mrs Hay,
Please let Sarah draw in class. It helps her to sit still, listen and focus.
Dianne Firth

FINALLY I COULD DOODLE FREELY!

I WAS ABLE TO FOCUS MY ENERGY and LISTEN.

AND OTHER KIDS LIKED MY DRAWINGS, which BOOSTED MY CONFIDENCE and COURAGE.

VISUALISING HELPED ME START TO UNDERSTAND NUMBERS MORE.

SLOWLY I GOT BETTER AT DRAWING WORDS and WRITING PICTURES.

AND OVER THE YEARS I DEVELOPED VISUAL STUDY SKILLS and MNEMONICS TO HELP MYSELF.

DESPITE my WRITING, READING and ARITHMETIC STILL being WEAK, I DID BETTER than EXPECTED at SCHOOL.

COLOURFUL VISUAL NOTES WERE MY STRENGTH.

AND ALMOST a DECADE AFTER FINISHING SCHOOL, THIS SKILL LED ME TO WORK AS A GRAPHIC RECORDER.

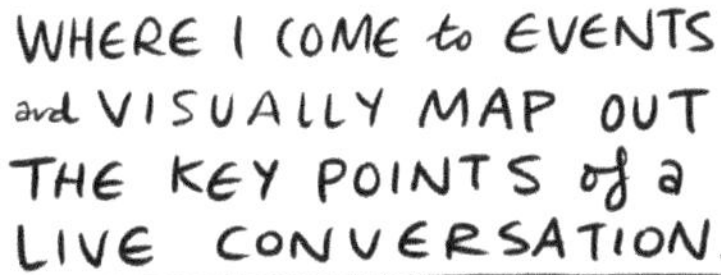

WHERE I COME to EVENTS and VISUALLY MAP OUT THE KEY POINTS of a LIVE CONVERSATION.

TO HELP MAKE DISCUSSION TANGIBLE and SHAREABLE.

STILL, I OFTEN JUMBLE UP LETTERS and SPELL THINGS WRONG.

MAKING MISTAKES in FRONT of GROUPS WAS VERY STRESSFUL, and I OFTEN FELT ASHAMED. SO I TRIED TO DEVELOP SOME WORK AROUNDS:

I WAS SO WORRIED THAT IF A CLIENT DISCOVERED I STRUGGLE with READING and WRITING, THEY JUST WOULDN'T HIRE ME.

AFTER a few YEARS OF TRYING SO HARD, I WAS EXHAUSTED.

UNSURE of WHAT TO DO I FINALLY SOUGHT OUT PROFESSIONAL HELP.

I'M SO BURNED OUT AND OVERWHELMED JUST TRYING TO BE A "NORMAL" ADULT.

I'M NOT COPING.

WE TALKED THROUGH CURRENT and PAST BEHAVIOURAL ISSUES.

AND I OPENED UP ABOUT MY CHALLENGES with READING and WRITING.

YOUR MOTHER CLEARLY HELPED YOU SO MUCH.

HI MUM. DO YOU HAVE a minute?
SURE!
SO MY PSYCH SAID IT LOOKS LIKE I HAVE DYSLEXIA AND DYSCALCULIA CLUSTERED WITH ADHD and AUTISM SPECTRUM SENSITIVITIES. IT MAKES SENSE!
OH, I'M NOT SURE WHAT THAT all MEANS?
I'LL NEED TO LOOK THAT UP!
I'M LEARNING TOO. DON'T WORRY. BUT, I AM CURIOUS, WHY DIDN'T YOU TAKE me TO GET HELP when I WAS STRUGGLING EARLY ON?
WELL... I ALWAYS KNEW YOU were DIFFERENT.
BUT BACK THEN I DIDN'T KNOW ABOUT THESE THINGS.
AND THE LAST THING I WANTED TO DO WAS MAKE YOU FEEL LIKE SOMETHING WAS WRONG.
I SAW HOW HARD THINGS WERE for YOU.
I DIDN'T want TO LIMIT YOU, PATHOLOGISE, or PUT YOU IN A BOX.
BUT... IF I HAD BEEN DIAGNOSED EARLIER maybe THINGS COULD HAVE BEEN A BIT EASIER?

MAYBE.
I'M SORRY IF I DIDN'T DO THE RIGHT THING by YOU.
NO! NO. MUM YOU DID SO MUCH and HELPED me FIND my WAY.
IT'S JUST THAT GETTING THIS PROFESSIONAL HELP NOW IS SO USEFUL!
IT'S LIKE I'M finally CONNECTING THE DOTS. I CAN SEE WHAT'S GOING ON and WHY. AND HOW TO BETTER SUPPORT MYSELF. IT'S BEEN REALLY EMPOWERING.
KNOWING I AM NEURODIVERGENT GIVES me A CONTEXT. I FEEL LIKE I DON'T HAVE TO HIDE OR PRETEND.
WELL, I'M GLAD YOU HAVE SOME CLARITY and I HOPE IT MAKES THINGS EASIER.
THANKS MUM.

SLOWLY, I'VE WORKED UP THE COURAGE TO OWN my DIFFERENCE at WORK.

UNEXPECTEDLY, DOING this HAS MEANT THAT CLIENTS and PARTICIPANTS engage MORE CLOSELY with MY WORK.

LOTS of PEOPLE ENJOY THE TASK of HELPING and FEELING INVOLVED.

BEING UPFRONT about HAVING DYSLEXIA feels LIBERATING.

AND GIVES OTHERS the PERMISSION TO BE OPEN ABOUT IT TOO.

Who Counts as Disabled Anyway?

Astrid Edwards

Let me give you the short list of what can go wrong with my body.

In 2013, in Melbourne, I lost feeling in most of my body, from the soles of my feet to just below my breasts.

In 2014, in Berlin, I almost drowned in a hot bath when my body, no longer able to regulate temperature, shut down. I remember stumbling out of the bath and nothing more until I woke up on the couch. My partner had spent hours wetting towels, cooling them in the fridge and covering me with them, trying to wake me up and wondering whether to call a German ambulance.

In 2015, in Sydney, I had a tonic seizure, a brief but intense fit in which the muscles suddenly stiffen. I woke up beneath my niece's high chair to see her peering down at me with a quizzical expression. I often wonder if she thought it was a game, and if she will remember it when she is older.

In 2016, in an airport, I found myself unable to remember how to get to the gate for my flight. I sat, ticket in hand, and waited for my brain to start working again. I missed my flight. I was too scared to ask for help, because cognitive disfunction (or cog fog, as I like to think of it) can look like intoxication. I didn't want to be mistaken as drunk – a conclusion commonly drawn about people with my disease when they are experiencing this intense brain fog.

In 2017, there were days I didn't leave home. My proprioception (my perception of the position and movement of my body) was off. I couldn't tell where my limbs were in relation to the rest of me. Moving objects – including other people – were terrifying. I found myself holding my arms to remind me where they were, and scratching myself until I bled to check I still had feeling.

In 2018, in the middle of a remedial massage for neuropathic pain relief, I had a paroxysmal tonic spasm – a fancy way of saying my hands, forearms, neck, mouth and tongue locked. I could not communicate. I could not form words; I could not gesture. I was semi-naked and fully conscious on a table, trapped in my own mind. If I didn't already identify as a person with a disability, I did from that moment onwards.

And these are just the annual highlights.

As I write this in 2019, I don't know what will happen to me next. A few weeks ago I walked face-first into a lift door because I couldn't get the timing right to enter it, and yesterday I stabbed myself in the nose with a mascara wand as I tried to put makeup on.

Multiple sclerosis, or MS, is a degenerative neurological disease of the central nervous system. Essentially, my body attacks itself, destroying the fatty layer – the myelin – around my brain, spinal cord and optic nerve. Imagine a phone charger, the rubber casing worn away to reveal the frayed wires within, and you'll see the problem. My body is unreliable and my nerves don't work. But, aside from ageing, I look the same as I did back in 2013, when I was diagnosed.

I don't look sick, but I am.

Not looking sick is a problem. It means people sometimes don't believe me about my illness, and they certainly don't offer to help me. Not looking sick makes it harder to describe to others what is going wrong with my body or to explain why I can't do something that most people can, or why I can do it sometimes and not others. It means people don't vacate a seat for me on public transport, and I often get off trams before my stop to avoid passing out. And those 'healthy' walking meetings at work? They are a nightmare.

At the same time, the fact that I look healthy means I can pass for someone who doesn't have a disability. There is an inherent privilege to this. Disability and disease both still come with stigmas, and I am spared much of that due to my appearance. This is not uncommon in the MS community: some people's symptoms are invisible, while others are visible. People with observable indications of MS definitely experience more discrimination than I do, as do many with other forms of visible disability, disease-related or otherwise.

As MS is progressive, the list of my symptoms will only grow as my disease advances. In a room of people, I often find myself musing that I am likely the 'sickest' person there, though no one would know this just by looking. When I was diagnosed, I was told I had a degenerative disease for which there is no known cause and no known cure. I was also told – and I kid you not, this was the line – that there was good news and bad news. The good news was that MS would not kill me; the bad news was that MS would not kill me.

The prognosis for me is much better than it would have been for someone in my position twenty, or even ten, years ago. Still, although the available therapies are improving at a rapid rate, MS is expensive to manage. When I am receiving my six-monthly infusion, at more than $35,000 a pop, the nurses check my identity every hour. They want to make sure I am who I say I am – and fair enough, too. These infusions are covered under the Pharmaceutical Benefits Scheme.

It took a while, but I have grown to accept a label. I am a person with a disability. I have a lifelong disease that will likely worsen. I will accrue disability over the course of my life. I will have visible symptoms one day. I may need mobility aids, either consistently or intermittently.

That message took years – and more neuropathic pain and public embarrassment than I expected – to sink in. But eventually the penny dropped. I have a disability.

That protracted reluctance to acknowledge my disability is funny when I think about it, because every time I see my neurologist (at best every six months, although often much more frequently) we discuss the Expanded Disability Status Scale, looking at where to place me, based on my symptoms, on a chart ranging from one to ten. The EDSS is a method of quantifying disability in MS and monitoring changes in the level of disability over time. There is nothing I or current medical science will ever be able to do to get me off the damn thing.

I am about a 1.5 as I write this. During an MS relapse – I have relapsing remitting multiple sclerosis, which means my MS symptoms flare and slowly recede – I have been as high as 4. But where I am officially on the scale is determined by my neurologist. It is not a one-way progression – I will go up and down as my MS peaks and troughs. This uncertainty is one of the reasons MS is so misunderstood. Having MS means a life lived in the unknown.

The problem is, not everyone thinks I have a disability. Or thinks I have the right to say that I identify as a person with a disability. I feel welcome in the MS community, but I have not always felt welcomed in the disability community. This was my motivation to contribute to this anthology. I'm writing because I fear that people like me will not be represented otherwise. But I am hesitant. What right do I have to assert that I have a disability, when others like me, who do not have a visible disability or who choose not to talk publicly about their invisible disability – decide not to identify this way?

My body went haywire as an adult, so I remember what it was like to trust my limbs and senses. Unlike someone born with a disability or who acquires a disability, I once had an identity that didn't involve chronic illness or disability, and I have had to grow as a person to include this new part of me.

I once had an identity that was trusted in the workplace. After my diagnosis, I spent two years unemployed, underemployed and working for free because no one wanted to employ such a sick-leave risk.

MS is not well understood. The stigma is profound. Reveal you have cancer and someone will give you a hug, buy you flowers and maybe even wear a pin in support or throw you a morning tea. Reveal you have MS and people avoid eye contact. Once, the person I told backed away slowly, as though it was contagious.

My condition is chronic. I would take a cure if there was one. But not only is there no cure for MS, there is disagreement over what would even constitute a cure. A vaccine, so no one in future gets MS? That doesn't help those of us who have it. A treatment that halts progression but leaves the damage? That wouldn't prevent the disease, nor would it fix the symptoms those of us with MS already have. The holy grail is remyelination, which would repair the lesions in our brains. Imagine that frayed phone charger again, and how much better it would work if the rubber coating was still in place and the wires intact. Maybe that will be possible in my lifetime. Maybe it won't.

*

There aren't many Australian role models for people with MS. The late Chrissy Amphlett spoke more about her breast cancer than her MS. Olympian Betty Cuthbert was also relatively private about her experience with MS. It is worth noting that both women were diagnosed years (and in Betty's case, decades) before the latest generation of MS therapies. They did name a rose after Betty, though, and my father dutifully grows one in her honour.

Since my diagnosis I've been looking for a role model. In late 2018 Selma Blair made her MS diagnosis public. She has received (mainly) positive media attention, and I am grateful for this. Representation matters. Even if this representation is limited (Selma is a beautiful, wealthy white woman, and I have no doubt this helps her avoid the stigma and engage others with the disease in a way they may normally not), it is a start. But I do wonder how the media coverage of Selma Blair may alter if her visible symptoms improve for a time, which is very common in MS. Will entertainment reporters understand, or will they think she was faking, hamming it up? Will they ignore her advocacy if she appears 'healthier' for a while?

I've always wanted Joan Didion as my MS role model. But America's greatest living essayist wrote two paragraphs about her diagnosis in 1979's *The White Album* and has revealed almost nothing since, despite writing about the most intimate of topics: her grief over the deaths of her husband and her daughter. Didion has revealed her emotional pain to the world, but not her MS. I often wonder why.

Many times I've watched the video of Joan Didion receiving the 2012 National Medal of the Arts from President Obama. Always diminutive, in this clip she looks incredibly frail and small. After a military chaperone helps her to the stage, Obama has to prop her up. Is that age or MS? Is that what I will be like one day? Is that why I never see people who have had MS for a long time in public?

I've been a National Advocate for MS Australia since 2015, and people with the disease have started to confide in me. MS is more common than you think. A surprising number of people have MS but don't talk about it openly. They – or their partner – will whisper about it to me. Many of this number don't look ill. Those who do often choose to disappear from public view. I know of one lauded individual who has detailed their lived experience with another disease (one of those ones you get a morning tea for), but not their MS. Their MS is visible; they live with visible symptoms. But they let people think those symptoms are due to the other disease they have.

People don't admit they have MS because of the consequences – the stigma, the fear, the lack of understanding.

I am still learning about my body and about this disease. And about how I fit – and do not fit – with society's expectations. I am privileged. I am Anglo, cisgender, heterosexual and highly educated. And I don't look ill, yet. But my central nervous system does not work properly. It misfires and causes different parts of my body to fail, and the damage it wreaks will likely worsen for the rest of my life.

MS is painful. The pain can be incapacitating. At its worst, I have lost time to the pain, blinded by the agony of misfiring nerves and unable to find a way back to myself.

Sometimes I feel like a healthy person with a chronic disease. More often I feel a stranger to my own flesh, tethered to this body I once trusted but now would rather trade in. I compare it to a used car: looks fine, but you wouldn't want to get behind the wheel. Some parts are broken, and others are likely to fail.

I broke my toe a few months ago because I experienced drop foot and couldn't control my gait. My left arm stopped working for a few hours this week, and for want of a better idea I wore a coat inside so I could carry my hand around in a pocket. No one noticed, as I didn't look sick. But I am. Which brings me back to my question. Do I belong in this anthology?

Curve

Jessica Walton

They say I'm too fat to run.
You should've seen me just after chemo:
all skin and bone,
small and pale and bald,
angles and shadows and scars.
Now my hair has grown back,
and I'm curved in places I never was before.
I'm well again,
but I've done it wrong.
You're not supposed to get *fat* after cancer.
Lose some weight, they say.
We'll give you a golden leg, a speedy blade.
I never lose it. I can't.
Instead, the fat grows and grows,
and every time I see them the shame grows, too.
My mouth shuts tight.
I don't ask again, knowing what the answer will be.
I am a child,
even years after I'm not.
I am a bad body, and I will never run again.
Sometimes I wake from sleep, face wet.
The wind in my thick brown hair,
the air in my lungs,
a smile on my face,
and both feet pounding the ground.
I wish it would fade away to nothing
and leave me alone,

but it visits me over and over,
over the years.
My painful old friend; my memory, my dream.
Until suddenly … it's gone.
The absence of it is an ache, deep and long.
Something grows slowly
in that ache:
an anger that opens my mouth.

I tell this story and find someone new.
She makes me a curve like a question mark,
only it's an answer instead.
You are not too fat. You were *never* too fat.
She takes me to a car park: RUN!
I run.
My fat, disabled body carries me forward;
strong curved legs, flesh and metal, pound the asphalt –
more real than any long-lost dream.
This gloriously bad body is what's real, and I am all in.
I'm practising being proud, like Laura told me.
The wheels I get are real, too:
Fat and fierce and fast.
The wind greets my face joyfully, daring me.
I'll race you! I shout,
and my children shriek with laughter as we speed across
the grass.

Notes on Contributors

Editor

Carly Findlay OAM is a writer, speaker and appearance activist. She is the author of memoir *Say Hello* and has been published in the ABC, *The Guardian*, *The Age*, *The Sydney Morning Herald*, *CNN* and *Vogue*.

Contributors

Alistair Baldwin is a writer and comedian based in Naarm/ Melbourne. He's written for *The Weekly with Charlie Pickering*, *Hard Quiz* and *Get Krack!n*, developed a play – *Lame* – for MTC First Stage, was a Wheeler Centre Hot Desk Fellow and has been published in *ACMI Ideas*, *un. Magazine*, *Art + Australia*, *Archer* and more.

K.Z. Barton is a Melbourne-based writer and primary school teacher. She studied creative writing at the University of Melbourne. While studying, she reviewed YA novels for the university's *Viewpoint* magazine. She's currently raising her one-year-old son, writing her first novel, and learning how to thrive while living with chronic illness.

Dion Beasley lives in Tennant Creek and is well known across the Territory as the artist behind the much loved t-shirt brand Cheeky Dogs. Dion has muscular dystrophy and is profoundly deaf. In 2019 he received the Australia Council National Arts and Disability Award for an Emerging Artist. He writes with the help of Johanna Bell.

Working with Dion has changed the way Johanna sees the world and tells stories. Johanna and Dion's books include *Too Many Cheeky Dogs* and the CBCA Book of the Year *Go Home Cheeky Animals.*

Marla Bishop is a poet and LGBTQIA+ portrait photographer from Perth. They were officially diagnosed in 2017 with fibromyalgia, a chronic pain condition that causes muscle aches and stiffness, brain fog and chronic fatigue. Marla's artistic emphasis is based on empowerment, and giving a voice to those in marginalised communities.

Chantel Bongiovanni is a writer and woman with disability. She is currently completing her PhD in the area of disability and policy, seeking to understand how people with disability experience policies relating to inclusion. She also writes about disability-related issues on her blog, *Cee's Thinking Space*.

Ricky Buchanan is passionate about disability and chronic illness and thinks and writes a lot about homebound/bedridden people and assistive technology. When Ricky's not designing new assistive technology for herself, she uses her computer to draw, listens to audio books, and takes photos of her cat.

Lucy Carpenter is an aspiring writer who has just completed her secondary education and hopes to continue her studies and work in the media industry.

Emma Di Bernardo is a bespectacled writer and speaker from Queensland. She is a women's rights, LGBTIQ+ and disability advocate. Emma's non-fiction work has been featured in *The Undergraduate Journal of Whedon Studies*, *Disability in Kidlit* and *One Woman Project*.

Belinda Downes is a language scientist and linguistics teacher who can be found via a quick internet search for 'Coffee with Belinda Downes' and occasionally on radio and television. She will never have too many Moleskine notebooks. Belinda is also the proud owner of a≈rare 1971 model Bilateral Tessier Cleft.

Sam Drummond is a lawyer and disability advocate. He has worked in community, commercial and public broadcasting, and written extensively on disability rights. Sam lives in Melbourne's north with his partner and child. He can often be found swimming laps of Fitzroy pool. His family hopes to get a dog soon.

Kath Duncan is a multimedia producer, performer and writer, a lover and a fighter, with a background in electronic journalism. Kath co-founded *Quippings: Disability Unleashed*, Australia's first all-disabled queer cabaret spoken-word troupe. Kath holds degrees from UTS, AFTRS and SCU and believes in lifelong learning.

Robin M. Eames is a queercrip poet and historian living on Gadigal land. Their work has been published in *Cordite*, *Overland*, *Meanjin*, *Lilith* and *The Deaf Poets Society*, among others. They are currently working on a PhD at the University of Sydney, examining trans pathologisation and histories of madness.

Astrid Edwards coordinates the Associate Degree of Professional Writing and Editing at RMIT University, serves on the board of Melbourne Writers Festival and hosts *The Garret: Writers on Writing*. She is a member of the Victorian Disability Advisory Council and a national advocate for MS Australia.

Yvonne Fein holds an MA in History (Monash University) and Diploma of Creative Writing (Prahran College). She has written three novels (*April Fool*, *The Torn Messiah*, *Rachel Running Time*) and a short-story collection (*Choose Somebody Else*). She has written for theatre and the screen. She conducted creative writing workshops for people with mental illness and advocates for those with mental and physical disability by performing stand-up to raise public awareness.

Sarah Firth is a comic artist, writer, graphic recorder and animator based in Melbourne. Recently she received a *Frankie* Magazine Good Stuff Award, was a finalist in the Incinerator Social Change Art Award, and her graphic essay on complexity was listed in *The Conversation*'s ten best literary comics in Australia. She has a fat stack of self-published comics and pieces in upcoming anthologies with Abrams Books,

Picador and Allen & Unwin. She is currently working on her debut graphic novel thanks to the Creators Fund program.

El Gibbs is an award-winning writer with a focus on disability and social issues. Her work has been published by the ABC, *The Guardian*, *Eureka Street*, *Croakey*, *The Sydney Morning Herald* and many more. El has an unhealthy interest in Senate Estimates and spends far too much time on Twitter.

Patrick Gunasekera is a queercrip Sinhala interdisciplinary artist who lives, works and plays on the Whadjuk region of the Noongar nation, disrupting white and settler epistemologies of art through writing, photography, visual arts, live art, theatre, and advocacy. He has been published in *Voiceworks*, *Australian Poetry Journal*, *Seesaw*, *Pelican* and the Centre For Stories's anthology *Wave After Wave*.

Fran Henke of Hastings, Victoria, is a retired journalist, now writer, artist and photographer. She was a media adviser for state and federal politicians, and a member of the Commonwealth Film Censorship Board. As Frances Kelly she wrote many books on gardening, then on polio issues, and three historical novels.

Isis Holt is a Paralympic athlete competing in T35 sprint events. She was born with cerebral palsy. She won gold medals in the 100 metres and 200 metres at the 2015 and 2017 World Para Athletics Championships. At the 2016 Rio Paralympics, she won two silver medals and a bronze medal.

Eliza Hull is a writer, audio producer and musician based in Castlemaine, Victoria. She produced the ABC series *We've Got This: On Parenting with a Disability*, an audio series on disability and relationships for Radio National, and *And Then Something Changed*, a kids TV drama for ABCME about a child's experience of having a disability. She is the access and inclusion coordinator at Arena Theatre, and a current member of the Victorian Disability Advisory Council.

Andy Jackson is a poet currently living in Castlemaine, Dja Dja Waurrung country. He has co-edited disability-themed issues of *Southerly* and *Australian Poetry Journal*. Andy's most recent collection,

Music our bodies can't hold, consists of portrait poems of other people with Marfan syndrome.

Kit Kavanagh-Ryan is a writer, librarian and academic interested in cripping your kidlit. She is based in Melbourne and currently completing a PhD on speculative young adult fiction, disability and secondary worlds. Her writing can be found in places like *Cordite*, *Southerly* and *Kill Your Darlings*, as well as David Bridie's *The Wisdom Line*.

Gayle Kennedy is from the NSW Ngiyaampaa nation. Her poetry collection *Koori Girl Goes Shoppin'* was shortlisted in 2005 for the David Unaipon Award, and she won the award in 2006 with *Me, Antman & Fleabag*. She's published eleven children's books and articles and poems in national and international publications.

Jessica Knight is a Melbourne-based writer and performer, and a conflicted heathen. Jessica wrote and performed *Mormon Girl* at the 2019 Melbourne Fringe Festival. Her writing has been published in *Meanjin*, *SCUM Mag* and *Archer*.

C.B. Mako is a non-fiction, fiction, and fanfiction writer. Winner of the Grace Marion Wilson Emerging Writers Competition, shortlisted for the Queensland Literary Awards – QUT Digital Literature Award, the Overland Fair Australia Prize, and longlisted for the inaugural Liminal Fiction Prize.

Kerri-ann Messenger lives in Adelaide and loves attending university to learn how, in the future, to better help others with a disability. Kerri says writing poetry is like painting a picture and she wants to use it as part of a therapy program for herself and other people.

Carly-Jay Metcalfe is a Brisbane-based writer and spiritual carer. Born with cystic fibrosis, she's had many medical adventures (and misadventures) including a double lung transplant in 1998 at the age of twenty-one and surviving a rare form of cancer in 2007. She is currently writing her memoir and is very, very bad at dying.

Tom Middleditch is an autistic/ADHD artist, currently working in theatre and slowly sliding into writing essays and stories. He only wears maroon clothes to save time dressing and shopping while still appearing dapper. It's working. He is balding gracefully.

Oliver Mills is a South Australian artist and poet who lives with cerebral palsy, a physical condition that affects muscle movement and verbal communication. Using specially designed equipment, and in collaboration with his poetry and art teachers, Oliver's works offer a written and visual expression of how he sees the world.

Fiona Murphy is a Deaf poet and essayist. Her work has appeared in the *Griffith Review*, *Big Issue*, *Kill Your Darlings* and *Overland*, among others. In 2018 she was shortlisted for the Richell Prize, and in 2019 the Monash Prize for creative writing.

Olivia Muscat is an emerging writer and critic. Her work has appeared in *Meet Me at the Intersection*, and her theatre reviews can be found on *Witness Performance*. She is co-creator and co-host of The YA Page writing community in Melbourne and has worked at the Encounters With Writing festival and the National Young Writers' Festival.

Jessica Newman-Marshall is a disabled woman living on Wathaurong Country. She is Mum to Golden Retriever Willow, and is studying a Bachelor of Health Science, majoring in Disability Inclusion. Jess has been writing creative non-fiction about living life with Marfan Syndrome & Co. for twelve years, and has been published locally and nationally. She volunteers to support programs that create opportunities for social inclusion and participation for young people living with chronic illness and disabilities. Jess lives by the motto that life is short, but she's not.

Khanh Nguyen is a writer and university lecturer. He has written for television, stage, and print. He wanted to write something witty here, but the deadline for submission is 5 p.m., and it's 4.52 p.m. right now. He wants to thank you for reading his bio, and hopes that you enjoy his chapter.

Sandi Parsons lives and breathes stories and has written several books for young readers. She is passionate about diversity in storytelling. She considers the guardianship of her gifted lungs one of her many victories in her ongoing battle with cystic fibrosis.

Lauren Poole is a word-lover and postgraduate student from New South Wales.

Melanie Rees is a dual transplant survivor and speculative fiction writer from South Australia. Her work has appeared in over 100 domestic and international publications such as *Nature: Futures* and *Cosmos*, and she was recently awarded The Hope Prize's Women's Writing Career Development Scholarship.

Jane Rosengrave is a proud Yorta Yorta woman and disability advocate. Jane lives with an intellectual disability and is widely respected for her fearless advocacy regarding violence against people with disability.

Iman Shaanu is a university student from Melbourne, studying psychology. In her spare time you'll find her reading, aggressively tagging her friends in memes, baking and eating chocolate. She is a proud Gryffindor. She is passionate about social justice and promoting the voices of people of colour, particularly disabled POC.

Jasmine Shirrefs is a zine maker, writer and social work student living on Boon Wurrung land. They were a Wheeler Centre Hot Desk Fellow 2019 and have been published in *Overland*, *Right Now* and *Lot's Wife*.

Tim Slade's poems have been published in *The Weekend Australian*, *Cordite* and *The Koori Times*. His debut collection of poems, *The Walnut Tree*, will be published by Bright South in early 2021. Tim lives in Pioneer, a tiny town in the forest in Tasmania's north-east.

Jordon Steele-John is a disability rights advocate and politician. He is currently a Greens senator for Western Australian. Elected to the senate at twenty-three, he was Australia's youngest sitting parliamentarian. In 2019 he was named the McKinnon Emerging Political Leader of the Year for his leadership as a disability advocate.

Jessica Walton is a white, queer, disabled writer and teacher living on Boon Wurrung land with her wife and two children. She is the author of the picture book *Introducing Teddy*. In 2017, Jess completed a Write-ability Fellowship with Writers Victoria focused on poetry about disability, cancer and pain. She is currently completing Writers Victoria's Publishability Fellowship, which continues this work. She co-wrote an episode of *Get Krack!n* focused on disability, which aired on ABC in February 2019.

Anna Whateley writes 'own voice' young adult fiction. Her debut novel, *Peta Lyre's Rating Normal*, was published in 2020. She holds a PhD in literature and lives in Brisbane with her husband, three children, two dogs and two rescue guinea pigs.

Natalia Wikana is a writer, book reviewer and freelance beta/sensitivity reader. While dealing with her terrifying stacks of unread books and writing her own, she champions diverse stories.

Todd Winther lives in Brisbane. He specialises in political leadership and policy-making in the disability sector. As a political commentator, Todd has been published in *The Conversation* and *ABC Ramp Up*. He has also taught subjects in politics and disability studies at university.

Tully Zygier is a qualified social worker, and a writer with an interest in food, movies and painting. She has worked in the disability sector for ten years. She works in communications at VALID. At the age of four, Tully was diagnosed with familial dysautonomia. Her condition is degenerative and she uses her trusty walking frame to get around.

Cover artist

Wendy Dawson is a painter whose art practice is one of repetition and structure: within her practice, she applies hundreds of linear marks to the paper using paint pens and markers. She has worked at Arts Project Australia since 2008, featuring in group exhibitions including FEM-aFFINITY, which toured nationally. Her work is held in private collections throughout Australia.

www.ingramcontent.com/pod-product-compliance
Ingram Content Group UK Ltd.
Pitfield, Milton Keynes, MK11 3LW, UK
UKHW021052270726
13967UKWH00012B/590